THE CARIBBEAN
AND ADJACENT COUNTRIES

The British Caribbean territories are shown in heavy type
and those which form The West Indies federation are underlined

70°

MILES

0   100   200   300

0 100 200 300 400 500
KILOMETRES

20°

CAICOS IS.
TURKS IS.

HAITI   DOMINICAN REPUBLIC

VIRGIN IS.
(U.S.)

VIRGIN IS.   LEEWARD IS.
ANGUILLA

PUERTO
RICO
(U.S.)

ST. KITTS
NEVIS   ANTIGUA
MONTSERRAT

GUADELOUPE (Fr.)

DOMINICA

MARTINIQUE (Fr.)

N SEA

WINDWARD IS.

ST. LUCIA
ST. VINCENT   BARBADOS

ARUBA (Neth) BONAIRE (Neth)
CURAÇAO (Neth)   GRENADA

TOBAGO

Port-of-Spain
TRINIDAD   10°

V E N E Z U E L A

George-
town

BRITISH
GUIANA   NETH.
GUIANA

OMBIA

70°

B   R   A   Z

THE BRITISH WEST INDIES:

THE SEARCH FOR SELF GOVERNMENT

THE BRITISH WEST INDIES

THE SEARCH FOR SELF-GOVERNMENT

―――――

MORLEY AYEARST

Ruskin House

GEORGE ALLEN & UNWIN LTD

MUSEUM STREET LONDON

FIRST PUBLISHED IN 1960

© 1960 *by Morley Ayearst*

PRINTED IN GREAT BRITAIN
in 10 *on* 11 *pt Times type*
BY EAST MIDLAND PRINTING CO LTD
BURY ST. EDMUNDS, KETTERING, PETERBOROUGH
AND ELSEWHERE

PREFACE

The writer would like to express his gratitude to the various committees concerned with the Fulbright awards who made possible this study at first hand of British West Indian politics. Thanks are due also to New York University for granting the author a leave of absence from his usual teaching and administrative duties. He is also indebted to the United States consular officers in the area, the officers of the British Overseas Service and the numerous West Indians of all parties and opinions who gave generously of their time to answer his questions. Special thanks are due to the officials of the University College of the West Indies at Mona, Jamaica, and particularly to the Institute of Social and Economic Studies and its Director, Dr. Dudley Huggins, for the facilities extended during his stay in that island. Such faults as this study contains cannot be blamed upon the officials, politicians or citizens of the West Indies who went out of their way to be of assistance and who were so hospitable to a passing stranger.

M.A.

CONTENTS

CHAPTER I

INTRODUCTION

THE British West Indies consist of two mainland colonies and a number of islands stretching in a great arc from British Honduras in Central America to British Guiana on the mainland of South America—a total distance following the island chain of nearly 3,000 miles.[1] They vary greatly in size. The mainland colonies are much the largest: British Honduras is about 8,598 square miles in extent and British Guiana 83,000 square miles (about the size of Kansas, and larger than Great Britain). Of the British islands, Jamaica, with 4,411 square miles is larger than all the rest put together. Trinidad is next in size with an area of 1,856 square miles. Some of the others are tiny. St Kitts is only 68 square miles in extent and Barbados, 166 square miles. Grenada is 133, St Vincent 150, St Lucia 233 and Dominica, the largest of the Windwards, 205 square miles.

All are tropical in climate. Most are mountainous. Both the mainland colonies have rugged and only partly explored mountain regions and flat coastal plains. Many of the islands are of volcanic origin including the western members of the Leeward group (St Kitts, Nevis and Montserrat) and the Windwards: (Dominica, St Lucia, St Vincent and Grenada). Antigua and little Auguilla, a small portion of Barbados, Tobago, and northern Trinidad are of limestone formation. Most of Barbados and southern Trinidad are coral covered with a thin layer of earth. The island climate and that of the coastal parts of the mainland colonies is one of permanent summer tempered by the trade winds which blow constantly. Especially in the north, Caribbean hurricanes are an annual menace. They rarely hit as far south as Barbados while Trinidad and British Guiana are considered below the hurricane belt. The damage to standing crops (especially serious in the case of tree crops—coconuts or cocoa) and to housing can be appalling. Most have ample rainfall which falls much more heavily on the windward (Atlantic) side. Antigua, however, suffers from a perennial water shortage and Barbados is occasionally plagued by droughts. The seasons appear

[1] Sometimes the Bahamas and even Bermuda are included as part of the British West Indies. In fact they are not thought of as such by most West Indians and are not members of the West Indies federation.

AREAS AND POPULATIONS OF BRITISH CARIBBEAN DEPENDENCIES[1]

Territory	Total Area (sq. miles)	Population (mid-1956 estimate)	
Barbados	166		228,000
British Guiana	83,000		499,000
British Honduras	8,867		82,000
Jamaica and Dependencies	4,677	Jamaica	1,564,000
		Dependencies	13,410 (1955
Leeward Islands:			
Antigua	171		53,000
St. Christopher-Nevis-Anguilla	153		54,800
Montserrat	32		14,400
Virgin Islands	67		7,680 (1955)
Trinidad and Tobago	1,980		743,000
Windward Islands:			
Dominica	305		63,800
Grenada	133		89,100
St. Lucia	238		89,000
St. Vincent	150		77,600

identical to the visitor except as to the amount of rainfall. To the West Indian they are distinguished also by the flowering periods of various plants and trees. The day shade temperatures vary between eighty and ninety degrees Fahrenheit, and the nights are pleasantly cool. As the principal towns and cities are invariably ports, they are located usually on harbours on the leeward coast and consequently occupy the hottest spot on the island. Both Belize in British Honduras and Georgetown in British Guiana, however, face the east and enjoy cooling breezes. The constant summer temperatures, although not excessive to anyone used to the climate of the eastern seaboard of the United States, seem to sap the energy and reduce the pace of activities.

Public health measures have improved greatly in recent years. Some tropical ailments are found, of course. Yaws, leprosy, filariasis (elephantiasis), tuberculosis, hookworm, malaria and yellow fever occur but are much less general than they were formerly. Mosquito control has proved effective in the sharp reduction and virtual elimination of yellow fever, filariasis and malaria, even in British Guiana where these, particularly malaria, were a very serious problem.

Except for Trinidad (which has nearly all the flora and fauna of northern South America save for the largest cat, the jaguar), most of the islands have few indigenous animals and plants. Most of the ornamentals and crop plants are exotics. Of the economically important trees possibly only the coconut is native. The beautiful and useful breadfruit was introduced by Captain Bligh of 'Bounty' fame. The Indian mango was also first planted in the eighteenth

[1]Table from British Information Services pamphlet 1282, December 1957.

century. Other trees were brought from Africa and India. The fauna, except for a number of varieties of lizards, is meagre. Snakes are almost non-existent in the islands with the exception of Trinidad and the former French islands where the deadly fer-de-lance is found—allegedly introduced by planters to discourage slaves from escaping into the forest.

An important factor in West Indian life is sheer distance. From Belize, British Honduras, to Kingston, Jamaica, is almost seven hundred miles. Jamaica in turn is widely separated from the nearest British islands to the east, the tiny British Virgins. The Leeward and Windward groups, as well as Barbados and Trinidad, are not so remote from each other but nevertheless suffer from a degree of isolation. Shipping services are occasional and consist chiefly of schooners and small motor boats. The ships of large American and British companies touch at the chief ports but seldom serve the smaller islands. The only practical passenger service for many of the islands, and for the mainland colonies is by aircraft, unavailable to most West Indians because of the cost. One result is a high degree of insularity. This insularity is fostered also by extreme difference in size and degree of urbanization. Jamaicans tend to feel superior to other West Indians and this attitude has made them unpopular elsewhere. Trinidadians also speak scornfully of the 'small island' people from Barbados and Grenada. It is difficult for the ordinary Kittitian or Grenadian to feel that he and the Jamaican he has never met are both part of the same West Indian community. Even within the colonies themselves transportation is often inadequate. The two largest islands, Jamaica and Trinidad, have a good network of roads and even short railroads joining principal towns. Engineering difficulties (almost insurmountable in British Guiana) combined with poverty have prevented the mainland colonies from securing an adequate highway or rail system. The logs from the British Honduras interior were floated out on rivers so the company had no interest in roads. Only recently have the two principal towns of Belize and Stann Creek been joined by a road that can take motor traffic. The interior of British Guiana is separated from the coast by formidable mountains and only air transport is available between coast and hinterland, even to take out the beef produced by the herds of the Rupununi savannahs. Of the islands, Dominica suffers most from lack of roads. This island, virtually a mountain peak jutting from the sea, has had roads only along the leeward coast although a road to the windward coast is now under construction and due to be completed in 1958. These conditions have been due to two factors: the high cost of road construction and the low income of the colonial governments, and the tendency of former governments to spend money upon the ports and concentrate their efforts upon the cash-crop export trade rather than upon local amenities. Present governments are trying hard to compensate for past neglect.

The colonies and ex-colonies in Africa and Asia present the familiar picture of native peoples ruled more or less benevolently by European powers and, as they acquire self-government, reviving or developing a local nationalism based upon their own historic culture. In contrast with such colonies, those of the West Indies contain no 'natives'.[1] Instead, their populations constitute an amalgam of non-indigenous peoples, chiefly of African and European origin, but also, especially in Trinidad and British Guiana, of East Indian derivation.[2] Smaller numbers of others, principally Chinese and Syrians are found in most of the colonies. Trinidad and British Guiana also have some Portuguese whose ancestors came from Madeira for the most part.

Because the entire population consists of immigrants and their descendants no question of direct versus indirect rule could ever arise. No native government was replaced. There are no native institutions upon which to base social and political life. The only significant culture is European. There would seem to be a few remnants, what might be termed faint memories of West African culture among the Negroes. Before emancipation the slave-owners were almost completely successful in stamping out the use of African languages and the traditional institutions of African tribal society. Having been de-culturized the Negroes assimilated the only available one, that of the Europeans. They did so the more readily as this culture was the only one with prestige. Indeed, African tribal culture was bound to disintegrate under the conditions of slavery and the plantation economy nor could it compete with that of the West except perhaps, in the fields of religion, music and the dance. The traces that remain are in these categories. There is, therefore, little culture-conflict as between European and African West Indians. This is not entirely the case as regards the post-slavery immigrants from India. No attempt was made to compel them to change their

[1] This is not strictly accurate. There is a tiny group of Caribs on Dominica and both mainland colonies have sizeable Amerindian minorities. In British Honduras most of these are Mayans of Yucatecan or Guatemalan origin. Many are Spanish-speaking mestizos. In British Guiana the Amerindians of the interior are genuine primitives. In neither colony are they as yet politically important.
[2] 'East Indian' is used here and throughout in its West Indian usage to mean a person of Indian ancestry rather than an inhabitant of the East Indian archipelago. The parents and grandparents of many West Indian East Indians hailed from the United Provinces. Most are Hindus but there is a Moslem minority.

customs or religion or to cease to use their own languages. They have tended to remain endogamous and even though many now have become educated and most have given up native Indian costume, have retained a high degree of communal feeling including some attachment to Mother India—manifested chiefly by a desire to preserve their religion. In rural areas they have tended to remain grouped in village communities with few, if any, African inhabitants. They constitute a vigorous and colourful but complicating element in the social and political life of Trinidad and British Guiana.

One might expect the political development of the British West Indies to differ somewhat from that, say, of the Gold Coast or Ceylon. This is indeed the case for their societies are very different. At the same time there are important similarities. All of these colonies and ex-colonies are underdeveloped in that they must live mainly upon export agriculture with a resulting low living standard. All are undergoing rapid 'Westernization' or what might better be called a transfer of authority from autocratic and official to democratically elected rulers, which took place in the West also at an earlier date. All are vividly conscious of their new nationality as they emerge from colonial status. But in the West Indies the new nationalism is conditioned and somewhat blurred by the mixture of races in the population, the absence of any truly local culture and the small size of the units. Even the larger colonies are too small to develop a meaningful nationality of their own. Nor, despite the ancestry of the majority, can the West Indian nation be African. The dominance of British culture would seem to make inevitable the evolution of a West Indian sub-nationality based upon the federation and sharing a British identification with the older Dominions within the Commonwealth of Nations.

This West Indian society rests upon an economy chiefly dependent upon a single crop: sugar. These islands were developed upon the mercantilist theory and sugar was for a long time the most profitable crop they could produce. Other crops as well were exploited in certain colonies, mahogany in British Honduras, for example, but in general the West Indian economy remains today, as it has been for three hundred years, tied to sugar. So complete is this specialization that the colonies produce only a portion of their own food.[1] In Barbados even citrus fruis is imported. The staple diet of the ordinary Jamaican contains a good deal of rice and salt

---

[1] Sugar is the most valuable export crop in: Jamaica, Barbados, British Guiana, St Kitts, Antigua, St Lucia. It is second to oil in Trinidad. It is not important in British Honduras, and the small islands of Grenada, St Vincent and Montserrat.

fish, as in the days of slavery. Both are imported, the salt fish mainly from Canada. Flour is also a principal import, of course, as are vottons, synthetic fabrics and manufacturers of all kinds.[1] Efforts are being made now to stimulate diversification of both food and cash crops but whatever is grown for export must be able to meet fierce competition in both British and foreign markets. In recent years oil exploitation in Trinidad has enabled that island to enjoy a greater degree of prosperity than is the case elsewhere. Grenada, at least until the hurricane 'Janet' of 1955, was fortunate in its high-priced cocoa production as well as enjoying a near-monopoly of the world nutmeg crop. Sea-island cotton is grown in some other islands and St Vincent has developed successfully the cultivation of arrowroot. But the general picture is still sugar and its by-products of rum and molasses. And, as is the case nearly everywhere in the world, sugar is a profitable crop only when it receives government subsidies. Were these to cease, the West Indies economy would be in desperate straits.

Even the largest of the island colonies (Jamaica) is small compared with British colonies in other parts of the world. Some of the British West Indies could be called miniature. This very quality makes it easier to study their social and political life and structure. In a sense they represent small-scale experiments in emergent democracy, enabling the student to examine the problems that beset such a development in a mixed, if not quite a plural,[6] society, and to judge, as well, the benefits and disadvantages of colonial tutelage during this social and political evolution.

[1] British Guiana produces an export surplus of rice. The chief imports in terms of cost (as of 1950) in order of importance were: Jamaica—flour, cottons, rice, dried fish; Trinidad—flour, pipes and tubes (for oil industry), cottons, condensed and dried milk; Barbados—machinery, flour, art silk, cottons, motor cars; Grenada—flour, cottons, wood, motor cars, dried fish; St Vincent—flour, cottons, hardware; St Lucia—flour, hardware, cottons; Dominica—flour, sugar, machinery, cottons; British Guiana—machinery, flour, cottons, hardware; British Honduras—flour, condensed and dried milk, cottons, gasoline, rice.
[2] 'Plural' is used in the sense coined by J. S. Furnivall, as meaning a society containing two or more groups living side by side under the same government but forming distinct communities with nearly all contacts between individuals of different communities confined to those dictated by economic necessity. See J. S. Furnivall, *Colonial Policy and Practice* (New York, 1956) pp. 303-312.

CHAPTER II

WEST INDIAN GOVERNMENTS FROM THE OLD REPRESENTATIVE PERIOD TO THE CROWN COLONY SYSTEM: A GENERAL SURVEY TO 1945

IN the seventeenth and eighteenth centuries West Indian history is an account of romantic adventures, piracy, privateering and dashing naval and military battles. During these centuries some of the colonies changed their allegiance several times and it was then that the forts were built which now add to the picturesque attractions of many of the islands. The importance to the imperial powers of these insular possessions is attested by the number and intensity of naval battles fought over them as well as the cost and extent of the forti-fications built for their defence.[1] But by the close of the Napoleonic Wars Europe had settled into an uneasy equilibrium destined to last for a century except for minor and limited wars. This equilibrium was maintained in the West Indies as well and the allegiance of the British colonies has not changed since that time. The 'expansion of Europe' in the West Indies had been completed. Any further changes were to be in the direction of American attachments (the Danish Virgin Islands and Puerto Rico) or to result in independence. The sole exception was the transfer of tiny St Bartholomew by Sweden to France in 1878.

Internally, the political establishment of the British colonies in the seventeenth and eighteenth centuries was first, the Proprietory and then the Old Representative System, the latter lasting, indeed, down into the century following the permanent allocation of owner-ship following the Napleonic Wars.

The Old Representative System was essentially similar to that used in the North American colonies. In the West Indies it became an oligarchy of white planters and merchants successfully keeping control of local affairs much of the time by periodic struggles with the Governor and the Colonial Office. Chiefly as a result of steady pressures from the British Government these oligarchies gradually were forced to permit more participation in elections by the growing

[1] One of these, the fortification system on Brimstone Hill, St Kitts, known as 'the Gibraltar of the West Indies' was virtually impregnable by eighteenth century standards.

middle class, both white and coloured. Then, afraid of expanding political democracy operated by a coloured and Negro electorate, the oligarchies surrendered their powers to the Colonial Office. Elected legislatures were abolished and the Crown Colony system established. Under this system, not only all executive powers were in the hands of the Crown-appointed Governor but he was in control of general policy and legislation because the legislature consisted of officials, subordinates of the Governor plus some colonists nominated by the Governor. This kind of government, the ex-oligarchs hoped, might operate so as to preserve the economic and social status quo. But then, as a result of continued local demands and, in time, a new British colonial policy, political democratization was speeded up. The official and nominated element in the legislatures was reduced, the elected element enlarged by stages, suffrage became universal and the fears of the nineteenth century planters at last were realized: colonial government had become almost complete self-government as regards local affairs in the hands of legislatures composed of persons elected by the Negro majority. This study is concerned with certain aspects of these developments and more particularly with their most recent manifestations.

For this purpose it will be unnecessary to examine in detail this history as it unfolded in the various colonies as has been well done elsewhere.[1] Nevertheless, a brief review is necessary to give perspective to a consideration of modern West Indian politics.

The beginning of British interest in the West Indies came early in the seventeenth century. Spain was predominant in the area, of course, but Spain was interested primarily in the mainland and secondarily in the Greater Antilles, so British settlers were able to slip into some of the smaller islands with a minimum of difficulty. Their first settlement was in the little island of St Kitts (St Christopher) in 1623. Thereafter landings on others of the Leeward group were attempted. There were armed clashes at times with the Carib Indians and with the French who, like the British, were trying to swallow these disregarded crumbs from the Spanish colonial banquet. In 1625, Sir William Courteen, a London merchant, sent an expedition to occupy uninhabited Barbados. At this time, the success of the Virginia tobacco plantations encouraged the West Indian settlers to try the same crop, and tobacco was planted in Barbados as well as St Kitts. But by 1670 sugar had taken first place. This shift to sugar was of enormous consequence to the subsequent

---

[1] For a quick survey, see Agnes M. Wriston and Lucy F. Horsfall *Britain and the West Indies* (New York, London & Toronto, 1948); W. L. Burn *The British West Indies* (London, Hutchinson, 1951) and Chapter I of the 'Moyne Report', *The West India Royal Commission Report* (Cmd. 6607) July, 1945.

history of the colonies. Sugar production is an industry as well as agriculture. The bulky cane must be processed as soon as it is cut. This requires a factory for expressing the juice and reducing it to sugar and molasses. Obviously this can be done efficiently only if the operation is conducted on a large scale with a heavy capital investment. The smallholding English farmers who had cultivated tobacco had no part to play in this new enterprise. The typical establishment of the sugar industry became a large plantation with its own factory. Quantities of cheap labour were needed too, and this labour could be supplied by the West African slave-dealers.

At first, white indentured servants were employed and treated, incidentally, exactly like slaves during their period of indenture. Later on, the back-breaking labour in the cane fields became exclusively the work of Negro slaves and the white servants were employed at more skilled and lighter work. During the period of slave importation, white indentured servants continued to be brought in but in smaller numbers. These poor whites subsequently became successful planters themselves in some cases. Others drifted into a life of roistering adventure with pirate and buccaneer bands. Sir Henry Morgan, sometime pirate and later Governor of Jamaica, had first come to the West Indies as an indentured servant. Others emigrated to the North American colonies. It was always difficult for the colonial governments to enforce the Deficiency Laws which required a fixed proportion of whites to Negroes to be maintained on the plantations in order that any slave insurrections might be suppressed. A Jamaican law of 1672, for example, required that each estate should have a minimum of one white to every ten Negroes.

The island colonies soon ceased to resemble those of the British American mainland which still consisted mainly of white settlers. Instead they became a mosaic of estates and plantations dominated by a small, white planter-class. The tiny middle class included the 'attorneys' for absentee landlords, and a few lawyers and merchants. There were also the overseers and 'book-keepers' on the estates and a handful of craftsmen and artisans. At the bottom was the black labouring class, constantly replenished from the slave-ports of West Africa.

When they could, the British enlarged their West Indian possessions. The big island of Jamaica in the Greater Antilles was captured from the Spanish in 1655. Later some Jamaican buccaneers found a convenient hiding place on the little islands off the desolate Central American coast in what was to become the colony of British Honduras. In 1762, the islands of Grenada, St Vincent and Dominica were taken from the French. St Lucia joined their number after the

B

Napoleonic wars. These islands were small, remote and very mountainous and discouraged white settlement as they were not as suitable for sugar production as the older possessions. Trinidad was taken from the Spanish in 1797, largely for strategic reasons—as a base from which to harry the Spanish trading ships. It was some time before there was much English enterprise here. The small neighbouring island of Tobago, after a series of conquests by various powers, was ceded to Britain by the French in 1815. The Dutch settlements on the South American mainland at Essequibo, Berbice and Demerara were captured by British privateers in 1781 and after changing hands several times, were finally ceded to Britain by the Netherlands in 1814-15 for a payment of three million pounds. The three settlements were united as the colony of British Guiana in 1831.

To begin with, as in the North American mainland, the British system of providing government for these colonies was to leave both the economic development and the political government of the colony to a proprietor or an exploiting company. Of course, the proprietor was not an absolute monarch. In the typical charter granting many of the smaller islands to Lord Carlisle in 1627 it was provided that local laws should have . . . 'the Consent, Assent and Approbation of the freeholders of the said Province, or the greater part of them' . . . In any case, the proprietory system did not survive beyond the seventeenth century. For one thing, the planters were anxious to run their own affairs and in particular, to have the right to tax themselves by a vote of their own representative assembly. As in North America there was frequent reference to the 'Liberties of the [British] subject' which he took with him wherever he went. This was a particularly strong argument in the colonies of settlement and cession. It was even advanced in Jamaica which had been a military conquest and in which, therefore, the Crown was free, legally, to design any government it liked. Whether or not Englishmen legally took their 'liberties' with them, wherever they went, it was surely true that they retained their attachment to representative government. When royalist Barbados was compelled by force of arms to accept Cromwell's Commonwealth in 1652, the little island was able to extract a promise that all taxes should have the approval of a General Assembly elected by the freeholders and that the government should be in the accustomed form of a Governor appointed in England, his Council chosen by him and the elected Assembly.

As the Old Representative System developed, the general plan of government in the colonies during the eighteenth century was as follows: The government was headed by a chief executive, the Governor, who was appointed by the Crown. He was assisted by an Executive Council, also Crown-appointed and by a Legislative Assembly elected by the freeholders. Local government was handled by parish vestries and local administrative officials. A court system was also provided, administering English Common Law plus local ordinances. As noted by E. Long in his *History of Jamaica* (1774),[1] the Old Representative System was a miniature of that of Great Britain itself, the Governor substituting for the monarch, the appointed Council for the House of Lords and the Assembly for the House of Commons. The history of these governments consists in large part of a struggle between Governor and Assembly over the control of the purse-springs and general policy. The Assembly always insisted upon its veto over money bills and managed in some times and places to get such control of finances as to compel the Governor's compliance with its wishes in purely executive matters. The Governor was in the unenviable position of being answerable to the Crown, meaning in fact, the British Cabinet and particularly the Lords of Trade and Plantations, and at the same time often unable to compel local acceptance of British policies. The situation was not helped by the custom of selecting Governors and lesser officials according to influence and connections rather than merit or experience. Many of the first Governors were able men, put particularly in the early eighteenth century some of the appointees were almost fantastically unsuitable. The British government seemed to regard the colonies chiefly as places to provide incomes for their friends and connections. Lesser officers sometimes did not bother to take up residence in the colony at all and collected large sinecure incomes from their poorly-paid deputies who derived them from fees paid by the colonials who needed their official services until this practice was forbidden by an Act of Parliament in 1814. In truth, a governorship called for more than ordinary abilities of a special kind. The most successful governors were those who were highly skilled in the arts of cajolery, the use of influence and with a feeling for political timing. They had to know when to stand firm and when to close their eyes to violations of British law. A similar state of affairs existed in the North American colonies at this time and there, the arrogance and stupidity of some eighteenth century governers made a solid contribution to the sentiments that were to find violent expression in the War of Independence. The West Indian colonists were able to overcome some of their difficulties by going around and above the governor via their London representatives who operated as lobbyists directly upon the Ministry. Then, too, many of the most successful planters soon left their estates in the hands of an 'attorney' and returned to England where some of

[1] Quoted in H. Wrong, *Government of the West Indies* (Oxford, 1923), p. 37.

them secured seats in the House of Commons. So 'the West Indian interest' was never without active representation at Westminster although the absentee planters, the resident planters and the West Indian merchants in London were not always in agreement as to government policies.

The late eighteenth century and early nineteenth century was the period of the planter aristocracy. Beautiful gardens and stately royal palms framed the great house, sometimes imposing enough to stand comparison with the noble mansions of England. Often the house was entered at one-storey height by a double flight of stairs in the 'welcoming arms' pattern. Ceilings were lofty and louvered windows and wall vents allowed a welcome sweep of breeze. Here, in relative luxury, lived the planter and his family, lords of the waving cane fields where hundreds of slaves laboured. Nearby would be the barracks or rows of cabins for the slaves and a little farther off the factory. In the older colonies the tendency was for the planters to remain permanent residents, sometimes for generations. Despite the wealth of the planters, however, there is contemporary evidence of the cultural poverty of the colonies. The upper classes seemed to be interested in money-making and little else beyond eating and drinking. Almost no art, music or literature was produced in this society. An early colonial theatre in Kingston, Jamaica is one of the rare exceptions. Government was a white oligarchy except that a certain number of coloured persons of property, self-identified with the whites, began to appear and take their places in the professions and the legislatures. Some of these were by origin the illegitimate offspring of the planters who not infrequently left them legacies and provided for their education. Many were the results of temporary unions between unmarried white overseers or 'bookkeepers' and female slaves. The Negro slaves remained unrepresented in any way except that the Governors and the courts sometimes tried to protect their legal rights against their owners. In fact a *modus vivendi* evolved in accord with which the slaves enjoyed certain perquisites, the right to cultivate 'ground provisions' for their own use or for sale, occasional holidays and so forth.

From the mercantilist viewpoint sugar was an ideal product—supplying the home market with a needed commodity, providing an opportunity for investment of British capital and a steady income to the British merchant marine that enjoyed a monopoly of the West Indian carrying trade as well as the vastly profitable trade in slaves. In turn, the West Indian interest made certain that their sugar was well protected in the British market. According to a correspondent of the *Gentleman's Magazine*, forty or more Members of Parliament in 1766 were the owners of West Indian plantations, the descendants of planters or had other ties and interests in the West Indies. In the single month of Juluy, 1757, one hundred and seventy-five ships arrived in British ports with cargoes from the West Indies valued at £2,000,000. Sugar was so profitable and fitted so well into the mercantilist economy that the British government actually toyed with the idea of trading Canada back to the French, after its capitulation, in exchange for Guadeloupe (area: 532 square miles)! Of course the West Indian influence was exerted against the acquisition of Guadeloupe with its competing sugar production.

The West Indies colonists were happy enough under this system except as the navigation laws interfered with their own shipping. However, they were able to evade the regulations to some extent and carried on some contraband trade with North America both during and after the colonial period there. With British approval they also traded, contrary to Spanish law, with the non-British islands and the Spanish Main, largely in British goods.

But the nineteenth century witnessed a triple blow to the British West Indies economy. The collapse of the Spanish American empire meant that British ships could and did go directly to the ex-colonies of Spain and the West Indian ports suffered from loss of business. The next disaster was emancipation. Already in 1897 the slave trade had been abolished. This was a serious matter, as, under plantation conditions and health standards, the slaves were not even maintaining their numbers by natural reproduction. Costs of maintaining a plantation had gone up because of the loss of the British North American colonies. Salt fish, the staple protein of the slaves' diet, now had to come from Canada and cost more than the New England product. The same was true of lumber. At the same time, West Indian sugar was faced with growing competition in the markets of Europe. The less efficient or 'marginal' estates were beginning to fail and some had been allowed to relapse into weeds as early as 1816.[1] This economic pinch seldom led to any attempt at increased efficiency in the use of labour. As Curtin points out,[2] the slavery system rendered it difficult for planters to see any advantage in labour-saving methods. Further, the method of growing, cultivating, harvesting and pressing the cane had become routine, even traditional, and changes were likely to meet with resistance from all concerned.

As time went on the slaves had become rather less amenable to

[1] According to M. G. Lewis, *Journal of a West Indies Proprietor, Kept During Residence in the Island of Jamaica* (London, 1835).
[2] Philip D. Curtin, *Two Jamaicas: The Role of Ideas in a Tropical Colony 1830-1865* (Cambridge, Mass., Harvard University Press: Oxford University Press, 1955).

slavery. The cessation of the slave trade had enabled the slaves to adjust themselves to their new condition and reconstitute the beginnings of a society of their own to replace the tribal society and culture destroyed by their owners. They could do this the more readily as they no longer had to absorb new, ignorant captives from Africa. They had come to prefer work on their own 'provision grounds' where they could raise produce for market, to their forced labour on the estates. Despite planter opposition, Baptist missionaries had entered Jamaica and had had much success in converting the slaves. The latter found leaders among these missionaries and especially among their own 'Native Baptist' pastors. Through these they learned something of the libertarian ideas now circulating in England. An annual Christmas festival had always been permitted the slaves, tolerated by their masters as a safety valve for emotional release. But this celebration in 1831 ended in some disorder and the burning by the slaves of a few plantation houses. The whites at once thought of what had happened in Haiti and organized prompt and cruel repressive measures including the hanging of numbers of slaves supposedly implicated. The incitors of this unorganized revolt were chiefly Native Baptist leaders and the Negroes referred to the uprising as 'the Baptist War'. Then in 1833 the first reformed House of Commons passed the Emancipation Act. Although compensation was provided the former slave-owners, it was considered generally by them to be far too meagre, amounting to about one-half of the current market value of slaves. Many of the ex-slaves took at once to the hills and left the plantations nearly bare of labour. Only in Barbados where almost the whole of the arable land was planted could this not happen. As they had nowhere to go, the ex-slaves remained as hired labour and the Barbados economy received the lightest blow from emancipation. The British law provided for a period of compulsory 'apprenticeship' to follow slavery and precede complete emancipation. This required the ex-slave to remain at his job under his old master for a period of years. The chief distinction from slavery was that he now received wages. In Jamaica apprenticeship was abolished abruptly in 1838 and nowhere did it work very well. The new freedmen considered it a trick to avoid the freedom they had been promised. Where possible some bought small holdings of their own, often a bit of a subdivided estate. In British Guiana many co-operative purchases were made by associations of freedmen. In Jamaica with its wild mountainous country, the freedmen tended to become squatters in some high valley or in remote parts in the 'back lands' of the estates. In any case they avoided working in the cane fields if they could manage to get away. Not even high wages would tempt them.

If they did accept employment it would be for the minimum period required by sheer necessity. The embittered planters made matters worse by refusing to continue traditional gratuities and by adopting hard bargaining practices while they continued to treat their Negro labourers with the same rough arrogance they had employed in their dealings with the slaves. The freedmen deeply resented this treatment. Furthermore, slavery had been the worst possible training for free wage-work. Slaves might work hard in their own garden plots but estate work had always meant working in gangs at a prescribed pace under constant and often brutal discipline. Above all, emancipation meant to them freedom from this kind of work, whether wages were paid or not.

Then came what seemed to the planters to be the final and catastrophic blow. In 1840 duties in Britain on sugar from India and Mauritius had been equalized with those on West Indian sugar. Free trade had triumphed completely by 1854. Meanwhile sugar prices had been falling. Only the most efficient producers with the best sugar lands could hope to survive and many West Indian planters were bankrupted at once or after a few additional crops.

It is possible that the free trade policy was not in fact the principal cause for the price decline, although it was so regarded by the planters. Sugar production in Cuba and elsewhere was increasing in quantity and efficiency. Jamaican production had fallen off before the adoption of free trade. In the period 1839-46 Jamaica had produced an average of only 4,775 tons per year as compared with the average of 7,607 tons during the years 1824-33.[1]

Emancipation of course did not herald the rapid arrival of political democracy in the colonies. The freedmen were not enfranchised. The Legislative Assemblies in the colonies continued to be the representatives of a very restricted class. Indeed the class enjoying representation had been shrinking in relation to the whole population. In many cases, the planters and their families had left the colony. Almost from the beginning of sugar production in the British islands, the most successful planters tended to return to England where they could enjoy their wealth in a cultivated society, buy themselves seats in Parliament and ascend the social ladder. They left their estates in the hands of resident 'attorneys' and were interested only in the revenue from them. England remained 'home' no matter how long a time was spent in colonial exile. Almost all planters wanted to return to England as soon as they could afford to do so. Hard times forced more of them out. In the end, the remaining whites were mainly poor planters, attorneys (some of them

[1] Figures based on statistics given in N. Deerr, *The History of Sugar* vol. II (London, Chapman & Hall, 1951) p. 377.

rich from the management fees of several estates) and lower-middle-class overseers and 'book-keepers' as well as a few merchants. These now comprised the dwindling electorate for there was little reason for any additional white immigration and most of the poorer whites were unmarried. At the same time the black proletariat had begun to multiply. In Jamaica (1861) the voters were considerably under one in two hundred of the population. In Barbados (1869) less than one in one hundred. The situation was even more extreme in some of the less populous islands. The Assemblies thus represented a small, disgruntled oligarchy—bitter at their 'betrayal' by the home government and almost disloyal to the British connection, indisposed to take an interest in the welfare of any class but their own and utterly unwilling to permit taxation for the benefit of the freed Negroes. The existing system had become nearly impossible to work under these conditions. The Governors found themselves permanently deadlocked with the Assemblies.

The Old Representative System, after all, was based upon the assumption that the colonies were and would remain areas of European settlement, whose inhabitants would be familiar with representative institutions and would form a fairly homogeneous society. This had long ceased to be the case in the West Indies. Nevertheless, the political implications of emancipation were not grasped immediately by either the Secretaries of State or the colonial assemblies. At first, the Whig solution was to imitate the Canadian pattern, as set by the Durham Report.[1] In 1849 the Secretary of State told the Governor of Jamaica (Sir Charles Grey) that it would be in order for Jamaica to follow the Canadian example, observing that in doing so the Jamaican Assembly would be giving up some of its money powers.[2] The Assembly rejected this proposal but shortly thereafter set up a committee to consider constitutional reform. The results of this study, which owed nothing to the Secretary of State or the Governor, were embodied in a bill which became law in 1854. This measure included two important reforms. In the first place, it set up a Legislative Council or persons nomin-

[1] 'I know not how it is possible to secure harmony in any other way than by administering the Government on those principles which have been found perfectly efficacious in Great Britain. I would not impair a single prerogative of the Crown; on the contrary, I believe that the interests of the people of these Colonies require the protection of prerogatives, which have not hitherto been exercised. But the Crown must, on the other hand, submit to the necessary consequences of representative institutions; and if it has to carry on the government in unison with a representative body, it must consent to carry it on by means of those in whom that body has confidence.' *Lord Durham's Report* (Lucas, ed., 1912) II, 278.

[2] This statement indicated a failure on the part of the Secretary of State to grasp the principles of responsible government, as noted in Wrong, *op. cit., p.* 64.

ated by the Crown for life as a second chamber without any executive functions and secondly it created an Executive Committee of four (three from the Assembly and one from the Legislative Council) to serve as a kind of quasi-cabinet. The Executive Committee would be salaried Crown officers, although picked from the legislature. They would concern themselves with financial matters chiefly, advising the Governor on revenue and expenditure and proposing all money bills in the legislature. In the legislature they would represent the government. They should be responsible to the Governor but *at the same time* dismissable by the Governor if failing to obtain the support of the legislature! It would be hard to imagine any scheme more likely to give trouble in a situation of continual struggle between the executive and legislative powers. This system could only work at all well under conditions of substantial inter-power harmony. However, the Jamaican plan was imitated promptly in a number of other colonies, possibly because of the great prestige of big Jamaica among the smaller islands.[1] Some thought it a brilliant compromise between the old system and full responsible government which would be unsuitable in the West Indian situation. But in any controversy between the legislature and the Governor, the Executive Committee was in a hopeless case. It could side with the Governor and have its proposals constantly rejected by the legislature, or it could defy the Governor and be dismissed. Only in Barbados did the system work with any degree of satisfaction.[2]

At the same time, full responsible government would simply have transferred all power in local affairs to the oligarchy of white and coloured landowners. Nor did these represent any sort of qualified governing class. Especially in the smaller islands, the governors were complaining constantly of the semi-literacy and total unfitness of their assemblies. The inability of these legislators to handle the business of government as well as their lack of interest in public affairs was well displayed in the scattered group of islets known as the British Virgins. There, in 1854 the the top-heavy bicameral structure was replaced by a single house of six elected and three nominated members presided over by a Lieutenant-Governor. Five years later the number of elected members was reduced to four and in 1867 elections were dropped and the entire legislature became nominated.

One would not expect the readiness of the Virgin Islanders to accept such drastic reduction and near-elimination of their powers of self-government to be reflected in the larger colonies. In Jamaica

[1] As suggested by Wrong, *op. cit.,* p. 67.
[2] For the controversy that led to its demise in Barbados, see below, p. 90.

it took the Rebellion of 1865 to compel the governing class to re-appraise the political situation.

In that year a number of Negro settlers in St Ann Parish were suffering from lack of food due to an unusually prolonged drought. Inspired by a Native Baptist pastor, they drew up a petition addressed to the Queen asking Her Majesty to open additional Crown lands to settlement. It has been suggested that they had not forgotten the fact that in West African usage such 'tribal' lands would have been free to any who could make use of them. To open such lands, however, would have been to encourage the freedmen to avoid work on the sugar estates whereas the planters were anxious to compel them to return to the cane fields. The planters persuaded the Colonial Office that it was necessary to force the freedmen back on to the estates and the reply to the petition was designed to give the impression of a royal order to do just what the planters wanted. Headed 'the Queen's Advice' it was printed in many copies and widely posted throughout the island. It was a patronizing homily on the virtues of thrift, submission to one's divinely-ordained place in society, and wage-work. Indeed, it was a typical Victorian pro-duction of its kind, not at all different in tone from the effusions of the pious, written for the edification of the British lower classes.[1] The Jamaican settlers believed it to be a message penned personally by the Queen, hitherto adored as their emancipator. They were out-raged and incredulous. They believed either that the Queen had been hoodwinked by their enemies, the estate owners, or else her-self had turned against them. Some time later they gathered at the Morant Bay courthouse with another petition. Warning of their approach had been given and guards posted. Shots were exchanged, the Courthouse stormed and several persons were killed, including the Custos (chief magistrate of the parish). There followed sym-pathetic outbreaks in several other places in the island and the Governor was highly alarmed as were the white landowners. The name 'rebellion' is a rather exaggerated term to describe what was, in fact, no concerted and planned affair but rather a spontaneous reaction against hunger and hopelessness. If unchecked it might indeed have developed into something really revolutionary. As for the whites the horrors of Haiti came to mind at once for they were outnumbered by the browns about six to one and by the Negroes about twenty-five to one. Severe repressive action was taken at once. About thirty persons had been killed by the 'rebels' but three hundred and fifty-four Negroes were hanged by order of the courts martial as well as many more shot without trial. Others were flogged

[1] See, for example, Mrs. Trimmer, *The Servant's Friend, an Exemplary Tale* (London, 1829).

without evidence of their participation in the uprising. One of the most outrageous incidents was the execution of a coloured man, G. W. Gordon, a well-to-do Kingston resident and a member of the Assembly. Gordon was arrested illegally, taken to Morant Bay, tried by court martial and hanged for speeches he had made which it was said had inspired the rebels. The whole affair was reminiscent on a larger scale of the 'Baptist War' of 1831. This time, however, the thoroughly frightened Assembly, after about a month of argument, accepted the advice of Governor Eyre and voted to surrender its powers to the Crown as well as to accept whatever constitution the Crown might choose to confer.

An Act of Parliament was passed (29 Vict. c. 12) authorizing an Order in Council which was duly issued on June 1, 1866, making Jamaica a Crown Colony. Elections were abolished and the Legislative Council was to consist of the Governor, six officials ex-officio, and such unofficial members as the Governor chose to nominate.

Other colonies followed suit at widely varying intervals. Antigua and Grenada did not become Crown Colonies until 1898 and British Guiana retained its Dutch semi-representative system until 1928. Among all the West Indian colonies here considered, Barbados alone kept its all-elected representative assembly. As noted previously, the labour shortage which had upset sugar production in other colonies did not affect Barbados and a relatively higher degree of general prosperity existed there. Nevertheless the Barbadian oligarchy did not differ in essentials from that of other sugar islands and the freedmen were not entirely happy in their lot. Late in 1875 a new Governor was sent to Barbados with instructions to establish the Crown Colony system there as well as a federation with the Windwards (then consisting of Grenada, St Vincent, St Lucia and Tobago). For some time the Governor of Barbados had also been Governor of the Windwards and there were other provisions of joint administration which might seem to foreshadow federation. But the plantocracy was strongly opposed to any real federation with the poverty-stricken Windwards, especially as they had become, or were on the eve of becoming, non-self-governing Crown Colonies. Federation clearly would mean similar reduction in the status of Barbados. The ensuing struggle between Governor and Assembly induced the whites to found a Defence Association for public agitation. The Negroes thought the anti-federation attitude of the 'bims'[1] must be due to the fact that federation would be in the interest of the Negroes. Feeling ran high and on April 22, 1876, there was rioting in Bridgetown and several persons were killed. The Secretary

[1] 'Bim' is a Barbadian Negro term for 'white man'. The Jamaican equivalent is 'buckra'.

of State was not prepared to force the Crown Colony system upon
Barbados but the government obviously needed more control over
money matters and spokesmen in the Assembly. To have officials
there, however, was contrary to Barbadian traditions and the idea
of nominated members in the Assembly highly offensive. In the end
a compromise was reached by way of the Executive Committee
system similar to the abortive device adopted in Jamaica is 1854.
In 1881 the General Assembly of Barbados accepted a bill which
provided that four Assembly members plus one from the second
chamber, the nominated Legislative Council, should work with the
Executive Council to prepare government bills. These five members
would then represent the government in their respective chambers
and enjoy the monopoly of the introduction of money bills. In
Barbados, this system worked reasonably well for a considerable
time.

The Secretaries of State for the Colonies did their best to induce
a general acceptance of the new Crown Colony system and acted
promptly to confer it whenever a colonial legislature could be
persuaded to accept it. The reasons for this preference are obvious
enough. The white oligarchies had proved to be incapable not only
of good government but even of stable and orderly government.
Their inability or unwillingness to meet pressing problems was a
constant incitement to riot and rebellion. On the other hand, a real
representative democracy based on the ignorant and inexperienced
Negro majority was unthinkable. The only remaining possibility
was a Crown autocracy. Not only did the new system free the
Governor to act positively for the benefit of the entire colony without a long struggle with his Assembly, but it enabled him to direct
the use of grants-in-aid received from the British Treasury in many
colonies, which otherwise might be diverted in their own selfish
interest by the oligarchs. Indeed if the Treasury were to provide
such grants, needed to forestall government bankruptcy, the British
government would insist upon a degree of control inconsistent with
the financial powers of the old Assemblies.

The new system was not a move in the direction of democracy,
of course, but it did represent a shift from a selfish, inefficient and
corrupt oligarchy to a relatively benevolent despotism. No West
Indian, instead of a few, now had any real voice in government. But
the officials in charge of the Crown despotism had a disinterested
approach to local interests and often were men of high ability as
well as integrity. Sir John Peter Grant, for example, as Governor of
Jamaica from 1866 to 1873 was able to reform the entire administration of the island and accomplish changes which had been overdue
for generations. He did this with the aid of his department heads

(all Crown-appointed officials) and a legislature with a majority of official members and a minority of unofficial members nominated by the Governor himself. Only the latter were Jamaicans and even if they acted in unanimity they could not block any of the Governor's proposals nor force any of their own against his will.

The governmental system for Jamaica, outlined above, remained in force until 1884, at which time nine *elected* members were added to the Legislative Council. In 1895 the number of elected members was increased to fourteen. This reform was extended to other colonies, but in most cases not until much later. In 1924, elected members were added to the legislatures of Grenada, St Vincent, St Lucia and Trinidad, and in 1936 to that of British Honduras and four of the five Presidencies of the Leeward Islands. These elected members were still not representative of the entire population because the franchise was limited to those meeting certain property qualifications. In Jamaica, for example, the vote was confined to men at age 21, paying rates (local taxes) of 10/- and women at age 30 paying rates of £2 or persons of either sex with a salary of £52 per annum. A candidate for the Legislative Council had to meet a higher property requirement: an income of from £150 to £400, depending upon the colony. There was little general interest in the elected members. Not all who could qualify bothered to register as voters, and such few political parties as attempted to organize remained of no importance.

As mentioned above, the small islands of the Leeward group were gathered into a loose federation in 1871. At first, they were divided into six 'Presidencies', later reduced to four: Antigua; St Christopher, Nevis and Anguilla; Montserrat; the British Virgins. Dominica was an original Presidency but was transferred to the Windward Islands in 1940. Each Presidency had a local representative of the Governor, an Administrator or Commissioner. The new federation was provided with a General Legislative Council and a Federal Executive Council. Each Presidency retained a legislature of its own and the unofficial members of these chose representatives to the General Legislative Council of the federation from their own number. Each Presidency also had delegates to the Federal Executive Council. The local legislatures had all become purely nominative in membership by 1898 and thereafter the General Legislative Council consisted of eight officials and eight unofficial nominees (three from Antigua, three from St Kitts-Nevis and two from Dominica). Subsequently in 1923, one was added from Montserrat and the following year one from the Virgins, as well as an additional official.

The islands remained parochial and mutually jealous. In particular, St Kitts, a small but relatively rich sugar island, objected to the fact that Antigua was the capital of the federation and, it was felt, exercised too much influence on federal affairs. This artificial federal creation did not represent any actual community of interest or feeling but rather an administrative convenience for the joint management of these little territories as regards those matters which could most efficiently be handled in this way. The original federal powers were narrow but Governors found small difficulty in getting the consent of the island legislatures to the extension of federal powers. It should be noted that all the legislatures contained an official majority and the Governor could always use this if needed to pass his bills. In fact, even the unofficial members seldom objected strenuously to the increase in federal subjects. Indeed, the Governor possessed the final authority in any case, whether the matter was handled in the local or the federal legislature. It was not until the presidency legislatures began again to contain elected members that objections were raised to the powers of the federal legislature which still retained its official majority. Then in 1956 the federation of 1871 was dissolved to the general satisfaction of all. According to the Governor, Sir Kenneth Blackburne, there were two reasons for this action: first, the Leeward Federation would be superfluous in view of the proposed British West Indies Federation; second, the introduction of the ministerial system in the several island governments. He mentioned also the wide variation in needs and viewpoints of the presidencies which had led to dissatisfaction with the federal government.[1]

The Windwards (Grenada, the Grenadines, St Vincent, St Lucia, and since 1940, Dominica) exemplified another system. Each of these colonies retained its own legislature and government and there was no joint legislature as in the Leewards. There is, however, only one Governor for the group. He resides in Grenada but is supposed to visit the other Windward colonies at least once a year and to take over active administration during his visit. In between his appearances, each, including Grenada, has an Administrator, who heads the official delegation in the legislature and steers government business there. Normally the Administrator remains in close touch with the Governor and secures his approval in matters of policy, but in emergencies, the Administrator may get in touch with the Secretary of State directly and in exceptional cases consent to a bill on his own responsibility. In sum, one might say that the Windwards are simply not big enough to support the full panoply of Crown Colony administration complete with Governor and staff. Accordingly they were given only one Governor among them but are

[1] See *Trinidad Guardian*, issue of January 29, 1956, p. 2.

administered as if they were completely separate colonies under their deputy-Governor, the Administrator. They have one other common institution which they share with the Leewards—the judicial system, consisting of a Supreme Court of the Windward and Leeward Islands whose puisne judges travel on circuit among the islands.

The system employed in the Windwards with each unit conducting its affairs as if it were a complete colony has avoided the inter-island friction found in the uncomfortable federal union of the Leewards.

World War I had important effects upon the West Indies. Sugar production expanded and there was a degree of war prosperity and inflation. Over fifteen thousand men and about four hundred officers served in the British West Indies Regiment during the war, the great majority of these coming from Jamaica but with sizeable numbers from Trinidad and Barbados and a scattering from the small islands. In their service overseas these men mixed with others from the Dominions and from England. They were introduced to the egalitarian and socialist ideals of the Labour Party now becoming more important year by year. When they returned, some of them brought home with them these new ideas.

The credit for starting the eastern islands of the West Indies on the road to self-government, however, belongs chiefly to a small group of Grenadian middle-class coloured men led by T. A. Marryshow, who formed a Representative Government Association in 1914. This group petitioned the Secretary of State to allow elected representatives in the Legislative Council. Favourable action in this petition was taken at the end of the war but only four out of fourteen members of the Legislative Council were to be elected. Marryshow went at once to England to protest the inadequacy of this reform. The small class of educated and politically interested persons in the various islands were stimulated by Marryshow's example to take similar action. Representative Government Associations were formed in several colonies and St Vincent and St Lucia also petitioned for elected representatives. At length the Secretary of State for the Colonies sent his Under-Secretary, Major the Honourable E. F. L. Wood (later, Lord Halifax) to make a personal survey. The resulting Wood Report became a landmark in West Indies constitutional history.[1]

Wood's suggestions may be summarized as advocating the cautious extension of the elected principle in the colonial legislatures. At first, the *official* element should remain in the majority but the *nominated* unofficials should be reduced in number, their

[1] *Report on the West Indies* Cmd. 1679 (1922).

places taken by *elected* members. Eventually the unofficial element, both nominated and elected should be in the majority. This would allow the electorate to become used to enjoying a constantly increasing share in government. This would be a safe procedure, however, only if care were taken to preserve ultimate authority in the hands of the Secretary of State. To do this the Governor should be empowered to act positively and legislate against the advice of the elected members with the approval of the official bloc and the nominated unofficial members, with reference for ultimate decision to the Secretary of State. This would be a safety device for use only in emergencies. Normally, the Governor would give the elected members as much leeway as possible in legislation. At this stage no elected members should be given seats in the Executive Council.

Wood did not approve of the representative constitutions of Barbados and British Guiana and thought it might be necessary to bring them under the Crown Colony System at some future date.

He found the colonies varied greatly in their demand for a representative element in government. In general, the Leewards were indifferent or actually hostile to such a reform. Dominica was enthusiastic for it as were the Windwards (St Lucia, St Vincent and Grenada). He was unsure of Trinidad because of the danger of frightening foreign capital needed for mineral exploitation and because of its lack of any informed public opinion. However, he recommended the extension of the representative principle to Trinidad as well as St Vincent, St Lucia and Dominica. It existed already, of course, in Barbados and British Guiana, and Jamaica had had elected members in the Legislative Council since 1884.

The suggestions of the Wood Report were accepted by the Secretary of State. Two new Acts of Parliament were passed relating to the Leewards in 1923 and 1924 providing Montserrat with an elected member in the General Legislative Council (to be elected from their number by the Legislature of Montserrat) and the Virgins with a nominated unofficial member in the General Legislative Council, which should also have one more official member. Dominica was given a new Legislative Council (Dominica Ordnance No. 21 of 1924) consisting of the Governor (if present), the Administrator, six officials and six unofficials, four of the latter to be elected and two nominated. Orders in Council established similar arrangements in St Lucia (six officials, three nominated and three elected unofficials), St Vincent (five officials, one nominated and three elected unofficials), Grenada (eight officials, three nominated and five elected unofficials) and Trinidad (twelve officials, six nominated and eleven elected unofficials).

The elections that followed would seem to indicate that the

general public had been little interested in the reforms and the possibility they gave for increased participation in government. Leadership was lacking. No political parties existed as yet and there were few among the politically alert minority who knew anything about the art of electioneering. In St Vincent there were no election contests at all and a minority of seats in Grenada and Trinidad were contested. Nor, with a single exception, did the elections throw up a new type of politician. Much the same kind of middle-class men of relative wealth and conservatism as had been nominated under the previous system now occupied the elected seats. The exception was Captain A. A. Cipriani of Trinidad who was himself a man of the upper middle class but whose appeal was to the common man, the 'barefooted man' as he put it. As an officer in the West Indian Regiment during World War I he had been popular with the men and after the war he had founded a Trinidad Workingmen's Association, rather along the lines of the old mechanics' institutes with emphasis upon educational activities. This was not a trades union and Cipriani insisted that it avoid union activities because of existing legal limitations upon unions. It did, however, provide him with loyal electoral support from 1925 onwards for a number of years. Cipriani was setting the pattern for most successful West Indian politicians of the future.

British Guiana, as noted above, had retained its Dutch colonial semi-representative system and had not been affected by the reforms following the Wood Report. But attention was soon drawn to this mainland colony because of the economic slump that had followed the prosperity of the war period. An economic survey of British Guiana was undertaken by two Members of Parliament sent out by the Secretary of State in 1926. They reported that much blame should be assessed against the constitution under which the government had control of only about one-fifth of the colony's revenue. The rest was at the disposition of the Combined Court, a body representing only the propertied class and tending to block the government's welfare plans.[1] The Governor then appointed a local commission to study reform proposals and the plan produced by this body was accepted by the British government. The British Guiana Act (18 Geo. V, c. 5) was passed authorizing the issuance of an Order in Council providing for a new legislature to consist of the Governor, two officials ex-officio, eight nominated officials, five nominated unofficials and fourteen elected members. The Executive Council, the policy-making body, was to consist of the Governor, the two ex-officio officials from the Legislative Council, four

[1] The report, Cmd. 2341 (1927) was made by R. R. Wilson (Conservative) and B. Snell (Labour).

C

additional officials, and three nominees and two elected members to be chosen by the Governor from the Legislative Council. Under this constitution the elected members of the legislature would be in a minority of one and unofficials in a minority of two in the Executive Council. This constitution was attacked vigorously by some elected members of the old Combined Court led by E. G. (later Sir Eustace) Woolford, who urged the granting of responsible government as a step forward instead of backward.[1] Their arguments were unavailing and British Guiana became a Crown Colony, at long last falling into line with the majority. This had been advocated mildly in the Wood Report and was hailed as a much-needed reform by Sir C. Clementi, a former Governor of British Guiana.[2] Now, it was argued, British Guiana had been led out of the blind alley of the Old Representative System and placed in the path towards gradual and orderly constitutional advance.

By 1930, then, the Crown Colony System had become universal in the British West Indies with the single exception of Barbados. There alone did the lower house of the legislature consist entirely of elected members. But the Crown Colony arrangements were soon to come under sharp attack throughout the area. The depression affected the colonial economy and caused much hardship. Prices of produce dropped, and exports fell. It should be remembered that the typical West Indian is not a subsistence farmer but a wage-worker or a grower of export crops and the depression was felt almost as keenly in the West Indies as in industrial economies. Under these circumstances the Colonial Governments came in for harsh criticism. Their tax revenues dwindled and they could do little more than carry on the minimum of services. The modest salaries of the officials seemed fantastically high to the unemployed West Indians and there was much grumbling in the legislatures about the high cost of government, The officials saw no way of securing revenue even for admittedly overdue improvements in government services. Any new enterprise was clearly impossible. The governments accordingly provided an obvious target for frustration and discontent. In some places the elected members of the legislature resigned in protest of the do-nothing policies of the government or refused to attend Legislative Council meetings.

Under these circumstances it is not astonishing that political reform should be advocated as offering a way out of economic stagnation. The Secretary of State tried to anticipate these demands by appointing a commission to look into the possible federation of the

[1] The Woolford plan is contained in Cmd. 3047 (1927).
[2] See Sir C. Clementi *Constitutional History British Guiana* (London), Macmillan, 1937), p. 402.

eastern islands (Leewards, Windwards and Trinidad). However, the commission advised against federation chiefly because no island wanted to give up its control of tariffs and because Trinidad was averse to throwing its lot in with much poorer small islands. Instead, they suggested that some economy might result from having a single Governor for the entire Eastern Group with an Administrator for each island. The commission recommended also some insignificant advances in self-government.[1] After the commission's appointment but before the publication of its report an informal conference had assembled at Roseau, Dominica in October and November, 1932. This conference advocated a general West Indies federation, the abolition of nominated unofficials in legislatures and the increase in number of elected members so that they would have a majority over the officials.[2] This report doubtless came far closer to representing West Indian public opinion in the matter of constitutional reform at this time than did the official report. It should be noted that 'West Indian public opinion' in the previous sentence refers to the opinions held by a small educated and politically active minority of the population. All the colonies contained large majorities who were still politically inert. Local leaders such as Marryshow in Grenada attacked the British suggestions as far too timid in political reform and failing to provide any answer at all to the economic depression. Owing to the unpopularity of the recommendations, the Secretary of State did not attempt to implement them. Instead, he asked the various legislatures to debate this resolution:

'That the official majority should be abolished; that only those officials whose presence is necessary for the conduct of business should sit as members of the Legislative Council; that an unofficial majority should be created with elected as well as nominated members, on the definite understanding that (in addition to his existing powers of veto) the Governor should be empowered in any stage to carry any measure which he considers necessary in the interests of public order, public faith, or other essentials of good government.'

The resolution was passed by the legislatures of St Vincent and St Lucia in November 1934. In Grenada, T. A. Marryshow tried to get it amended to provide an elected majority and requiring that in normal cases only the Secretary of State's decision could override the decision of the unofficial group. The Secretary of State stood

[1] *Report of the Closer Union Commission.* Cmd. 4383 (1933).
[2] See "Proceedings of the West Indian Conference held at Roseau, Dominica".

firm on the original motion and this was finally accepted by the Grenada legislature.

The new constitutions were provided by Orders in Council in June 1935. They provided that the official and nominated members together should equal the elected members with a casting vote remaining in the hands of the Governor or Administrator. In Grenada the legislature was to consist of the Governor, three officials, four nominated unofficials and seven elected; in St Lucia and St Vincent of the Administrator, two officials, three nominated unofficials and five elected. Again it may be noted that the debates in the Legislative Councils and the proposed constitutional changes were of interest only to a small minority of the population. The electorate was unexcited over the opportunity to elect more members and paid no more attention to the proceedings of the new legislatures than it had to the preceding bodies which had been heavily loaded in favour of the official side.

But the economic depression continued with no end in sight. The new legislatures were quite as helpless as their predecessors to do anything fundamental about the economy which depended upon exports for prosperity and which therefore could scarcely be revitalized by local political action. Times were getting harder. There had been little attempt to diversify the economy of the islands with the help of capital derived from the temporary war boom in sugar. By unfortunate and remarkable coincidence the depression period was also one of plant disease epidemics affecting all the principal export crops (sugar, cocoa, limes and bananas). The high birth rate remained unaffected and the population was increased also by the return of workers who had been employed in Cuba, Panama and elsewhere. Their remittances from abroad ceased at the same time as they came home to swell the numbers of unemployed, along with other members of their families formerly supported by the remittances.[1] The inevitable result was labour disturbances. Strikes occurred even though, as the North American unions found out, the strike weapon is useless in time of depression. Often a strikers' march would be the start of a disturbance or riot. The parading workers would become more and more excited and end with stone-throwing and window-smashing and occasional bloodshed. There were also some cases of arson on the sugar estates.

The first of these disturbances occurred in Trinidad in 1934. During the following year there were similar outbreaks in St Kitts,

[1] The importance of the remittances has been pointed out by Dr Eric Williams, *The Negro in the Caribbean* (Manchester, 1946), p. 43. He estimates that in 1930 Barbados residents received from relatives working abroad a sum equal in value to one-third of the island's exports.

Jamaica, British Guiana and St Vincent. Further rioting took place in Trinidad, Barbados and Jamaica in 1937 and 1938. As Dr Williams points out, the year 1935 might well be regarded as a significant date in West Indies political history.[1] Previously the politically conscious and active group in any of the colonies was very small, and consisted of a few members of the coloured middle class wanting a real share in government for themselves, but differing little from the white officials in their view of the Negro working class as still unready for self-government.

The labour disturbances were to usher in a new era. Some of the returned labourers had become familiar with trade unions in other places as well as ideas, political and social, in sharp contrast with those current in the islands. The Negro working class had been compelled by economic distress to look for leadership to give direction to their efforts and to spell out their needs and objectives. This they found in a new type of leader, new, that is, in the West Indies. Conceivably an upsurge of black racism might have occurred under the stimulus given by the Jamaican Marcus Garvey's United Negro Improvement Society which had been founded in the USA after World War I. Garvey's inflammatory writings had been suppressed in the colonies and his conviction for fraud led to the collapse of the movement although traces of it remain, especially in Jamaica. In fact, however, racism was little involved in the riots. Simey saw them as amounting almost to a 'West Indies social institution', enabling the release of pent-up frustrations and aggravations. He described the typical riot in these terms:

'There are many features in common between all these disturbances; few deaths are caused other than those resulting from armed intervention by the police and military; destruction of property is usually light, no element of racial conflict appears; and the whole affair generally collapses after a demonstration of force on the part of the government concerned.'[2]

The new type of leader produced by the labour riots is exemplified by Tubal Uriah Buzz Butler of Trinidad. He was a former member of the Trinidad Labour Party who had withdrawn to form his own organization which he named the British Empire Workers' and Citizens' Home Rule Party. His speeches were highly spiced with Biblical references and quotations but were also inflammatory. A strike in the oil fields in June 1937 led to his being charged with

[1] See Williams, *op. cit.*, p. 91.
[2] T. S. Simey, *Welfare and Planning in the West Indies* (Oxford, 1946), pp. 23, 24.

incitement to violence. An attempt to arrest him while he was addressing a meeting of his followers led to a riot and subsequent disturbances at Fyzabad and elsewhere. Butler became the idol of many Trinidadian working men and the inspiration of other would-be leaders in Barbados, Grenada and elsewhere. One of these, Clement Payne, a member of Butler's party, went to Barbados in July 1937 and began agitation along Butlerite lines. His claim to be a native of Barbados was challenged by the immigration authorities who moved to deport him. For this purpose he was arrested and his arrest along with rumours of police brutality led to a serious three-day riot in which fourteen persons were killed.

In Jamaica too, unemployment and general economic distress bred disturbances. Here, as well, the numbers of unemployed were increased by returnees from Cuba and the Canal Zone. In 1938 there were disorders at the great Frome sugar estates as well as in Kingston. These labour troubles provided the opportunity for one of the most remarkable politicians in the West Indies to emerge from obscurity. Alexander Bustamante, as he now called himself, who had worked in Panama, Cuba and New York, had returned to his native island where he engaged in the business of money lender. He began to make public speeches and almost overnight he was accepted by the Jamaican labouring class as their spokesman. In May, 1938, a demand for increased wages by Kingston longshore-men led to a strike which became city-wide and was accompanied by violence. The police jailed a number of rioters but six were killed and several injured. As the acknowledged spokesman for the longshoremen, Bustamante and his lieutenant, Grant (a Garveyite from New York), were arrested and charged with 'sedition and incitement'. At this point, a noted barrister, Norman W. Manley, who happened to be a first cousin of Bustamante, began legal proceedings for the release on bail of the arrested labour leaders. From this point forward for some time there was close association between Manley and Bustamante. Shortly the dock workers organized themselves into the Bustamante Industrial Trades Union with some two thousand founding members.[1] From the start this was a 'blanket' union accepting all categories of workers. By November, 1938, its membership included four thousand agricultural workers, mainly

[1] This is probably the only labour union in the world to be named after an individual. The Governor (Sir Arthur Richards) was much opposed to this nomenclature and it took considerable persuasion on Manley's part to induce him to accept it and permit the registration of the union, which was not registered officially until January, 1939. This was not the first general all-purpose union in Jamaica. Its predecessor was the Jamaica Workers and Tradesmen's Union (registered, 29 June, 1937) in which 'Busta' had held office. See Trades Unionism in Jamaica 1918 to 1946, pamphlet issued by Central Bureau of Statistics (Kingston, 1946).

sugar estate labour, as well as over two thousand waterfront labourers. In 1938 also, Manley founded his People's National Party which was shortly challenged by the Jamaica Labour Party founded by Bustamante upon his release from internment for 'subversive' activities. This internment had lasted from September, 1940, to February, 1942, and the new party was formed at once to contest the elections held that year. Manley was in many ways typical of the older type of respectable, educated, middle-class West Indian politician except for his attachment to West Indies nationalism and socialism. 'Busta' was typical of the new leadership, appealing to the uneducated masses and skilled in emotive oratory.

All these disturbances led to two more official investigations, the first by the Secretary of State's Labour Adviser, Major Orde-Browne, who analyzed the root causes of discontent and predicted further disorders.[1] Then the British government decided on a full-scale survey of the entire problem. A Royal Commission was appointed in August, 1938, under the chairmanship of Lord Moyne and including such well-known public men as Sir Walter Citrine, Sir Reginald Stubbs and Sir Percy Mackinnon. The Commissioners spent about five months in the area, spending time in every colony from British Honduras to British Guiana. The resulting report was the most complete and penetrating study ever made of the British West Indies.[2] The Commissioners were interested in all aspects of the problem, including the political, on the ground that many West Indians believed their troubles to stem from lack of self-government.[3]

They examined the Crown Colony System, which they described as 'neither an autocracy nor a democracy'. The Governors, they found, were not pure autocrats but benevolent despots who considered the views of their legislatures and other elements in colonial society before deciding on a policy. The trouble with this system they found to be not any incompetence or malevolence on the official side but the inescapable tendency of the elected element to form a *permanent opposition to the government*. The elected members could never hope to enjoy power on the executive or policy-forming side. They tended, therefore, to assert themselves in finding fault with government policies and this without any responsibility to formulate and develop practical, alternative policies. The Commissioners accordingly advocated the introduction into Executive Council of the unofficial element without destroying the Governor's initiative as policy-leader in the Executive Council, or his reserved

[1] Cmd. 6070 (1939).
[2] Cmd. 6607 (1945).
[3] Moyne Report, p. 73.

power to legislate contrary to the wishes of his legislature in case of necessity. They suggested also that in the larger colonies it might be desirable to assign the unofficial members of Executive Council to committees which would be concerned with various departments of the administration. The permanent department heads would also be members of these committees and the unofficial members of the Executive Council would thus have a chance to acquaint themselves with the details of departmental problems. The unofficial member on the committee, although without authority over the department or its functions, would be in a position to represent 'his' department in the legislature as a kind of quasi-minister. Official representation in the legislature could then be reduced to the minimum of the Colonial Secretary (as chief spokesman for the government), the Attorney-General and the Colonial Treasurer. The places formerly occupied by other officials could be filled by nominated unofficials chosen by the Governor for individual merit and usefulness as well as to represent important elements in the colony's life not otherwise represented. At this stage the Commissioners did not advocate any expansion of the elective element in government although they did recommend broadening the suffrage with universal adult suffrage as the ultimate goal, perhaps to be attained at varying times in the several colonies.

Another very important recommendation was that the already existing Colonial Development fund be enlarged and its uses expanded to include welfare spending. It was suggested that £1,000,000 per annum be spent on West Indian welfare projects by an official directly responsible to the Secretary of State. This recommendation resulted in the passage of the Colonial Development and Welfare Act (1940) appropriating £5,000,000 for the whole colonial empire of which about one-fifth was allocated to the West Indies to be administered by the Comptroller of Colonial Development and Welfare for the West Indies.

CHAPTER III

PROBLEMS OF THE AREA

BEFORE proceeding to examine constitutional and political developments in the individual colonies it might be well to give additional consideration to some of the economic and social factors mentioned briefly in the introductory chapter for only in social perspective can the purely governmental side of a society be seen in depth and reality.

It is hard to start a discussion of Caribbean area problems without quoting the famous remark of Professor W. M. Macmillan who wrote more than twenty years ago: 'A social and economic study of the West Indies is . . . necessarily a study of poverty.'[1] Some significant economic developments have occurred in recent years and yet the remark is scarcely less true today than when it was written.[2] That this is the case cannot fairly be attributed to any single factor nor is there a villain to receive the major share of the blame.[3] Basically, the situation is simple enough. As in most tropical countries, the West Indian economy is based principally upon the export of agricultural products. The exploitation of forest and mineral resources has been important in certain colonies, notably oil and pitch in Trinidad, bauxite in British Guiana and Jamaica, and timber in British Guiana and British Honduras. It is possible that further discoveries may extend or diversify the list of exploitable minerals but only unexpected developments can alter the picture radically.

The West Indies, therefore, must be classed as an underdeveloped area so long as it must rely upon export agriculture and consequently dependent upon the industrial economies which buy its produce and supply it with manufactures. Of all the natural resources, oil, as long as it lasts, is the most spectacular wealth-pro-

---

[1] *Warning from the West Indies: A Tract for Africa and the Empire* (London, Faber & Faber, Ltd., 1936).
[2] Cumper points out that real wages have tended to remain almost constant in the sugar industry over a long period, the wage increases achieved by collective bargaining corresponding to the increased cost of living. See G. E. Cumper, 'Labour Demand and Supply in the Jamaican Sugar Industry 1830-1950', *Economic and Social Studies*. 2, 4 (March, 1954), 84.
[3] For a discussion of British economic policies in relation to the colonies, see *below*, Chapter VI, pp. 129 ff.

ducer. Trinidad, therefore, is the most prosperous of the colonies. The small Dutch islands have enjoyed an even higher prosperity and for the same reason. Indeed, the oil industry in Curaçao and Aruba required more labour than these islands could supply, and, as a consequence, provided lucrative work for many British West Indians, mainly from the Windwards. The small businessmen of St Lucia, St Vincent and Dominica in many cases acquired the capital needed to start their enterprises by means of savings accumulated while working in the Dutch colonies. This would have been impossible in their home islands.

Except for a fortunate few, most West Indians depend directly upon agriculture for a living and of these, a majority do not farm their own land but are wage-workers on sugar estates or other farms or plantations. The crops produced on these are nearly all for export and face sharp competition in the world market. Most of them are not susceptible to a high degree of mechanization. Sugar cane is rarely harvested in any way but by the age-old method of the cutlass wielded by a strong black arm. Whether the product be coconuts, limes, cocoa, cotton or chicle it still requires a preponderance of hand labour. Not only is mechanization difficult of application in the case of such crops but it has not been applied as widely as it might have been. It is estimated that the fullest use of chemical weed-killers and reaping machines might reduce by as much as fifty per cent the amount of labour needed on sugar estates.[1] But the industry has been slow to adopt labour-saving devices and methods because of the serious unrest this would create in communities suffering from chronic underemployment. In British Guiana, at least until very recently, the large sugar estates were managed according to a system that might be described as semifeudal paternalism. An estate there may cover ten thousand acres and employ about ten thousand workers. The management actually did not know the precise number of employees and many of the older workers had no specific job. There was no work classification system and overhiring was common. Many estate workers also cultivate rice lands and customarily have been allowed to divert water from the irrigation ditches of the sugar estates.

So far, the principal technological advance in West Indian cane and sugar production has been the replacement of oxen and mules by tractors. Even this is not universal. Many of the small-holding East Indian cane farmers of Trinidad still haul their canes to the mill in two-wheeled carts drawn by oxen.

Under such circumstances it is impossible to predict a high

[1] G. E. Cumper, 'Two Studies in Jamaican Productivity', *Social and Economic Studies*, 1, 2, (June, 1953), 70.

VALUE OF EXTERNAL TRADE[1]

	Imports (c.i.f.)		(£ million) Exports (f.o.b.)	
	1948	1956	1948	1956
Barbados	6.35	12.7	3.05	7.47
British Guiana	10.0	20.9	7.71	19.8
British Honduras	2.0	3.99	1.53	2.49
Jamaica	19.9	58.3	11.5	38.8
Leeward Islands	1.89	4.71	1.46	3.44
Trinidad	27.5	62.8	27.6	68.9
Windward Islands	3.17	6.65	1.90	4.04
Total	70.8	170	54.75	145

DIRECTION OF EXTERNAL TRADE

	Imports			(percentages) Exports		
	1936-38	1948	1956	1936-38	1948	1956
United Kingdom	38.0	34.5	37.3	44.0	43.6	39.7
Other Sterling Areas[2]	11.7	9.3	10.5	7.1	8.6	9.7
United States	18.1	18.2	16.7	9.8	6.2	10.1
Canada	14.9	21.3	10.9	21.6	17.1	16.6
Central and South America	4.3	11.3	11.4	1.2	7.6	3.0
Others	11.6	4.7	11.7	11.4	7.8	12.7
Unclassified	1.4	0.7	1.4	4.8	9.2	8.1
Total	100	100	100	100	100	100

standard of living, by industrial standards, for most West Indian labour in the foreseeable future. Industrialization, which must raise living standards is hard to accomplish. Capital is not readily available, for various reasons. Local accumulations of investment capital in the hands of wealthy individuals, banks and insurance companies, tend to find investment elsewhere. Despite tax remission inducements, investment in local industry is not highly attractive to the capitalist, foreign or domestic. The buying power of the colonial community is low, for the bulk of the population lives at or near the subsistence level. Local needs have created small industries found in all the colonies to manufacture cotton or rayon clothing. Rum is distilled for domestic consumption as well as for export. There are breweries in several colonies. But industries that can find an export market are rare.[3] Distance, poor transport facilities, lack of local raw materials, few skills and low productivity of local labour discourage the introduction of export industries. It is also a fact that

---

[1] Tables from British Information Services pamphlet I.D. 1282, December 1957.
[2] Including trade between colonial territories in the West Indies group.
[3] As Albert Gomes put it in his column in the Trinidad *Sunday Guardian,* issue of July 14, 1957, p. 24: 'The West Indian manufacturer has readymade markets nowhere. Wherever he sells, he sells against tariff barriers, and, until inter-island trade is rationalized under Federal auspices, the West Indian manufacturer's domestic market will continue to be as large as the island in which he manufactures'.

many labour unions are led by inexperienced leaders who feel it necessary to be aggressive and unreasonable and who do not understand the principles of collective bargaining and the proper use of the strike weapon. This, together with poor union discipline, makes it difficult to establish sound labour-management relations. Most union members have no real conception as to what a union is and what it can and cannot do. A union may be organized in a burst of enthusiasm only to lose most of its members if they do not receive tangible benefits at once. Some will come to the union office a week after joining and demand their money back. Few union leaders have made much effort to educate the members or even to keep them informed of what the union is doing or intends to do. Membership rises and falls suddenly. Needlessly aggressive and noisy union leadership has its excuse in the attempt to keep members interested and consequently 'financial'. While there are well-organized and well-led West Indian unions, there are also many that could be described as semi-fraudulent and organized principally to serve the financial and political ambitions of the leaders.

Labour productivity is low in the West Indies. There are several 'pat' explanations for this: the tropical daytime heat, African 'laziness', the bad traditions of the slavery period. Even sympathetic observers assert that lack of enterprise and self-reliance are only too characteristic of West Indian labour. Many are inclined to say: 'Somebody owes me a bread'. A labour party leader at a political street meeting in 1954 remarked that England is the Mother Country and as a good mother should nourish her children. This dependent attitude may derive in part from the economic and social conditions of slavery when the ordinary man could not plan his own future and expected to be taken care of, after a fashion, by the master-class. But this is pure speculation. It seems far more probable that the two factors of most significance in the low productivity of West Indian labour are: the high incidence of underemployment and unemployment which induces the employed man to make the job last as long as possible, and the colour-class social complex which tends to stifle ambition by making economic or social advance appear hopeless for the uneducated Negro.

As a labour economist has pointed out, the transition to industrial work from agricultural work is not easy. The field worker's day is often only five or six hours and his work-week three or four days during the six months or so of employment. He finds it difficult to adjust to the long hours and constant activity of industry.[1] Hence

[1] See W. H. Knowles, 'Social Consequences of Economic Change in Jamaica' *Annals of American Academy of Political and Social Science*, 305 (May, 1956) 134-144.

the high rate of turnover, high percentage of absenteeism, tardiness and lack of responsibility which discourages capital investment.[1] Knowles notes that when labour is given a real incentive the attitude towards the job changes and the worker is far more productive. This has been proven by the experience of employers of West Indians in the United States, and by some local employers who have raised wages above the going rate in return for increased production.

The picture is not entirely gloomy. Some industrialization is taking place and improvements in transport should render enterprise in the West Indies more attractive to outside capital. The mainland colonies may have important mineral wealth, oil in particular, as yet undiscovered. Certainly the tourist industry has considerable possibilities of expansion when West Indian hotel men are able to provide the facilities demanded and as the cost of air travel decreases. The completely reliable winter climate of the islands and the truly magnificent scenery many of them possess make them ideal places for a vacation. Jamaica has, so far, profited most from the tourist industry and it is also important in Barbados. There is no reason why it cannot become a principal 'invisible export' for many others.

The colonial governments of course are well aware of the economic problem and are taking what steps they can to encourage new industry. The Colonial Development Corporation created by the Overseas Resources and Development Act, 1948, has underwritten a few projects[2] and local insurance companies are attempting to find local investments. Economic co-operation between the colonies is of growing importance and should become more important when federation is complete. There can be little doubt that capitalization of new industries would be a minor problem if such industries were likely to be profitable. Even if transportation costs and the need to import raw materials were not involved, Caribbean industries to become important must be export industries and so be able to hurdle tariff walls and compete with the products of industrial economies

[1] The need for increased capital investment with government encouragement was stressed in the study made by the International Bank for Reconstruction and Development, *Economic Development of Jamaica* (Baltimore, 1952).
[2] According to the UN *Special Study on Economic Conditions in Non-Self-Governing Territories* (NY, 1955) a summary of CDC operations in the West Indies to the end of 1952 shows that some £7,178,000 had been invested in agricultural, manufacturing, electric power and other projects. This is in addition to the estimated C.D. & W. expenditure of £5,378,000 under the 1940 Act and £9,922,000 under the 1945 Act up to March, 1952. According to the report by Sir Stephen Luke, Comptroller for Development and Welfare in the West Indies, 'Development and Welfare in the West Indies, 1955-1956' (Col. No. 335) p. 6, the grand total of C.D. & W. grants to the British West Indies for the sixteen-year period ending March 31, 1956, came to £35,978,508 or $BWI 172,696,838.

COLONIAL DEVELOPMENT AND WELFARE GRANTS AND LOANS*
Commitments from 1st April, 1946–31st March, 1957

(£ thousand)

	Development and Welfare Grants	Loans	Research Grants	Total
General	4,999	10	1,743	6,752
Barbados	1,335	nil	11	1,346
British Guiana	6,684	384	119	7,187
British Honduras	3,234	53	38	3,325
Jamaica	6,747	293	128	7,169
Leeward Islands:				
General	362	nil	15	377
Antigua	1,147	33	nil	1,180
Montserrat	272	nil	nil	272
St. Christopher-Nevis-Anguilla	318	7	nil	325
Virgin Islands	166	nil	nil	166
Trinidad	563	nil	240	803
Windward Islands:				
General	511	nil	10	521
Dominica	1,410	nil	1	1,411
Grenada	858	nil	1	859
St. Lucia	2,191	26	nil	2,217
St. Vincent	831	29	1	861

REVENUE AND EXPENDITURE

(£ thousand)

	1939 Rev.	1939 Exp.	1952 Rev.	1952 Exp.	1956 (est.) Rev.	1956 (est.) Exp.
Barbados	612	627	2,866	2,593	3,939	3,577
British Guiana	1,312	1,357	6,759	6,468	8,629	8,575
British Honduras	441	441	1,230	1,227	1,882	1,256
Jamaica	3,082	3,164	13,925	14,153	20,597	20,369
Leeward Islands:						
Antigua	127	152	878	868	1,504	1,520
St. Christopher-Nevis-Anguilla	148	180	769	707	1,034	1,179
Montserrat	29	35	123	137	247	249
Virgin Islands	9	11	80	66	155	151
Trinidad and Tobago	2,796	2,708	13,914	13,019	18,343	19,591
Windward Islands:						
Dominica	79	79	495	369	622	554
Grenada	158	174	808	789	962	1,051
St. Lucia	130	133	850	723	715	707
St. Vincent	102	100	432	439	710	710

These figures include receipts from and expenditure by United Kingdom Colonial Development and Welfare funds and grants-in-aid from the United Kingdom.

* Tables from British Information Services pamphlet 1282, December, 1957.

DEVELOPMENT PLANS IN 1956

	Total	CD & W Funds	Loan Funds	Local Resources
		(£ thousand) Sources from which financed		
Barbados	10,421	724	6,061	3,636
British Guiana	19,000	4,375	12,125	2,500
British Honduras	3,405	3,010	280	115
*Jamaica	—	—	—	—
Leeward Islands:				
Antigua	1,111	796	167	148
Montserrat	254	234	20	nil
*St. Christopher-Nevis-Anguilla	—	—	—	—
Virgin Islands	159	127	32	nil
*Trinidad and Tobago	—	—	—	—
Windward Islands:				
Dominica	1,109	909	200	nil
Grenada	687	687	nil	nil
St. Lucia	1,280	1,280	nil	nil
St. Vincent	954	594	360	nil

*Plans for Jamaica, St. Christopher-Nevis-Anguilla and Trinidad are being revised and no figures are available.

that enjoy mass markets. Size is important in this connection. The total population of the British West Indies even if it were concentrated in a single territory is insufficient to support, for example, a motor car industry even if there were a strong local demand for the product.

The success achieved in Puerto Rico by the industrialization programme called 'Operation Bootstrap" cannot be duplicated in the British West Indies. The Puerto Rican achievement is due in part to the large amount of American capital available, possibly also to a relatively larger number of skilled workers among the population, and, of key importance, the nearby continental market open to Puerto Rican products. Without these advantages Puerto Rico could hardly hope to do better than the Dominican Republic where the average income and literacy remain at the low Caribbean standard.[1] It is pertinent to note that the American Virgin Islands, while enjoying a larger tourist trade income than the British Leewards, and an American market for rum, have essentially the same economic problems as the Leewards and have not been able to achieve the measure of economic advance found in Puerto Rico.

[1] UNESCO *Basic Facts and Figures* (Paris, 1956) indicates percentages of adult *illiteracy* based on census enumerations as follows: for the British colonies of Barbados, British Honduras, Jamaica, the Leeward Islands, Trinidad and Tobago, an average of 19.4%. The lowest is Barbados with 9% and the highest Jamaica with 28%. This compares favourably not only with 57% for the Dominican Republic and 89% for Haiti, but even with 22% for Cuba and 25% for Puerto Rico.

SUGAR PRODUCTION AND EXPORTS*

(thousand tons)

	Production		Exports		Commonwealth
	1948	1956	1948	1956	Agreement Quota
Barbados	78.2	151.0	72.0	141.0	163.0
British Guiana	163.0	263.0	137.0	246.0	225.0
Jamaica	193.0	362.0	160.0	369.0	270.0
Antigua	11.9	28.5	12.4	27.0	32.0
St. Christopher-Nevis-Anguilla	31.3	49.8	28.6	47.9	40.9
Trinidad	116.6	162.0	95.1	148.0	157.85
St. Lucia	9.2	10.9	6.6	9.13	11.25
St. Vincent	2.35	3.94	0.4	1.25	1.5

TRINIDAD PETROLEUM*

(thousand tons)

		Imports		Exports	
	Production	Crude	Refined	Crude	Refined
1936-38 average	2,078	65	1.69	76	1,923
1948	2,697	1,188	3.21	280	3,330
1956	4,074	2,759	111.0	556	6,084

BAUXITE EXPORTS*

(thousand tons)

	British Guiana	Jamaica Bauxite	Alumina
1936-38 average	282	nil	nil
1948	1,873	nil	nil
1953	2,115	1,139	28.8
1956	2,108	2,604	207

In some colonies extractive industries have added considerably to government income but, except in the case of Trinidad's oil, have had relatively little effect upon general living standards. The bauxite extraction and refining industries in Jamaica and British Guiana employ too few to have much effect upon the labour surplus. The three companies operating in Jamaica gave direct employment to about five thousand persons in 1956. Some of these were used in construction work and it is estimated that the companies will give permanent employment to a maximum of four thousand workers. Government revenue from the companies is of much greater significance. New arrangements were completed in March, 1957, under which the companies agreed to a greatly increased rate of income tax (40%) and a royalty of four shillings per ton for production over one million tons, the rate to be lowered for production over two million tons. It is estimated that the government

* Table from British Information Services pamphlet I.D. 1282, December, 1957.

will receive about one quarter of its total income from this source, as compared with 1.7% in 1956-57, an amount sufficient to wipe out the unfavourable balance of trade.[1] The fact remains that for some time the population growth has regularly outstripped the increase in production, while at the same time opportunities for emigration have shrunk. There is less chance than in former times to get work in the Canal Zone, Cuba, the Netherlands West Indies or elsewhere nearby. The handful of farm labourers recruited each year for seasonal work in the United States represent a minute proportion of the surplus labour and almost none of these can hope for permanent emigration to the USA. Permanent emigration is possible for the great majority only to Great Britain. The cost of travel is a handicap in this case and many have been discouraged by the British climate and what they have heard about living conditions for West Indians in England.[2] Of course a good many come to the United States as students or visitors. According to the Trinidad and Tobago Central Statistical Office report for the year 1953, 4,376 persons left the colony for the United Kingdom in that year and 30,584 went to the USA.

Emigration remains far below the rate of population growth. The birth rate remains extremely high.[3] This would seem to be due to several factors. All poor, rural people have high birth rates. The West Indian pattern of sexual behaviour tends to employ all or almost all of the fertility period of women in the production of children. Whether Herskovits is correct in assuming a persistence of West African mating habits or whether Henriques is right in regarding these practices as a heritage of the slavery period, the fact remains that loose and temporary unions as well as those of greater duration are socially tolerated, that little or no stigma attaches to illegitimacy among the poor and that in some communities there are, indeed, social pressures tending to induce girls to prove their

[1] See Ministry Paper No. 2 (March 21, 1957) issued by the Jamaica Ministry of Development. (Additional information from the Central Planning Unit of the Chief Minister's Office).
   In March, 1958, one of the two companies (the Kaiser Co.) paid £1,270,712 income tax for 1957, having shipped 2,331,838 long dry tons of bauxite during that year. Altogether 3,644,253 long dry tons of bauxite were exported in 1957 as well as additional alumina.
[2] See G. W. Roberts, 'Study of External Migration Affecting Jamaica', *Social and Economic Studies,* Supplement to Vol. 7, No. 2 (June, 1958).
[3] The United Nations Statistical Yearbook (1956) lists Singapore as having the world's highest reported birth rate with 48.9 live births per 1,000 population. Mexico and the St Kitts-Nevis group in the Leewards have 46.2, British Guiana 43, St Vincent 42.5, British Honduras 42, Trinidad and Tobago 41.9 The USA birthrate is 24.6. These figures differ slightly from those given in the table prepared by the Colonial Office.

D

VITAL STATISTICS*

		Birth Rate per '000	Death Rate per '000	Infant Mortality Rate per '000 live births
Barbados	1937	29.9	18.5	217.0
	1951	32.0	14.2	136.0
	1956	30.8	10.6	96.7
British Guiana	1937	35.0	21.9	121.0
	1951	42.5	13.5	76.8
	1956	42.4	11.2	63.8
British Honduras	1937	32.9	18.5	122.6
	1951	41.4	11.4	94.6
	1956	45.5	10.0	69.0
Jamaica	1937	32.4	15.3	118.5
	1951	33.9	12.1	81.2
	1956	37.3	9.5	54.0
Leeward Islands	1937	37.5	21.8	161.3
	1951	35.8	13.6	87.5
	1956	38.9	10.4	55.2
Trinidad and Tobago	1937	32.9	17.4	120.5
	1951	36.7	12.0	78.2
	1956	36.6	9.6	63.5
Windward Islands	1937	33.8	14.6	112.0
	1951	38.1	15.9	116.6
	1956	41.4	12.8	103.1

* Table from British Information Services pamphlet I.D. 1282, December, 1957.

womanhood by early pregnancies.[1] While legal marriage is generally admired, this seems to be because it is associated with higher social status. Many women refuse marriage and prefer 'faithful concubinage' because husbands may become tyrannical and cannot, like lovers, be turned away at will. All of these statements apply to the lower class, including the large majority of the population. The middle class has accepted European standards in this as in other matters and has a lower birth rate.

In any case, as noted by a demographic specialist, a reasonable forecast is that the population of the British West Indies may double within a twenty-three year period unless there is large-scale emigration. In the case of crowded Barbados this would bring about a population density of approximately 2,500 persons per square mile within twenty-five years—this is an agricultural area![2]

The very high birth rate means that children of the poorer

[1] See M. J. Herskovits, The Myth of the Negro Past (New York, 1941) and Fernando Henriques, Family and Colour in Jamaica (London, Eyre & Spottiswoode, 1953). See also Raymond T. Smith, 'The Family in the Caribbean' and 'Discussion' by John V. Murra, Caribbean Studies: A Symposium, Institute of Social and Economic Research, UCWI, Jamaica, 1957, pp. 67-79.

[2] See G. W. Roberts, "Some Demographic Considerations of West Indian Federation' Social and Economic Studies, 6, 2 (June, 1957) 274, 276, and David Lowenthal, 'The Population of Barbados', ibid., 6, 4 (December, 1957) 445-501.

families, especially in rural areas, obtain little schooling. Many of them will attend school from one to three days a week for a time, the absences occurring in the latter part of the week because of lack of clean clothing or the need to help the mother prepare her provisions for market. After leaving school, the low degree of literacy learned is often forgotten as no further use of this skill is made. As they mature, these children swell the ranks of the under-employed and begin to play their part in maintaining the high birth rate. No serious attempt is made to enforce school attendance nor could the schools begin to accommodate the entire school-age population were attendance enforced.

A by-product of poverty and unemployment is the universal incidence of crimes against property. Most of these are petty theft including much 'praedial larceny'—the theft of growing crops. Despite severe punishments inflicted upon all who are caught by the police, the crime wave is permanent. Although starvation does not occur, there is much undernourishment. The diet of the poorest is deficient in proteins. Animal foods are mainly of poor quality and rarely available to many. Even among peasant proprietors the tendency is to sell the chickens in the market and eat only the oldest and toughest hens. Price controls have militated against breeding cattle for quality although there have been recent private as well as government attempts at stock improvement. Fish are not abundant in commercial quantities except near Trinidad and off the coast of British Honduras and British Guiana. Elsewhere the beautiful, clear, blue water of the Caribbean is not well enough stocked to supply a sufficient quantity of fish at low prices for the majority of the population. Fishing methods are primitive and entail some danger on wind-swept waters. Only recently has there been an attempt by the Barbadian government to assist in the motorization of the Barbadian flying-fish boats. In some of the islands freshwater fish culture is being encouraged in ponds constructed on waste lands. This is a recent development and it is too soon to say whether it is likely to result in any substantial increase in the protein food available to the very poor.

The distribution and use of land is not always such as to produce the best results. As Cohen points out, a Jamaican hill village is likely to contain one or two families with a surplus of land which they may not cultivate over long periods while others must work their land to death, hire their own labour to larger landowners and send their older children to try to earn a living in Kingston.[1]

[1] See *Social and Economic Studies*, 2, 4, 104-133 (March, 1954) article by Yehudi Cohen, 'The Social Organization of a Selected Community in Jamaica'. See also *ibid.*, 5, 3, 295-312 (September, 1956) article by M. G. Smith, 'Community Organization in Rural Jamaica'.

Economic striving is continuous and fiercely competitive and arouses feelings of envy and anxiety to a morbid degree, even though in such villages of smallholders actual want is uncommon. Money is desired, not to invest but to hoard in anticipation of some disaster, particularly illness. There is little mutual aid or co-operation even as between members of the same family, except as to the custom of trading work-days, done on a *quid pro quo* basis. There would seem to be no truly cohesive social group in the community, which presents a picture of rugged individualism to an extreme degree. Any community organization that exists is due to the influence of outsiders. Altogether the social climate of such a community is inimical to the development of leadership or group spirit. To such people, the government remains an outside power and the implications of this for the operation of political democracy are obvious. At the same time, the existence of a large proportion of peasant proprietors among the rural population militates against the acceptance of collectivistic panaceas.

It is also true that population pressure is mounting in most of the islands and that there is no immediate or simple solution. The two mainland colonies alone have considerable areas of unexploited land although its development is far from easy because of transportation problems and other considerations. The governments of the colonies are well aware of their problem and in almost every case have attempted to tackle it in one way or another. Where religious objections are not insurmountable, as in protestant Barbados, there has been some government support of birth control clinics. It is still too early to assess the impact of such measures on the problem. Public health has improved to such an extent in recent years that the infant mortality rate has dropped considerably and this in turn, has stepped up the unemployment and general population pressure.

A by-product of this general poverty is the natural tendency on the part of the 'barefooted man' to blame 'colonialism' and the selfishness of the small propertied class for his wretched condition. This means that the average man will be attracted politically by leaders and parties promising a rosy economic future to their supporters. Nor is the ordinary voter able to discriminate very well between competing political programmes or to access the practicability of the politician's promises. His electoral choice is likely to result from an emotional response to skillful oratory or to pressures from his social group. His lack of education, however, insulates him from intellectual radicalism which is confined to a very small number of educated urbanites. Sometimes he may follow and vote for a crypto-Communist leader but only because this leader's appeal is couched in terms of local nationalism, anti-colonialism and higher income.[1]

Colonies in which there are differences of race between the governing class and the governed majority are certain to develop some of the characteristics of a plural society. In the case of the West Indies, as compared with the Asiatic colonies, there was the additional fact that for a considerable period the society consisted mainly of Negro slaves, dominated and governed by a white planter class and white officials. Additional complications ensued with the emergence of an intermediate class of free coloured persons. Under such circumstances it was impossible to have a coherent society in which differences of class or status would be less important than membership in a single all-embracing community. Indeed, there was no really significant all-colony community feeling in the West Indies until, perhaps, very recently. The whites regarded themselves as Britons in exile. Their interest in the colony was entirely economic. England was still 'home'. The Negroes were without much in the way of community feeling or organization even at the village level. Such organized groups as they had were mainly religious. Their attitudes towards their white employers and rulers varied all the way from subservience and an acceptance of low status to bitter anti-white prejudice. As Barbara Ward has written: 'the three ways of looking at white-skinned peoples—veneration, equality, hatred,—can still be found in Asia and Africa.'[2] Miss Ward might have included the West Indies. The tensions of the slavery period found expression occasionally in riots, house-burnings and retaliatory action by police and military.

After emancipation it was necessary for both whites and freedmen to adjust themselves to a changing society and one in which the intermediate coloured class was destined to play an increasingly important part. Unlike the Eurasians of India the West Indian coloured group early became a socially and economically important minority in most of the colonies. The whites continued to occupy many high places, to represent the dominant culture and to set standards of dress, behaviour, and so forth. But they were too few to fill all the professional and mercantile middle-class posts. In time, therefore, the middle class was recruited largely from among creoles who had managed to secure a professional education, or sufficient schooling to secure 'white collar' employment, or who were shrewd enough to succeed in business. Naturally such middle-class recruits were found most frequently among the coloured people who had, in some cases, received inheritances from their

---

[1] See *below*, Chap. IX, for a fuller treatment of this paragraph.
[2] Article in *New York Times Magazine*, November 11, 1956, p. 69.

white ancestors. The Negro rarely had such advantages and it was only in unusual instances that brilliance, tenacity and luck would enable him to secure acceptance in middle-class society. He was not readily received socially, had fewer chances to make good in a business enterprise, and at the start of his career had to overcome the serious disadvantage of his colour even if his native ability was superior to that of his lighter-skinned competitors.

West Indian social stratification can be summarized in general terms as follows: the *upper class* consists of the principal British officials, white landowners, some professionals and businessmen, especially those of old, established colonial families and, in some colonies, a very few coloured families of considerable wealth or high eminence in the professions.[1] The *upper middle class* consists of whites of lesser wealth and importance, the local representatives of British banks and firms and coloured people of equivalent or higher economic status and education including professionals and upper civil servants. The *lower middle class* includes the bulk of the clerical and civil service employees, both coloured and Negro, self-employed small businessmen, some skilled artisans, some Negro peasant proprietors and elementary schoolteachers. The *lower class,* including as many as ninety per cent of the total population is made up of propertyless labourers, rural and urban, poor peasant small-holders, some artisans and semi-skilled workmen. In Barbados and some other places it also includes small enclaves of poor whites.[2] Illiteracy, underemployment, and unemployment are highest among this class but there is much variation in this respect among the colonies.

The East Indians, a few in Jamaica but mostly located in Trinidad and British Guiana, are still generally of the lower class although many have begun the social ascent through business success, the acquisition of education and professional eminence. The Portuguese of British Guiana and Trinidad and the Chinese found in all the colonies are mainly small shopkeepers and clerical employees of the lower middle class.

Class and social status are very important in the eyes of West Indians, especially those of the middle classes. Some exhibit an unhealthy preoccupation with this. Few middle-class families or individuals feel entirely secure socially and strive hard to ensure

[1] The word 'coloured' is used here and throughout in its West Indian meaning of a person of mixed European and non-white ancestry. The mixture may include Indian or Chinese as well as Negro forbears.
[2] The largest such group is the Barbadian 'Redlegs'. These people are said to be descended from the Duke of Monmouth's soldiery, exiled to Barbados after the rebellion of 1685. They have seldom mixed with the Negroes but live like poor Negro peasants.

or advance their social position. The small and somewhat ingrown nature of the community, even in the larger colonies, increases the awareness of social acceptance or rejection. The ambitious Negro can sometimes improve his status not only through success at a respectable vocation but by marrying a socially acceptable wife. Preferably the wife should be white or at least of very light colour. An unfortunate by-product of this situation is that educated women of dark colour are doomed to spinsterhood unless willing to marry men who are much their inferior in status and education.[1]

The development of such a class-society in the West Indies was inevitable. Colonial areas, even without a class-tied racial complex, tend to remain provincial and to display social lag in comparison with metropolitan countries. Victorian class prejudices were bound to persist in the West Indies even as they did in other 'provinces'. Of course the reinforcement of class by race consciousness was bound to stiffen the class structure and make class barriers higher. It is also the case that societies with a rigid class structure are conservative because class-motivated behaviour is often devoted to the preservation of the status quo. The individual is anxious to defend his own social position and protect that of his class from dilution by mass incursions from below. Class, when accepted without question and without envy, is a social stabilizing instrument and in its extreme form of caste was defended by Gandhi for this reason. But the individual may also be strongly motivated to achieve improved status, to identify himself with his 'betters' and secure general acceptance of this identification. A class-society, therefore, always contains many persons who are socially very competitive and ambitious. If anything happens to increase social mobility, social tensions are likely to show a corresponding increase manifested in the resentment of those who feel their positions challenged by the social climbers.

While class and colour are closely associated, colour is not the exclusive or even sometimes the dominating factor in status. No colour bar of the 'Jim Crow' sort with a colour barrier between whites and all others is practical in colonies in which whites are a small minority and the middle class is largely coloured. The non-existence of a class of poor whites means the absence of the bitter economic competition and jealousy between poor whites and Negroes which is a constant exacerbator of race relations in the Southern USA.[2] At the same time the coloured middle class is very

[1] The problems and conflicts arising from class and colour are explored in the novels of the British Guianese writer, Edgar Mittelholzer. See his *Sylvia, A Day at the Office,* and others.
[2] See 'The Negro in the United States of America', *International Social Science Bulletin,* IX, 4, 1957, 435.

colour-conscious. 'Colour' in the West Indian sense includes all physical traits indicative of race such as shape of features and hair texture as well as skin colour. The European ones are the 'good' ones and are admired as suggesting a greater proportion of white ancestry. It has been observed that West Indian beauty contests are won invariably by white or near-white girls who are pretty by European standards. African beauties are disregarded. The elders of a coloured family will frown upon or forbid marriages between their children and those of a darker colour. The known proportion of black and white antecedents may be of some importance but more significant is what M. G. Smith calls 'associational colour', that is, the colour level of the group with which one normally associates, as well as 'cultural or behavioural colour' based upon the conformity of an individual's dress, speech and manners with the norms usually associated with the white, brown or black segments of society. Smith quotes Broom's observation that census takers are prone to classify as 'coloured' an upper civil servant who is a Negro, and a dark brown peasant as 'black'.[1] The following story is told of an incident in Grenada during a strike by market women against the whites. When the women refused to sell their produce to the servant of a Negro physician, the doctor himself came to protest this treatment only to be told, 'Yu de whites' mahn in town'.

Smith observes also that attempts on the part of the upper class of a plural society to acculturate the lower classes (such as Lady Huggins's scheme to increase the incidence of formal marriage among Jamaican Negroes by the donation of wedding rings) are bound to fail because they try to change a culture pattern to that of a higher class without any corresponding improvement in social status.

Colour discrimination exists quite generally throughout the West Indies as regards employment, especially in connection with 'white collar' jobs in offices and stores. In many such establishments Negroes are not hired and the entire staff will be white or coloured. The discriminatory line is drawn between coloured and Negro and not between white and coloured. To be sure there are private clubs in the West Indies that admit whites only to membership and one case at least of a club which does not allow members to entertain coloured guests. On a single Barbadian beach one may find

[1] M. G. Smith, *Caribbean Affairs, A Framework for Caribbean Studies* Extra-Mural Department, UCWI (Mona, Jamaica, n.d. 51 ff., and L. Broom, 'The Social Differentiation of Jamaica', *American Sociological Review*, XIX, (1954) 115-123. See also, Lloyd Braithwaite, 'Social Stratification in Trinidad', *Social and Economic Studies*, Vol. 2, Nos. 2 and 3, (October, 1953) 5-175.

two clubs, one 'lily white', one mixed (chiefly coloured), and an open stretch of beach used by Negroes. Such segregation is rare today except in Barbados which has clung to some old colonial traditions as well as to its Old Representative constitution. The Barbadian Premier, Mr (now Sir Grantley) Adams thought it advisable on the eve of his departure for federation discussions in London to secure passage of a law in January, 1956, requiring all business establishments to serve customers regardless of race or colour. This law, which would have been superfluous in most West Indian territories, was directed mainly at hotels and liquor-selling 'clubs' which had been enforcing a 'membership' rule only against would-be customers of colour. The Barbadian colour-bar tradition was an important consideration in the vigorous opposition of other territories to Barbados as a possible site for the federal capital.

Since World War II social mobility in the West Indies has increased sharply in comparison with its former rigidity. Basically this has been due to the economic and political organization of the lower class resulting in the rapid growth of labour unions, triggered by the depression of the 'thirties, and to electoral reforms culminating in the general adoption of universal adult suffrage. These developments made possible the rise to eminence and power of labour leaders of humble origin. Butler of Trinidad, Bradshaw of St Kitts, Bird of Antigua, and Gairy of Grenada represent the Negro of working-class origin and little education who has reached eminence through union leadership and mass voting. This has had its effect upon politics. Such politicians are conditioned by their background to assume and maintain a pose of combativeness against the 'government' even when they themselves have come to form part of the government. They must continue to press for constitutional advance, for the socialization of industry and for social welfare activities even when these are beyond the means of the community. There are exceptions to this pattern but it is a fairly general one and for obvious reasons. The leader who has reached his goal of a ministerial post through attacks upon the colonial system, white domination and so forth, cannot afford to accept the system he has been fighting so vigorously. They must continue the fight or lose prestige with their supporters.

What is the political role of local whites? Formerly it was considerable. Even when the franchise had become broad enough to give the vote to a large number of non-whites, the white candidate enjoyed a distinct advantage because of his colour. In cities and towns the white candidate attracted the middle-class coloured vote because the members of this class tended to identify themselves with and admire whites. In rural constituencies no Negroes as yet had the qualifications, financial or educational, for candidacy and coloured candidates were at a disadvantage because of the anti-coloured attitude of the Negroes. Equally important, perhaps, is the fact that in competitive corruption (the purchase of votes) the white candidates were generally better able to meet the cost.

This situation changed abruptly in most places with the coming of universal adult suffrage. Everywhere white candidates began to fade out of the picture although it was not until after the 1944 electoral reform that they became a minority in the Barbados Assembly. There are several reasons for the eclipse of white leadership in West Indian politics. Almost no whites were associated with the rise of the union-based labour parties. The older type of white politician who could attract conservative coloured middle-class support could win few votes among the much larger lower class. Furthermore the middle class began to reject conservative leadership as they felt the intellectual appeal of socialism or the emotional appeal of local nationalism. Such white politicians as might have been willing to undertake the exhausting business of an endless succession of street meetings and the rough-and-tumble of West Indian electioneering knew that they had little chance against the new coloured and Negro nationalist and labour leaders. There were rare exceptions such as Cipriani, Rienzi and Gomes in Trinidad, all associated with labour. White conservative politicians had to withdraw from electoral contests and find a place in the legislature only by grace of a gubernatorial appointment to a nominated seat. In general the attitude of the white propertied class has been one of unwilling acceptance of the new political leadership. Along with their loss of political dominance the white colonials have suffered a general loss of prestige in the community. Colin Hughes has summarized their reactions in these words:[1]

'Knowledge of this position along with the lack of economic possibilities, the gradual rise to economic and social prestige of a mixed and Negro middle class, and the increasing feeling of political futility, has produced a deep psychological malaise which is all too often overlooked by external critics.'

In some places the businessmen and planters have refused to give financial or other support to conservative parties on the ground that the electoral failure of these parties is certain. They have preferred to court the new leaders and by 'lobbying' and personal favours to

[1] Colin Anfield Hughes, 'Politics and Constitution-Making in the Eastern Group of the British West Indies, 1922 to the Present Day', unpublished Ph.D. thesis, University of London, 1952, Ms. p. 16.

try to influence policies. Quite possibly they are correct in believing this method to be a more effective means of securing governmental action they desire, than by any direct appeal to the mass electorate which certainly would be indifferent or hostile to their leadership.

To a considerable extent, therefore, the old political leadership has abdicated in many of the West Indian colonies. It is still represented in some places by the appointed members of the Legislative and Executive Councils but obviously these nominated seats are certain to be abolished before long. Some of the younger men among the creole white population already have accepted the new situation and have attempted to convince the electorate that they are truly whole-hearted members of the local community and as such are seeking election. But this is still rather exceptional and withdrawal from public politics is the more general response. The colonies thus are denied the use of such political talent and service as white members of the community may possess and at the same time there is an increase in pressure-group politics as the commercial and other monied interests seek to influence policy in non-public ways.

The attitudes, social and political, that have been summarized under the heading of 'the colonial complex' have affected West Indian society as they have all colonial and many ex-colonial communities.[1] The colonial complex is a community-wide inferiority complex stemming from the relative unimportance and subordinate status of the colony as contrasted with the metropolitan country. Many individuals react to this situation in one of two contrasting ways. Some make a complete self-identification with the mother country. They become 'more British than the Queen'. England is idealized and everything colonial is denigrated. Others react by a self-conscious and sometimes fanatical colonial nationalism and a tendency to dislike and depreciate everything British. In the West Indies this attitude sometimes includes an element of anti-white racism.

Both attitudes were found from the beginning of West Indian history. Antagonism between creoles and newcomers is a universal phenomenon. In early Spanish America it resulted sometimes in small-scale civil wars. Thomas Handasyde, Governor of Jamaica in 1702 wrote of his legislature: 'They being this session most of them Creolians are at a great variance with those born in England as if they themselves were not descended from English parents.' Strong traces of this feeling still exist in the French Caribbean possessions on the part of the old creole white families in their

[1] See M. Ayearst, 'The Colonial Complex', *The Canadian Forum*, 14, 157, 14-15 (October, 1933).

attitude towards the metropolitan officials of the Republic. But with the development of mass voting and mass parties the attitudes of the small minority of creole whites became of little importance. Of significance now was the pro- or anti-British stand of the coloured and Negro emergent leadership and the attitudes of their followers. The colonial officials made a distinct effort to gain the good will and preserve the loyalty of outstanding members of the new elite. They were received at Government House and given recognition by the same Crown-conferred honours as customarily were given to the officials themselves.[1] Some among them owed their professional education to government scholarships for study in England. By these means friendly relations were maintained with the coloured middle class who tended to identify themselves with Great Britain and have feelings of British loyalty much like Canadians, Australians and New Zealanders of pure British stock.

It was much harder to employ this technique with the labour party and trades union leaders who rose to eminence and legislative leadership by beating the drums of local nationalism, home rule and anti-colonialism, and some of whom often expressed anti-British sentiments. These leaders voiced the emotional attitudes of their supporters including resentment at social rejection which may be as powerful a motive as economic misery in the political behaviour of the lower-class West Indian. The leaders had to be careful not to permit themselves to be identified with the old ruling class if they hoped to retain the loyalty of the masses. Only after attaining un-questioned party dominance and establishing a long record of repre-senting the aspirations of the ordinary West Indian could such leaders as Bustamante and Adams afford to accept knighthood. Because these leaders are now so firmly identified in the eyes of their followers with the aspirations of the ordinary West Indian, the latter may find some reflected glory in the honours conferred upon them.

Another matter of some importance to West Indian political development is the multi-racial situation in some territories. In all of them there are minority groups of varied origins. In none except the mainland colonies are there many Amerindians and there they have not as yet shown much disposition to take an active part in

---

[1] The junior honours generally given are MBE (Member of the Order of the British Empire), and OBE (Officer of the Order of the British Empire) ranks in the Order of the British Empire, created in 1917 particularly to honour services in the Colonial Empire. Governors during or after a success-ful career are usually made KCMG (Knight Commander of St Michael and St George) an honour also associated with overseas service. Knighthoods for colonials are normally of the knight bachelor variety, not associated with any order of knighthood.

politics. The Mayans of local, Guatemalan or Yucatecan derivation in British Honduras are mainly Spanish-speaking Roman Catholics. Those voting in general elections have tended to support the People's United Party which is nationalist and dominated by coloured leaders from Belize. However, they appear to be voting communally in local government elections. Much the same is true of the curious 'Black Carib' group located in Stann Creek, the colony's third town. This is a small, clannish community of mixed African and Carib ancestry who were exiled to British Honduras from their original home in St Vincent and whose first language remain Carib.[1] The Arawak and Carib-speaking tribes of British Guiana are still living for the most part in their own primitive societies and are still largely indifferent to colonial politics.

Chinese are to be found in all the colonies but in none do they compose a large minority. It would appear that in Jamaica and British Guiana the first Chinese immigrants were villagers uprooted by the Taiping Rebellion of 1851-64.[2] One evidence of this is the fact that the Chinese of British Guiana were most numerous in 1866 when they numbered about ten thousand. The Chinese of Jamaica display one of the characteristics of communalism, namely, the tendency to monopolize a particular occupation, in this case the retail grocery trade. But Jamaican Chinese are found in other occupations as well and occupational concentration is not found in connection with the Chinese of other colonies nor do they congregate in 'Chinatowns'. Chinese immigration has virtually stopped and the Chinese communities appear to be in process of assimilation. Of course the Chinese still retain some cultural traits of their own. There are Chinese clubs and many continue to prefer the Chinese cuisine but, in contrast with the East Indians, and with the Chinese of Southeast Asia, they have not established Chinese schools. There are few, if any, remaining traces of the clan system or ancestor-worship. Such secular festivals as the Chinese New Year are celebrated and there is a natural interest in China but there is no evidence of any special interest in Communism nor any tendency for Chinese, as such, to join the West Indian crypto-Communist parties.

As elsewhere one aspect of Chinese communalism is the disposition of Chinese to settle quarrels among themselves without recourse to the courts. Tongs play no part in this but eminent

[1] See D. M. Taylor, *The Black Caribs of British Honduras*, Viking Fund Publications in Anthropology, No. 17 (New York, 1951).
[2] See Morton H. Fried, 'The Chinese in British Guiana', *Social and Economic Studies*, 5, 1, (March, 1956) 54-73. See also Andrew W. Lind, 'Adjustment Patterns Among the Jamaican Chinese', *Social and Economic Studies*, Vol. 7, No. 2 (June, 1958) 144-164.

DISTRIBUTION BY RACIAL ORIGIN AT LAST CENSUS
(1943 in Jamaica; 1946 in all other territories)

(*thousand*)

	Total	African	E. Indian	American Indians	European	Mixed	Others
Barbados	192.8	148.9	0.1	*	9.8	33.8	0.1
British Guiana	375.7	143.4	163.4	16.3	11.0	37.7	3.9
British Honduras	59.2	22.7	1.4	10.0	2.3	18.4	4.4
Jamaica and Dependencies	1,249.9	971.4	21.4	*	16.0	232.2	8.8
Leeward Islands:							
Antigua	41.8	35.4	*	*	0.7	5.4	0.2
Montserrat	14.3	13.3	*	*	0.1	0.9	*
St. Christopher-Nevis-Anguilla	46.2	40.0	0.1	*	0.9	5.1	0.1
Virgin Islands	6.5	5.7	*	*	*	0.8	*
Trinidad and Tobago	558.0	261.5	195.7	*	15.3	78.8	6.7
Windward Islands:							
Dominica	47.6	11.9	*	*	0.1	35.5	0.1
Grenada	72.4	53.3	3.5	*	0.6	14.8	0.2
St. Lucia	70.1	40.6	2.6	*	0.3	26.3	0.2
St. Vincent	61.6	45.0	1.8	*	1.9	12.6	0.3

*None, or insignificant numbers

personages in the local Chinese community are accepted as arbitrators and judges. Recalcitrants can be coerced by several means including the influence of important Chinese with official authorities and even, if necessary, the extra-legal use of force. Wives of Chinese nativity are prized as giving prestige and as evidence of the husband's wealth, but *t'usheng* (creole) girls prefer creole husbands. There is little racial exclusiveness and intermarriage with Eurafrican coloured individuals is not unusual.

Such social communalism as exists among the Chinese does not extend to politics nor could it well do so in view of the relatively small size of the Chinese community and its lack of concentration geographically. The Chinese are either non-political or enter politics as members of the general community. Individuals among them vary as widely in political affiliation as do other West Indians. There is no political 'Chinese problem'. When the Honourable Solomon Hochoy became Chief Secretary of Trinidad and Tobago in 1956, his appointment was hailed in the colony as a West Indian success story.

In both Trinidad and British Guiana there are minorities of Portuguese derivation. Many of their ancestors came from Madeira as indentured labour in the post-emancipation period. The Portuguese immigrants did not long continue to work in the cane fields

* Table from British Information Services pamphlet I.D. 1282, December, 1957.

but gravitated quickly towards small-scale commercial enterprise, groceries, rum shops and the like. They have displayed no significant social or political communalism and have often intermarried with the general population. As in the case of the Chinese this minority has remained too few in numbers to exert influence as a group or remain permanently unassimilated. In this respect they resemble the old Sephardic Jewish group in Jamaica, permitted by Diego Columbus to settle in the island. Many of these have been important in the economic life of the colony but they have long been assimilated and have intermarried with the non-Jewish population, both white and coloured, for many generations. Most colonies also have a few Syrian businessmen of recent immigration.

The only racial community to display a tendency to behave communally in politics is the East Indian community in both British Guiana and Trinidad. The original East Indian immigrants were recruited in India as indentured labour to work in the cane fields after emancipation. A few were taken to Jamaica but the majority went to Trinidad and British Guiana. The last shipload of these people arrived at Georgetown, British Guiana in 1917 so that some of the older East Indians are of Indian birth. A few of the original immigrants chose to return to India at the termination of their indenture but the great majority remained as free labour. During the indenture period the Indian 'coolies' were treated much as the slaves had been. Floggings were administered as punishment for attempts to run away. Because of the kind of work they did and their inability to speak English they were looked down upon by the Negroes who now in many cases were landowners and a few of whom had begun to acquire education and middle-class or professional status.

By the beginning of the twentieth century the class system in British Guiana might be said to have four strata: the white officials and propertied class, the coloured middle class of civil servants and professionals, the Negro peasant proprietors, urban employees and schoolteachers, and at the bottom, the East Indian field hands and drivers who were the labour force on the vast sugar estates. Substantially the same situation existed in Trinidad. But as the East Indians began to finish their stint and leave the estates, they were able sometimes to buy a small piece of rice land or undertake a little commercial enterprise. They proved on the average, to be thriftier and more ambitious than the Negroes and before long had begun to educate their children and in some cases to acquire riches. It was not long before East Indians began to enter the professions, the civil service, the teaching field and other areas long considered a coloured and Negro monopoly. Naturally this was resented by the

Negroes who felt their status threatened and the result was the development of anti-East Indian sentiment. The situation was exacerbated by the tendency of the East Indians to congregate in their own villages, retain their own religion, avoid the use of the ordinary (Christian) schools and cling to the endogamous rules of the caste system. Negroes allege that they display a 'clannishness' in all business and interpersonal relations, discriminating against non-Indians. When they began to enter the political arena they displayed a strong tendency to vote East Indian. Because they were a large minority and increasing at a faster rate than the rest of the population, fear of their domination of the social and economic life of the colony was added to Negro resentment at their success in achieving an improved social and economic status.[1]

Indian communal sentiment was stimulated by post-war developments in India and the independence of India and Pakistan. A new sense of racial and national pride was felt by West Indian East Indians. This was not discouraged by the activities and speeches of the High Commissioners sent out by the Government of India. The first of these, S. C. Shastri, publicly advocated the employment of more East Indians in the civil service. Another High Commissioner, S. B. N. Nanda, who was recalled after about eight months in the post during 1954, was charged with interfering in the local political debate over West Indian federation. A prominent local politician, B. S. Maraj, gained prestige with his community by securing government subventions to aid in the establishment of Hindi-language schools.[2] Maraj also succeeded in becoming the president of the Sanatan Dharma Maha Sabha with more than one hundred branches in Trinidad and an affiliation with the Maha Sabha organization in British Guiana.

The Moslem minority among the East Indians were not much affected by the India-Pakistan controversy and, having shared a

---

[1] By 1948 the East Indians composed 45% of the total population of British Guiana as compared with 36% Negro and 12.9% coloured. In that same year the East Indian crude birth rate was almost 14 per 1,000 higher and the crude death rate 3 per 1,000 lower than that of the Negroes.
The racial composition of British Guiana (estimated, December, 1955) was:

		%
East Indian	230,840	46.8
Negro	171,960	34.9
Coloured	55,260	11.2
Chinese	3,320	.7
Portuguese	8,070	1.6
Other European	4,130	.9
Amerindian	19,400	3.9

[2] At a meeting in 1954 Maraj observed that the Maha Sabha had enabled the erection of 23 Hindu schools within a three-year period.

history with the Hindus as indentured labour and despised 'coolies', continued to feel themselves a part of the East Indian community. A Moslem leader in British Guiana, M. A. H. Hack, issued a statement in 1955 in which he referred to any expectation that the East Indians should allow themselves to be assimilated with a foreign civilization as 'gross injustice'.[1]

Political communalism can be a serious obstacle to the successful operation of parliamentary democracy. The elected representatives of a racial or religious sub-community cannot afford to subordinate the interests and prejudices of their people to those of the larger community. Whether elected as independents, members of a communal party or even as members of a party professing to transcend communal lines, they must never accept party discipline in a way to offend the group upon whose support their political future depends. For this reason their position upon matters affecting their community tends to be rigid and uncompromising. A bloc of such representatives may be able to force their special views upon a government needing their support. At the worst, a legislature seriously divided among competing communal blocs is likely to waste much time in futile debate while failing to come to grips with urgent problems of general importance. This impasse may continue indefinitely as successive elections return similar communal delegations to the legislature.

Fortunately the West Indies has no communal problem of this magnitude. East Indians do not concentrate their economic activities within a single occupation. Although the majority are still cane farmers and oil-field workers in Trinidad and sugar estate labourers and rice farmers in British Guiana, they are tending more and more to leave the villages and move to the towns and cities where they are compelled to learn English and where they come into contact with the general population. (Trinidad has at least one East Indian calypsonian!) Their numbers are not longer increased by immigration to make up for those who enter the wider community. Many are now loyal supporters of non-communal political parties as well as members of the leadership-group of such parties. There were two East Indians (one Hindu and one Moslem) among the eight ministers in Dr Eric Williams's PNP 'cabinet' of 1956. It may safely be assumed that slowly but surely the East Indians will be assimilated with the general West Indian community in all important social and political aspects.[2]

[1] See *New York Times* despatch by Sam Pope Brewer, issue of February 10, 1955.
[2] The present writer has treated this subject elsewhere. See 'Political Aspects of Federation', *Social and Economic Studies*, 6, 2 (June, 1957) 249 ff.

E

CHAPTER IV

CONSTITUTIONAL AND POLITICAL DEVELOPMENTS IN THE ISLANDS

A L T H O U G H the constitutional suggestions of the Moyne Report were far from radical, its authors did advocate an increase in the representative element in government. Their argument against complete self-rule based on universal suffrage was the time-honoured assertion that such a gift would . . . 'render impossible the financial control necessary if, as we consider to be inevitable, substantial assistance is to be afforded by His Majesty's Government' . . . Indeed, the conditions of war emergency held up certain changes and required the Governors to impose something approaching an executive autocracy for the duration of hostilities. West Indian nationalist views were not encouraged and any sort of political agitation tended to be regarded as approaching the subversive.[1] It may have seemed to many that political and constitutional reaction rather than progress was in store for the colonies. It is true that no Secretary of State had yet indicated that self-government for the West Indies was a goal in the foreseeable future, despite the acceptance of this objective in the case of India and Ceylon. The West Indies had at least as good a case as the Asiatic colonies in respect of literacy level and the existence of a responsible and educated middle class. But the inability of many of these West Indian colonies to pay their own way year in and year out seemed, in the British view, to postpone any serious consideration of responsible government. Even so, the war period produced not only a temporary executive dictatorship in the colonies but also reiterations at high levels in the British government of the intention to foster self-

[1] In Jamaica, for instance, Alexander Bustamante and five officials of the People's National Party were detained under the Defence Regulations. Roger Mais, a locally well-known writer, was given a jail sentence in 1945 for an article highly critical of the proposed constitution. In this article, entitled 'Now We Know', in *Public Opinion* (the PNP organ) July 13, 1944, Mais wrote as follows: '[We are asked to fight] . . . that the sun may never set upon aggression and inequality and human degradation, . . . upon repressions and exploitation . . . upon urchins in rags and old men and women in rags . . . upon insolence and arrogance of one race toward all others . . . For the great ideas of democracy which relegates all 'niggers' of whatever race to their proper place—For such things as these we are fighting. . . . Now we know'.

government throughout the Commonwealth at the earliest possible moment.[1]

JAMAICA

It will be remembered that Crown Colony government was given Jamaica in 1866 with a wholly nominated Legislative Council.[2] The Jamaican middle class, white and coloured, contained many who were dissatisfied with such an arrangement from the beginning. As the years went by, agitation for reform increased and in 1877 a petition was laid before the British Government asking for an enlarged Council with an elected majority. This was denied, but in 1884 the Legislative Council was re-formed to consist of nine elected, four ex-officio, and five nominated members.[3] The Governor would preside and have both an original and a casting vote, thus ensuring a government majority because the nominated members were appointed only upon the clear understanding that they would always support the government. However, the elected members were given financial powers over both taxing and spending, other than the fixed administrative expenses, by a provision that if six or more of them opposed a financial measure, the official votes should not count. This reform did not long satisfy the Jamaicans who continued to press for an elected majority which was finally granted in 1895 by increasing to fourteen the number of elected members. At the same time, the nominated members were increased to ten in number, although only six were appointed to the Council. The custom of leaving vacancies among the nominated members had begun in 1884 in order to placate Jamaican opinion and provide a working majority of elected members while the Governor still retained the right to appoint nominated members in emergencies. When the

[1] See below, p. 134.
[2] Colin Hughes notes that Crown Colony governments may be classified into eight categories: 1. The Governor as the sole executive and legislative authority (used temporarily or in places that are simply military bases). 2. The Governor advised by an entirely official Executive Council, either ex-officio or nominated. 3. The Governor, an Executive Council of officials plus a Legislative Council of officials and unofficial nominees (unofficials appearing for the first time as part of the governmental machinery). 4. As No. 3 but with some elected members in the Legislative Council and/or the addition of nominees and elected members to produce an unofficial majority. 6. (An important stage) Elected members added to Legislative Council to produce an elected majority and so, representative government. 7. The placing of policy-making in the hands of representatives of the elected chamber in the Executive Council with a safe-guard in the Governor's reserve powers: semi-responsible government.—'Semi-Responsible Government in the British West Indies', *Political Science Quarterly*, (Sept., 1953) 338-353.
[3] (Jamaica) Order-in-Council, 19 May, 1884. For the historical background of this 1884 constitution and the recommencement of representative government see Ronald V. Sires, 'The Jamaica Constitution of 1884', *Social and Economic Studies* 3, 1, (June, 1954) 64-81.

Governor ran into legislative difficulties over a tariff in 1899 he appointed nominated members to the four vacancies. In effect, the nominated members voted as part of the official bloc although this had not been the Colonial Office concept of their function as was pointed out by Major Wood in his 1922 Report.

Unwise government expenditure plus a sharp decrease in the price of sugar created a financial crisis for the Jamaican government as the nineteenth century drew to a close. The elected members complained that they were not fully informed as to government finances and that while they could embarrass the government by refusing to vote money, they had no control over its use once it had been voted. At the same time the Governors shrank from the use of their reserved powers because of the resentment and agitation this might cause. When the four vacant nominated seats were filled in 1889, the elected members protested strongly, and when the Secretary of State declared for their permanent installation in February, 1900, all the elected members save one walked out of the House. The protests were unavailing and the legislature continued to function under the domination of the government although Jamaican reformers also continued to agitate from time to time for more representative government.

It was not until the 'twenties of this century that the British Government was disposed to consider any significant changes. Correspondence took place between the Governor and the Secretary of State on this subject in 1922 and 1923.[1] This resulted in a constitutional proposal by the Secretary of State which was discussed in the Legislative Council in 1926 and rejected.

There followed the labour disturbances and riots of the 'thirties and the subsequent organization of mass political parties. The first of these, the People's National Party, was the outcome of movements in both Jamaica and the USA. A group of New York City residents of Jamaican origin founded the Jamaica Progressive League in 1936. This had political objectives: universal suffrage at once, party activity in the island and the final goal of Dominion status for Jamaica. The League's three most active members were Adolphe Roberts, Wilfred A. Domingo and the Reverend Ethelred Brown[2] One reason for establishing the League's headquarters in

[1] See *Jamaican Gazette,* issue of November 8, 1923, for this correspondence.
[2] See Adolphe A. Roberts, *Self-Government for Jamaica* (New York, 1936) and other books and articles by the same author as well as pamphlets issued by the Jamaica Progressive League. The part played in island politics by West Indians in the USA is mentioned in Roi Ottley, *New World a-Coming: Inside Black America* (Boston, 1943), pp. 43-48; T. S. Simey, *op. cit.,* pp. 75-78; section by C. Augustin Petioni, 'West Indians and the Post-War World' in E. Franklin Frazier and Eric Williams, eds., *The Economic Future of the Caribbean* (Washington, 1944), pp. 33-36.

New York was that it could operate there more freely than within the jurisdiction of a hostile Jamaican government. It did attempt some agitation and organization in Jamaica itself in 1937. Also in 1937 the periodical, *Public Opinion,* was founded in Kingston by a group of middle-class Jamaicans including G. T. Fairclough, H. P. Jacobs, Frank and Ken Hill, V. L. Arnett, Richard Hart and Edna (Mrs. Norman) Manley. The ideas of the League at first seemed too radical to some of the *Public Opinion* group, but the disturbances of 1938 and their indignation at the government's reaction led them to accept the League's nationalist objectives. Many of these same people belonged to the National Reform Association, a middle-class organization. It was at a meeting sponsored by this association on September 18, 1938, that Norman Manley founded the People's National Party with the objective of achieving self-government for Jamaica. In his inaugural address Manley advocated universal adult suffrage at once, a strong trades union movement and rapid constitutional advance.[1] Although Sir Stafford Cripps who was visiting Jamaica at the time, also addressed the inaugural meeting, it was not until August, 1940, that the PNP declared itself to be socialist officially. 'Nationalist' rather than 'Labour' was chosen as the working adjective in the party's name because it was Manley's hope that the party might be broader in its appeal and might unite Jamaicans of all classes behind its objectives. Manley himself and other leading figures in the party employed an intellectual approach in their arguments for their nationalist and socialist objectives but Manley believed, nevertheless, that the PNP could attract the vote of organized labour. He might have been correct in this assumption had he continued to receive the support of Bustamante and through him the mass voting power of the large Bustamante Industrial Trade Union. But upon his release from detention, as noted in Chapter II, Bustamante immediately founded the Jamaica Labour Party which was victorious in the elections of 1944, the first held under universal suffrage. Although polling only 41.4% of the total vote the JLP won twenty-two seats out of thirty-two. The PNP, its voting strength heavily urban, won only five seats for 23.5% of the vote. The remaining five places were won by independents.

In the meantime constitutional discussions had continued at the legislative and official level. A select committee of the legislature under the chairmanship of J. A. G. Smith had come up with a proposed constitution in 1939. This 'Smith Constitution' amounted virtually to the restoration of the Old Representative system. It called for a broadened but still not universal electorate and a

[1] N. M. Manley, *This Jamaica* (Kingston, Ja., 1938).

bicameral legislature with the lower chamber entirely elected. Lord Moyne, then Secretary of State, turned down this proposal and countered with one retaining the mixed unicameral legislature of the Crown Colony type but with an enlarged representative element. Governor Richards strongly urged acceptance of the Moyne constitution, refusing to consider any changes in it. His aggressive advocacy of this reform annoyed the elected members and they voted unanimously against it and defeated it in August, 1941. At this time the Legislative Council contained ten officials, six nominated unofficials and fourteen elected members. Despite the wartime imposition of virtual executive autocracy, discussions of constitutional reform continued and finally, in 1943, the Secretary of State, Oliver Stanley, after consulting with the Governor, Sir Arthur Richards (now Lord Milverton), accepted the chief elements of the Jamaican proposal of 1939, and granted them by the Jamaica (Constitution) Order in Council, 1944, as authorized by the Jamaica Act of 1866.

This 1944 constitution, created a much modified Crown Colony government of rather elaborate kind. The Governor was assisted by a *Privy Council* consisting of four officials (the Colonial Secretary, the Officer Commanding the Troops, unless below the rank of Lieutenant-Colonel, the Attorney General, the Financial Secretary) and two unofficial nominees of the Governor. This Privy Council advises the Governor as to the exercise of the Royal Prerogative and the administration of the Civil Service. The 'principal instrument of policy', however, was the *Executive Council* with the Governor as Chairman, the three top officials as ex-officio members (Colonial Secretary, Attorney General and Financial Secretary), two unofficial nominated members of the Legislative Council selected by the Governor and, to begin with, five elected members of the House of Representatives, elected by the House. The Executive Council was given the authority to approve by majority vote all the government and all financial bills to be introduced into the House of Representatives and consequently to act in relation to the latter pretty much as the British Cabinet acts in relation to the House of Commons as regards control of business. It will be noted that a majority of the members were now elected by and responsible to the House. Of course, the usual safety provisions were made: the Governor to have the right to legislate contrary to the wishes of the legislature, with the consent of the Secretary of State or, in emergencies, without such consent, but only with the approval of his Executive Council.[1] This meant that the Governor had an emergency power to act positively to pass bills

[1] Jamaica (Constitution) Order in Council, 1944. Section 47, sub. section (2).

against the will of the entire elected element providing he could obtain the consent of the two Nominated Members in the Executive Council. He might be assured of this because of his authority to dismiss these members at will and appoint others. The Governor also was given an effective veto power to be used either directly or at the discretion of the Secretary of State by reserving bills for the royal pleasure. Certain types of bills, notably those concerning constitutional changes or those affecting the legislature or its members were required to be reserved. Even if the Governor approved a bill the Secretary of State was empowered to exercise his veto upon it.[1]

The ingenuity of this device of 'semi-responsible government', in Hughes' terminology, lies in the freedom it gives to the elected quasi-ministers, chosen by and responsible to a popular legislature, to formulate government policies in the ordinary course of events, while it retains for the Governor the possibility of effective control if the situation requires. It provided responsible government on a leash.

Despite this limitation, it was a most significant advance in that it represented a real departure from all previous Crown Colony systems wherein the right to formulate policy belonged strictly to the colonial officials no matter how numerous the elected element in the legislature. Under the 1944 constitution the Governor would tend to become less and less a prime minister and more and more a constitutional monarch giving advice when asked and intervening with warnings and guidance according to his best judgment but allowing the final decision in policy matters to rest with the ministers.

The legislature consists of two chambers. The second chamber, the *Legislative Council,* is much like an old Crown Colony legislature in composition. It contained, as of 1944, the three chief officials other than the Governor, ex-officio, plus a minimum of ten unofficial persons nominated by the Governor to hold office 'at pleasure' or until the dissolution of the Legislative Council. Such nominees might not be elected members of the other chamber. The Governor was empowered to appoint not more than two additional officials, but this power was not exercised. Two unofficials, members of the Legislative Council, were appointed by the Governor to sit in the Executive Council. The Legislative Council has only a one year suspensory veto over legislation.

The real legislative authority rests with the *House of Representatives* or lower chamber, consisting of thirty-two members elected by universal adult suffrage from single-member-district constituencies. No property or literacy test determines the suffrage. The House elects its speaker from its own membership and also elects the

[1] Jamaica (Constitution) Order in Council, 1944. Sections 48, 50.

Elected Members of the Executive Council. The 1944 constitution provided that there should be five Elected Members in the Executive Council. Responsibility of these quasi-ministers to the House was assured by requiring that they must resign after a general election or if their election to the Executive Council is revoked by a two-thirds absolute majority of the House. (This requirement was criticized by Governor Foot as making it possible for the opposition to compel the retention in the Executive Council of a minister who had lost the confidence of his own party.)

The 1944 constitution was frankly transitional as regards the relationship between executive and legislature. The five original elected members of the Executive Council were assigned specific areas of the administration for which they would be spokesmen in both House and Executive Council. But they were not ministers in the full sense of the term. They had no authority over 'their' departments and of course had to share the power to make policy decisions with the non-elected members of the Executive Council. This system was intended to provide them with training in the work of a minister and prepare them for full ministerial responsibilities at a later date. Additional training was provided by their duties as members of the two committees of the Executive Council: the Estimates Committee and the Administrative Committee. Their mentors here were the Financial Secretary and the Colonial Secretary. The real responsibility for administration still rested with the permanent Secretariat and the Colonial Secretary was responsible to the Governor and not to the Ministers for the conduct of administration and its personnel. All matters of defence and local security remained within the Governor's province.

This 1944 system worked fairly well for a time though not to the satisfaction of some Jamaican political leaders, particularly those of the opposition People's National Party. The quasi-ministers had no real power to act within their departments in policy matters and far too many details had to be decided in Executive Council, which fell behind in its work. The Secretariat too was overworked in its job of running all the departments. Bustamante is said to have liked the system well enough. He was not yet convinced that Jamaica was ready for responsible government and he could always blame mistakes in policy on that old whipping-boy, the permanent official, whether or not the officials were at fault.[1] But even if Bustamante

[1] The tendency to avoid responsibility by blaming the permanent officials may not yet have disappeared entirely. In October, 1956, the Speaker of the House rebuked the Honourable A. G. S. Coombs (PNP) Minister of Communications and Works, for refusing to answer a question by an Opposition Member regarding an alleged offence by a civil servant and for referring the inquirer to the Colonial Secretary for an answer. See Trinidad *Sunday Guardian,* November 4, 1956, p. 25.

was less than enthusiastic about further changes at this time, others were impatient for more self-government. In July, 1947, the House chose a select committee to report on the constitution. It did so in February, 1949, and proposed modest advances: an increase in the elected members in Executive Council from five to eight, giving an elected majority. The other members of the Executive Council would be the Governor, the Colonial Secretary, and two nominated members. It was proposed also to reduce the suspensory veto power of the second chamber from one year to six months. Attacked by the PNP as far too modest, the proposals were adopted by the House on a strictly party vote.

The next elections (1949) were fought over the constitutional issue, the PNP demanding full responsible government at once and the JLP attacking the PNP as radicals, socialists and possibly Communists. This time the PNP did better, receiving 43.5% of the total vote to 42.7% for the JLP. Nevertheless the distribution was such that the JLP won seventeen seats to thirteen for the PNP. Two independents were elected. The constitutional argument that followed was complicated by party politics. The PNP, believing that it could win the next election, wanted one as a prerequisite to further change. The JLP, of course, did not relish another electoral trial of strength at the moment and wanted no changes that would require one.

The new Governor, Sir Hugh Foot, took the view that his function was not to put the brakes on constitutional advance and not even to take a passive attitude but rather to promote the growth of self-government as much as possible within the limits of his instructions. As he wrote in 1950, before taking up his post as Governor of Jamaica:

'As a member of the British Colonial Service I would sum up my main beliefs by making three general propositions. First, that we can only succeed in the great tasks ahead of us in the British Colonies—in the crusade against ignorance and superstition and disease and poverty—if we secure the whole-hearted co-operation and participation of the peoples of the Colonial territories. Second, that the principles of democratic government are just as sound in Jamaica or Nigeria as they are in England or America. And third, that the only way to train people in responsibility is to give it to them—not reluctantly and grudgingly but confidently, as a matter of positive policy.'

In August, 1951, Sir Hugh inaugurated a series of conversations with individual political leaders of both parties and the unofficial members of the Legislative Council. Basically, he proposed that details of administration should be left to the various departments rather than settled in Executive Council meetings, while the ministers, increased in number to eight, should be given real responsibility for policy decisions and be the working political heads of their departments. Foot presented these proposals on the basis of a needed reform in administration rather than an increase in self-government. The Secretary of State agreed to the suggestions including the principle that the Governor should appoint and remove ministers on the advice of the leader of the majority party in the House. He noted that, as the Governor no longer would have voting control in Executive Council, it would be necessary to allow him to use his reserved powers without the approval of that body. In selling this point to Jamaican politicians, Sir Hugh noted that this would place full responsibility for any use of these powers on the Governor alone. Sir Hugh was very active in advocating his constitutional reforms and even appealed directly to the public.[1] In the house the JLP backed the plan but Manley opposed it as too timid an advance and one 'dictated' by the Governor. Notwithstanding this, the House, including the PNP members, accepted the reforms.

The Governor and the Secretariat worked hard at the job of initiating the ministers into their duties. It is generally the case that the experts, that is, the permanent civil servants, tend to have a covert lack of respect for the politician-minister who heads the department for the time being. This may have been particularly true in Jamaica, for certain of the new ministers were scarcely of ministerial calibre and were outstanding in their proved loyalty to the Chief Minister, Bustamante, rather than in ability or background suited to their new positions. This may have been due in part to the tendency displayed by Bustamante to surround himself with lieutenants who would obey him without question. Bustamante himself worked hard to make the new constitution a success and refrained from any attempt to use the higher ranks of the civil service for patronage purposes even though he was well aware that most of the upper civil servants were PNP supporters. The most obvious weakness of some of the new ministers was a failure to live up to high standards of probity in public office. Several cases of corruption were uncovered during the life of the 1949 House, one of which involved the sale to businessmen on a regular subscription basis of the secret minutes of Executive Council meetings. Bustamante instantly dismissed the minister whose guilt was implied plainly by the evidence uncovered.

---

[1] See *Constitutional Reform, Three Broadcast Talks* by H. E., Sir Hugh Foot, etc., January, 1953 (Government Printer, Kingston, 1953). The Governor announced that the reforms would become effective on May 1, 1953.

This provided the PNP with an issue and Manley hammered away at corruption in the House and at street meetings as did his lieutenants, Nethersole, Isaacs and the rest. Recognizing the need to enlarge the base of the party, especially in rural districts, the PNP began to devote much attention to the organizing activities of the National Workers' Union, in which effort Manley's son Michael took a prominent part. Some progress was made among sugar estate workers to the disadvantage of the BITU. Although the NWU was not able to catch up with the BITU in membership it did make considerable gains, replacing the Trades Union Council as the island's second largest union. In the relatively light poll of the 1955 elections (approximately 75% of the electorate voted) the PNP won control of the House for the first time with eighteen seats to fourteen for the JLP.

One of Manley's first acts as Chief Minister was to initiate a conventional development in the constitution. This was the 'Ministers' Conference', a meeting of the ministers alone to agree upon united action at forthcoming Executive Council meetings. If a new policy problem was introduced at an Executive Council meeting by an official or a nominated member, decision might be postponed to allow the Ministers' Conference to come to an agreement. Because the united action of the elected ministers would determine the result in Executive Council, this convention tended to reduce the latter to a rubber stamp. Apparently this development took place with the tolerance of the Governor but not with the express consent of the Secretary of State.[1]

As Chief Minister, Manley pushed as far as possible in the direction of complete self-government by the use of extra-constitutional devices. In addition to the Ministers' Conference, noted above, he created the office of Chief Economic Adviser to the Chief Minister, responsible solely to the Chief Minister and not a member of the colonial service. The holder of this post, nevertheless, sits as a member of the Economic Committee of the Executive Council, the other members of which are four ministers and the Financial Secretary.

Before the 1955 elections Bustamante had been converted to the advocacy of complete self-government. He could no longer oppose the overwhelming popularity of the 'self-government' slogan. This enabled the House to adopt unanimously a report of a Select Committee advocating a completely elected Executive Council presided over by the Chief Minister instead of the Governor and an enlargement of the ministry to include responsibility for the judicial

[1] Compare this with the PPP 'Council of People's Ministers' in British Guiana. See *below*, p. 122.

system, police and security. These reforms were not at once pressed by Manley following his election as Chief Minister. It would seem that a possible shift in party strength, if the constituencies were to be redrawn to make room for more members, may have been a reason for the delay. Nor did there seem to be any great public demand for immediate further reforms of a radical nature. On April 16, 1956, a ninth minister was added under an authorization made by Order in Council of July, 1955. The non-elected member-ship remained constant at three official and two nominated members. Subsequently, however, the matter of constitutional advance to the point of complete self-government was again considered by the House and both sides agreed that such an advance would be desir-able. It has been Manley's position that the West Indian Federation should, at the outset, be a federation of fully self-governing units and Bustamante has been compelled to agree because of the un-popularity of any contrary stand. On November 3, 1956, the House appointed a bi-partisan seven-man Committee to work out the details. Chief Minister Manley and three other ministers, Glasspole, Lloyd and Nethersole represented the PNP, and the leader of the opposition, Bustamante, with Messrs. Sangster and Edwin Allen, the JLP.

The following March, Governor Foot, in his opening address to the legislature, proposed constitutional changes which the com-mittee approved subsequently. These included the replacement of the Executive Council by a *Council of Ministers* to meet at the call and under the presidency of the Chief Minister, the Governor re-serving the right to summon and preside over extraordinary meet-ings of the Council. The Council of Ministers consists entirely of unofficials, ten ministers from the House and two nominated members of the Legislative Council to be appointed by the Governor on the advice of the Chief Minister. The Legislative Members are ministers without portfolio and take charge of govern-ment business in their chamber. This second chamber now con-tains the only official with remaining legislative duties, the Attorney General. The Colonial Secretary's title was changed to Chief Secretary. These reforms were approved by the two chambers and went into effect on November 11, 1957, and gave Jamaica essen-tially complete internal self-government with the Governor reduced to the function of a ceremonial executive except in emergencies.

The nominated Legislative Council has quietly assumed the role of a House of Lords as a chamber of revision but rarely of opposition. On May 4, 1956, it took little more than an hour to pass seven bills of eight submitted, including the all-important appropria-tions bill. The eighth bill was amended on a detail of drafting.

TRINIDAD

At the opposite end of the island chain, Trinidad has also appeared, in some respects, to be Jamaica's political opposite. Trinidad never experienced the Old Representative System although the nearby island of Tobago had it, following its final acquisition by Great Britain in 1803. The British settlers in Trinidad, a tiny minority, agitated for representation but they were outnumbered by the free coloured inhabitants. To enfranchise the latter group was considered inadvisable but it was considered equally inadvisable to exclude them from a general franchise. The solution was the establishment of a Council of Government in 1831 containing six officials and six unofficial nominees of the Governor under the chairmanship of the latter who had both original and a casting vote. This Council had little more than advisory powers. The Governor was, in effect, the Government. One reason for the unwillingness of the Colonial Office to permit more self-government in Trinidad at this time was the fear that a truly representative assembly with actual authority might block the humanitarian policies of the home government and especially its determination to end slavery. But as time went on and this issue became historic, pressures mounted for an increase in local representation in government. Gradually the nominated unofficial element was enlarged and by 1900 the Legislative Council contained ten officials and eleven unofficial nominees. Its president, the Governor, had an original and a casting vote so an official majority was certain in the event of an even split.

By the close of World War I the agitation for constitutional reform found generally in the British West Indies also occurred in Trinidad and it was now voiced not by the white planters but by the increasingly important Negro and coloured middle class. In Trinidad the social and political situation was complicated by the presence of large numbers of 'East Indians' who had been brought in as indentured labourers, and who had remained a fairly coherent and separate group. Indeed, at this time, some Indian leaders opposed any constitutional reform, fearing the domination of the coloured and Negro majority. Others advocated communal representation. The white minority too opposed reform, also fearing the possibly ill-advised actions of a coloured legislature. Reform was urged by a Legislative Reform Committee, largely coloured in membership, and by Captain Cipriani's Trinidad Workingmen's Association. Cipriani, a white man of Corsican descent, whose family had been settled in Trinidad for generations, was founder and first president of the Trinidad Workingmen's Association which he regarded not as a labour union but rather as a political pressure group and a means of advancing the general and political education of the working class. His principles included the use of Trinidadians instead of foreigners for managerial posts and the conferring of real power upon the Legislative Council.

The Wood Report advocated a very slight advance for Trinidad: the increase in the unofficial element in the Legislative Council from eleven to thirteen of whom six should be nominated and seven elected thus providing for elected members for the first time in Trinidad. At the same time the official representation should be increased from ten to twelve, which with the Governor's two votes would maintain the official majority if the entire unofficial side combined against the government. This recommendation was carried out and the Trinidad Legislative Council was so comprised from 1924 to 1941.

This change did not affect the autocratic power of the Governor who was not bound to accept the advice of his Executive Council, and which was under his control in any case because official in membership except for one or more unofficials nominated by the Governor from the nominated unofficial members of the Legislative Council.

It will be observed that the Governor, with the aid of his official bloc, dominated both the executive and legislative arms of government and that the elected members who took their places after 1924 could never hope to influence policy except as they might persuade the Governor to accept their views. Even when the entire unofficial side, both elected and nominated, combined against a government proposal the result would be no more than a suspensory veto, the matter being referred to the Secretary of State for final decision. This happened upon one occasion, in 1938, concerning the income tax regulations. There were high property qualifications for eligibility to membership in the Legislative Council and a property qualification for the franchise so that something under six per cent of the total population could qualify as electors. There was no literacy requirement, almost half the population being illiterate, but candidates for the Legislative Council had to be able to speak and understand English and prospective voters had to be able to sign their names to an application for inclusion on the voters' list and this prevented a number of East Indians from qualifying.

Under this 1924 constitution Trinidad was governed by its successive Governors who ruled as benevolent despots. Some chose to preside in the legislature as more or less impartial chairmen, leaving it to the principal official members, the Colonial Secretary, Attorney General and others, to expound and defend government policies. Other Governors combined the role of speaker with that of prime minister and took active charge of government bills in debate.

The high property qualifications for elected members ensured the absence from the chamber of any but well-to-do persons who were unlikely to entertain radical views.[1] For some time the only member who might be described as radical in his opinions was Captain Cipriani who was an elected member for Port-of-Spain from 1925 until his death in 1945. Cipriani advocated various reforms, and did secure the adoption of one or two after years of agitation. But after the disorders of the 'thirties, Cipriani was no longer acceptable as the leader of the 'barefooted man'. His political approach was to be replaced by that of the union negotiator who would secure election as a result of his success, or appearance of success, in fighting union battles with the employers.

The difficulties of Crown Colony government in a period of social and economic crisis were displayed plainly in Trinidad following the riots of 1937. To be sure, the root cause of the trouble was the world-wide depression about which no Trinidad government could do very much, but the fact that this government was not truly representative and that the nominated unofficial members of the Legislative Council were chosen from the propertied class, gave the Trinidad labourer the firm conviction that his government was an agency of the rich to be used for his suppression and exploitation. It made little difference to the public that, in this situation, the Governor, Sir Murchison Fletcher, chose to defend the rioters and blame the employers for sub-standard wages. This led merely to bitter conflict between the official and unofficial nominated side in the Legislative Council.

The Moyne Report suggested for Trinidad the use of fewer officials in the Legislative Council, only the ex-officio ones to be present (the Colonial Secretary, the Attorney General and the Financial Secretary). Other official heads of departments should work with committees of the Legislative Council to give the unofficial members some understanding of administrative problems. It was also suggested that the franchise be extended and property qualifications for members be lowered.

The Moyne Report was discussed in Executive Council and also in conversations between the Governor and unofficial members of the Legislative Council. The result was a constitutional change effected by the Order in Council of 25 April, 1941. This increased the number of elected members from seven to nine and confined the Governor to a casting vote only in the Legislative Council. The previous year the Governor had stopped nominating minor officials

---

[1] Property worth £2,500, or income from real estate of £200 or income from any source of £400 per annum.

to the Legislative Council. With the increase in elected members there were also new letters patent authorizing the Governor to act positively to overcome the veto of a bill in the Legislative Council which now had a large unofficial majority, fifteen to three. Of the fifteen unofficials, nine were elected and six nominated, so, if the Governor as president be included, the legislature now had nine elected and ten non-elected members.

From 1940 onwards the Executive Council had an unofficial majority. It now consisted of the Governor and his three top officials plus five members of the Legislative Council (three nominated and two elected members). This was not an altogether happy arrangement. The Governor still retained ultimate power and responsibility but he could not, in actual practice, constantly override his Executive Council. On the other hand, Executive Council members felt responsible for the acts of the Governor whether they approved of them or not. After a short time as a member, Cipriani resigned from Executive Council for this reason.

The next important reform was the introduction of universal adult suffrage without any property or language limitations. Along with this the property qualification for membership in Legislative Council was reduced by half.[1] This was in accord with the recommendation of a Franchise Committee of the Legislative Council which had worked from 1941 to 1944. As is usual when universal suffrage is introduced, there was considerable public response. Previously, with less than seven per cent of the population eligible to vote, only about eighteen per cent of this tiny electorate had bothered to do so. Now some forty-five per cent of the entire population registered and well over half of these actually voted in 1946. Stimulus was given to party development but the most successful politicians were those associated with labour. Actually the 'labour' label was assumed by some candidates who had little or nothing to do with the unions. Parties were little more than vote-catching names given to the temporary alliance of a few candidates without any real organization or fixed programme.

Even the more serious attempts to base a permanent party upon a political philosophy were not successful. The West Indian National Party, for example, was founded at San Fernando in South Trinidad in November, 1943, by Dr David Pitt who had been elected previously to the San Fernando Borough Council as a socialist. The WINP was organized as a socialist party and in its early history grew rapidly in importance and attracted the allegiance of a number of Trinidad's active politicians. Some of its candidates were elected to municipal councils but it never managed to organize a corps of

[1] Both changes by Order in Council of 3rd August, 1945.

voters whose first loyalty would be to the party. Successful WINP candidates owed election to personal qualities rather than to party designation. Lacking an island-wide following, the WINP tried to ally itself with organized labour under the name of United Front. Some union leaders came in but the best-known of all, T. U. B. Butler, refused to do so. Only three UF candidates were successful in the elections of 1946. These included two WINP members, Dr. Patrick Solomon, a coloured physician, and Roy Joseph, a Syrian with a large personal following in San Fernando. The other was Albert Gomes, an ex-socialist and trade unionist of Portuguese descent who had been expelled from the WINP but who joined the UF and gained celebrity by defeating the famous Butler. The ephemeral nature of parties at this time is indicated by the fact that in 1950 all three UF candidates again sought election but under different designations. Gomes was now sponsored by the Party of Political Progress Groups, a rather conservative, middle-class organization. Dr Solomon was now president of the Caribbean Socialist Party, successor to the WINP, and Roy Joseph ran as an independent.

Universal adult suffrage now brought a new set of elected members into the legislature, only three of the old ones retaining their places. The most striking change was the increase in the East Indian element, East Indians winning four of the nine elected seats. The new members varied in their attitudes towards the policy leadership provided by the executive, still dominated as it was by the officials. In general they were readier to oppose government measures than had been the case in earlier Legislative Councils and a few were consistently in opposition. Even the elected members of the Executive Council were sometimes uncomfortable, as Cipriani had been, in their compulsory alliance with the officials. It seemed that the chief result of the reforms might be to turn the legislature into a permanent opposition body, as in the days of the Old Representative system, the chief difference being that the members now represented the general population rather than the planters.

Constitutional reform in the direction of some elected control over policy was the next obvious step. A legislative committee of unofficials was appointed to make proposals. A minority of this committee advocated complete responsible government and the removal of ex-officio members from the legislature. The majority report, less radical, suggested that a majority of the Executive Council consist of unofficials, chosen by and responsible to the legislature. After considerable debate the majority plan was accepted in the Legislative Council by the close margin of three votes. Six nominated and two elected members voted for it and five

F

elected members were opposed. The officials abstained. Accordingly Trinidad was given a new Legislative Council of three ex-officio, five nominated and eighteen elected members, presided over by a nominated speaker without a vote. The Executive Council consisted of the Governor with a casting vote, three officials, ex-officio, one nominated member of the Legislative Council chosen by the Governor, and five elected members of the Legislative Council chosen by secret ballot in the Legislative Council and removable by a two-thirds vote in the Legislative Council. Except for the retention of a mixed unicameral legislature, Trinidad now had approximately the same amount of self-government enjoyed by Jamaica under its 1944 constitution.[1] The significant feature of both was that, except in unusual circumstances, the elected members in the Executive Council would actually determine government policies.

The Governor's power of certification was enlarged so that he could use it to overcome opposition in both the legislature and the executive branches. This reserved power was a principal cause of the objections to the new constitution raised by the elected members who opposed it. Another feature they disliked was the power of the Governor acting alone to assign departmental responsibilities to the ministers elected by the legislature. Some also objected to the continued presence of nominated members. The Secretary of State had insisted that the nominated element was still needed because the existing bad feeling between employers and unions together with the political innocence of the mass voter might lead to an elected delegation consisting of extremists and demagogues who might wreck the colony's economy if given a free hand. He referred also to the fact that Trinidad so far had not developed a stable, responsible set of political parties.

The colony was divided into eighteen single-member districts, one being Tobago, and elections were held in 1950. There were one hundred and forty-one candidates contesting the eighteen seats. Ninety of these were independents and the others had some kind of party affiliation although it would be a mistake to assume that this had much significance as to programme or even general agreement on policies. The largest and most successful party was Butler's BEW and CHRP. Six affiliates of this group were elected as well as Butler himself and they were joined by another who had been elected as an independent. Evidence of the fact that party affiliation was chiefly a matter of expedience on the part of the candidates is dis-

[1] Changes made by Letters Patent of 16 March, 1950, and Royal Instructions and Order in Council of 31 March, 1950. The Secretary of State also sent a memorandum on the ministerial system.

played in the case of the successful Tobago contestant who claimed to be allied with both the BEW and CHRP and the Caribbean Socialist Party, which had been founded in 1947.

Despite the fact that Butler's group was the most successful, neither he nor any other member of it succeeded in securing a place in Executive Council. Instead, the Legislative Council voted for three independents, one member of the Caribbean Socialist Party and one who had been sponsored by the Political Progress Group. Obviously the majority of the Legislative Council, including the ex-officio, nominated and elected majority, were determined to exclude Butler and his party and had the necessary votes to do so. As a result Butler denounced this action as "Capitalist conspiracy" and continued to oppose the Executive Council in the same way and using the same language as when all had been nominees of the Governor. As in Jamaica, the ministers operated their departments as political policy-makers and represented them in the legislature. Much government business, however, was still introduced and defended by the ex-officio members, the Colonial Secretary and the Financial Secretary. There was no 'premier' nor could there well be one while the Executive Council consisted of officials and independent elected members and the responsibility for introducing government bills still remained largely in the hands of the officials. The nearest approach to such a personage was Albert Gomes who defended Executive Council policies in debate ably and volubly and who engaged in frequent and acrimonious exchanges with T. U. B. Butler, the leader of the Opposition Bloc, which suffered defections until it came to consist of Butler himself and two others.

Constitutional advance continued to be discussed at intervals. It is doubtful if the general public except on rare occasions has been greatly excited by the constitutional issue. But the small, politically active minority and especially the elected politicians have occasion to encounter official opposition to their plans. It is a constant aggravation to know that one will be compelled to defer to official judgment, even if serious differences occur but seldom. There is always the subtle implication of inferiority which cannot be detached from colonial status, however advanced. Under the 1950 constitution the elected ministers were still uncomfortable sometimes in their close association with the official side. Gomes spoke of this in debate, referring to the Executive Council as an "anachronism" which compelled the ministers to divide their loyalties between the Governor and the legislature.[1] Another reason for the unremitting drive for constitutional advance has been inter-

[1] *Trinidad and Tobago Legislative Council Debates*, 22 November, 1946, pp. 43, 44.

colonial competition and jealousy. It is felt to be derogatory to the pride and dignity of an important colony if it fails to receive at once a measure of increased self-government conferred elsewhere.

So once again, in January, 1955, the Governor, Sir Hubert Rance appointed a Constitutional Reform Committee consisting of all unofficial members of the Legislative Council, both nominated and elected plus eleven other eminent persons. This committee reported to the new Governor, Sir Edward Beetham in September. The report was accepted in large part by the government and by the Secretary of State with the result that more elected members were added to both Legislative Council and Executive Council.[1]

In brief, the Executive Council retains the Governor as chairman but consists now of only two other ex-officio members (the Colonial Secretary and Attorney-General) and seven elected members instead, as formerly, of the Governor, three ex-officio, one nominated and five elected members. The Legislative Council was enlarged to a total of thirty-one members (formerly, twenty-seven). Twenty-four, instead of eighteen, are now elected. The non-elected portion now includes two ex-officio members (the Colonial Secretary and the Attorney-General) and five nominees. This is a reduction of one ex-officio member (the Financial Secretary) now replaced by a Finance Minister from the elected membership. In addition the Speaker is chosen by the elected members instead of being a nominee of the Governor. He may be an elected member or someone not in the legislature. Furthermore, the elected members choose a Chief Minister who directs the time and business of the chamber, as well as serving as Government leader in the Executive Council, a function performed formerly in large part by the Colonial Secretary.

One difference between the position of the Chief Minister and a normal parliamentary prime minister is that the Chief Minister in Trinidad does not have a free choice in picking his team. They, as well as he, are chosen by the Legislative Council but he does have the right to advise the Governor in the assignment of portfolios to the various ministers, as well as the assignment to the specific ministries of four Parliamentary Secretaries appointed by the Governor to assist the ministers and represent them in the legislature when they are absent. The Chief Minister can advise the Governor to withdraw a portfolio from a minister but the ex-minister remains a member of the Executive Council unless removed by a two-thirds vote of the Legislative Council. Under this rule the votes of the opposition might be used to keep an ex-minister in the Executive Council against the will of the Chief Minister. Such

[1] By Constitutional Instruments published June 7, 1956.

a provision is not truly compatible with party government. The Chief Minister is also unable legally to force a dissolution. The Governor is free to reject his advice on this point. Of course, as a practical matter, the Governor might find himself in serious political difficulties if he refused the Chief Minister's advice and so compelled his resignation while the Chief Minister still retained the support of a majority in the Legislative Council.

The most important event of 1956 in Trinidad was political rather than constitutional. For the first time in the colony's history a single political party won a majority of the elected seats. This was the People's National Movement which had its inception when Dr Eric Williams resigned his post as Deputy Chairman of the Research Council of the Caribbean Commission and decided to become active in politics. Dr Williams is an historian and former university teacher who was educated at Oxford on an Island Scholarship. The PNM was launched officially in early January, 1956, its organization patterned after that of the Jamaican People's National Party. Dr Williams was fortunate in securing as party chairman, Learie Constantine, perhaps the most celebrated cricketer in the West Indies who had become a professional player and had used his earnings to finance his studies for the bar. Williams himself was named Political Leader. The party's General Council was inter-racial and included three women and four trades union officers.

Williams began his public campaign with a series of lectures in Woodford Square, Port-of-Spain, the traditional forum for open-air political meetings. These meetings were sponsored in part by the People's Education Movement of the Teachers' Educational and Cultural Association, Limited, which Williams had sponsored. He lectured on constitutional reform and other subjects including education, repeating the lectures in other towns throughout the island and publishing them as 'Public Affairs Pamphlets'. He was careful not to attack denominational education directly nor to discuss birth control.[1] His lectures were literate, well-reasoned and must have been over the heads of many in his audiences. But the PNM was the best-organized party Trinidad had yet seen and attracted a number of well-known supporters including politicians not connected with the existing ministry. Williams himself caught the imagination of the poor and ignorant who decided that he was their champion. They thronged his meetings to cheer him and refused to listen to other speakers. By midsummer, 1956, the growing popularity of the PNM had led to mergers of several other parties, the withdrawal of a number of independents and the announcement

[1] This did not prevent some of his Roman Catholic opponents from asserting that the party initials, PNM, stood for 'prenatal murderers'.

of the People's Democratic Party, led by B. S. Maraj, that it was supporting Gomes, Joseph and Butler. These four were curiously ill-assorted, having little in common except their united opposition to the PNM. At the polls the PNM won thirteen of the twenty-four elected seats. The PDP won five, the Trinidad Labour Party two, the Butler party, two, and there were two successful independents.

This meant that the ministers, instead of a collection of independents as heretofore, were all chosen from this victorious party and the party leader, Dr. Eric Williams, became Chief Minister.[1] Furthermore, this one-party victory, unprecedented for Trinidad, was followed by a remarkable constitutional innovation. The nominated seats in the legislature had been filled traditionally by persons chosen as representatives of important economic interests or else because they could be depended upon to support the government, that is, the official bloc. Now, for the first time, nominations were made deliberately to increase the working majority of the *elected* leadership. This was done in accord with instructions from the Secretary of State (Lennox-Boyd). This is an interesting example of the flexibility of parliamentary institutions. Having begun as a means of providing a check upon the elected element, this institution of nominated members is now, as regards Trinidad, used in reverse fashion, to give the elected majority a greater number of votes than it won in the elections. From one viewpoint, this change is less revolutionary than might appear at first glance. The nominated members had often been chosen to strengthen the government and this is still their function even though the government is now an elected rather than an official group.

BARBADOS

As remarked in Chapter II, Barbados alone among the British West Indian colonies retained an unbroken line of constitutional descent from the Old Representative System. In general, the population was politically apathetic and there was little interest in elections under the severely restricted suffrage. Very often a single candidate would be elected in his constituency without opposition. From 1891 to the first of February, 1954, the real executive power in Barbados was in the hands of the Executive Committee consisting of the Governor, the Colonial Secretary and the Attorney General (all ex-officio) plus such other persons as the Governor chose to appoint.

But between the World Wars, Barbados like the other colonies, began to feel the need for constitutional advance. One of the earliest manifestations of dissatisfaction was the Democratic League

[1] See below, pp. 206, 208, for a discussion of Dr. Williams and his party.

founded in 1923-24 by Dr Charles Duncan O'Neale, some of whose followers had been inspired by the racist ideas of Marcus Garvey. In 1932 Dr O'Neale secured election to the House of Assembly. The efforts of the League, however, proved to be abortive. Possibly its approach was too exclusively political to appeal to the unenfranchised and unorganized majority and too radical to attract the small voting public. A young barrister, Grantley Adams, had been elected to the House of Assembly in 1934 and gained celebrity in 1937 as the defender of Clement Payne, the leader of the 1937 riots. When the Progressive League was founded in 1938 by Hope Stevens (a Barbadian returned from the United States) Adams soon became prominent in this organization and was elected president in 1939. Barbadian students in England became interested in this new movement which stood for a broader franchise, social welfare and even some practical socialism. One of these, Hugh Springer, on his return from Oxford, urged the founding of a strong labour union. Accordingly, the Barbados Workers' Union was founded in October, 1941, and Adams became its president. The first election in which the League ran candidates was that of 1940. It was highly successful; five of its six candidates secured election. But the first political results of the new union were not encouraging and the elections of 1942 saw the reduction of the League members from five to four. Nevertheless, Adams and his colleagues were successful in inducing the House to accept several of their measures, and Adams was appointed to the Executive Committee early in 1942. The Progressive League had now become the Barbados Labour Party with the Barbados Workers' Union as its right arm. Adams, as president of both, was able to dominate the political scene, pick his candidates and throw the voting power of the union behind them. The Labour Party increased its House representation to eight in 1944 and Hugh Springer joined Adams as a member of the Executive Committee. This victory was due to the success of Adams and his supporters in putting through a bill reducing property requirements for voting by almost one-half and extending the franchise to women. Even though cane-field workers were still unable to meet the property requirement,[1] this bill increased the electorate from about six thousand to nearly thirty thousand. Although the Labour Party did not have a majority in the House, a coalition with the West Indian National Congress Party (a socialist, ultranationalist group led by W. A. Crawford) was formed which gave the coalition a two-to-one majority over the conservative Electors' Association, each party having won eight seats. Subsequently Adams was able to induce several Congress Party members to join his party and by

[1] An income of £30 per annum. Most field workers earned about £25.

the 1951 election the Congress Party had become unimportant.

The next constitutional advance came about because of a crisis arising from a peculiarity in the Barbadian constitution. The law allowed the Attorney General to be an *elected* member of the House of Assembly. Attorney General Keith Walcott (a Barbadian) secured election to the House supported by the conservative Electors' Association and in accord with Barbadian tradition became the usual spokesman for government (Executive Committee) measures. A bill to restrict the operations of Pan American Airways in Barbados was desired by the government. The Attorney General, as an official, duly introduced the bill, and then, as an elected member, spoke against it. The anomaly of an official member (even if not ex-officio) acting independently as an elected member became obvious. The Governor, Sir Henry Grattan Bushe, subsequently withdrew permission from the Attorney General to stand for election and proposed that the House permit him to name an ex-officio member to sit and speak even if not permitted to vote. The House, proud of its Old Representative tradition, regarded this as a retrograde step in the direction of Crown Colony government and rejected the proposal. The Governor next announced that he proposed to send for the elected member who was a party or coalition leader able to command a House majority, and ask him to nominate the other Elected Members of the Executive Committee.[1] He proposed also to ask these members to familiarize themselves with the work of specific administrative departments in order to represent these departments in Executive Committee discussions and House debates. Governor Bushe, that is, proposed to introduce a quasi-ministerial system with the Executive Committee evolving by usage towards becoming a cabinet without any change in the Governor's legal power to intervene if necessary.

The 'Bushe Experiment', introduced in 1946, was continued by the next Governor, Sir Hilary Blood, who said in November, 1948, 'In practice I accept as a general though not as an absolute rule, the advice given by the House of Assembly Members [in Executive Committee] if they are unanimous.' From 1946, therefore, Barbados was governed under a system which gave the elected majority party leadership the handling of executive decisions on policy matters except in unusual circumstances.

But the 'Bushe Experiment' was not entirely satisfactory to

---

[1] This announcement came in his speech proroguing the House on October 1st, 1946. He said, 'The defect of the constitution lies in the imperfect distribution of power and responsibility. The Governor has the whole responsibility of government but he is given no power. The House of Assembly possesses the power but has no responsibility."
—*Barbados House of Assembly Debates*, 1 October, 1946.

Adams and his colleagues. It did much to provide a link between the House of Assembly and the Executive Committee (hitherto almost totally lacking), but the quasi-ministers were not given salaries which would enable them to devote full time to departmental business, nor did they have any real authority to direct departmental policies. The House of Assembly in September, 1949, passed an address requesting the establishment of a full ministerial system and this matter was discussed by Adams with the Governor, Sir Alfred Savage. Subsequently universal adult suffrage was introduced, property qualifications for membership in the House were abolished and the life of the House extended to three years. These changes were noted by the Acting Governor (Colonial Secretary), R. N. Turner, as justifying a further advance because ensuring that the new ministers would be genuine representatives of the people and with sufficient time (three years) to operate a ministerial system efficiently. Turner noted further that the Barbados Labour Party had announced the rapid achievement of 'full responsible government' as a prime objective and had won the ensuing (December, 1951) elections by seating sixteen members in a House of twenty-four.[1] Accordingly it was proposed to establish five salaried ministerial posts, each to be assigned a group of departments, one to be occupied by the Principal Minister or Premier.[2] The Secretary of State agreed to this proposal and Adams became the first Premier of Barbados on February 1, 1954.

This was accomplished by *convention* rather than by changing the legal requirement. It was agreed that the Governor would henceforth ask the leader of the majority party in the House, or the member able to secure majority support in that body, to become Premier. He would then ask the Premier to suggest the names of the four other House members to be made ministers. This would in fact give the ministry almost complete control of policy because only through them can government bills, including all financial measures be introduced in the House of Assembly. And because Barbados has escaped the Crown Colony stage in its constitutional progress the Governor has no reserved power of certification to enable him to legislate despite an adverse vote in the legislature.

On the other hand, there remain some limitations upon full self-government. These include the presence in the Executive Committee of the three top officials as well as a member of the nominated Legislative Council (the second chamber) who is almost

[1] See Message No. 25/1953. *His Excellency the Governor to the Honourable the Legislative Council.*
[2] Adams preferred the title 'Premier' to 'Principal Minister'. 'Prime Minister' has been denied to chief ministers within the colonial system, although allowed in the new West Indies Federation.

certain to be out of sympathy with some Labour Party policies. The Executive Committee, therefore, falls short of the Jamaican Council of Ministers in its resemblance to a cabinet.

The Barbadian legislature resembles the British Parliament in miniature. The Barbadian 'House of Lords' is the Legislative Council, a second chamber of fifteen members appointed by the Governor for five-year terms. In this chamber the principal spokesman for the government remained the Chief Secretary, as the Colonial Secretary has been called since 1954. When day-to-day executive and policy decisions were in fact made by the Governor it was logical that his chief subordinate should expound and defend these policies in the Legislative Council. But when the policy-making function passed to an elected Premier it seemed anomalous that a permanent official, neither appointed nor dismissable by the Premier and directly responsible to the Governor, should continue to discharge this duty. A Chief Secretary not in sympathy with government policies might, at the least, fail to show the energy and resource in debate demanded by the Premier and the latter would be unable to do anything about this. Mr (now Sir Grantley) Adams made these points in a House debate in March, 1956, and subsequently the Governor and the Secretary of State agreed to a constitutional change which would permit the Premier to nominate a member to the Legislative Council to act as leader of government business. Accordingly, in 1959 the Executive Committee Act of 1891 was amended to enable the appointment to the Executive Committee of more than four members of the House. At the same time it was provided that the member appointed from the Legislative Council to sit in the Executive Committee should be a Minister Without Portfolio who would be nominated by the Premier and who would act in the Legislative Council as leader of government business. It was provided that he would retain his seat in the legislature only so long as he remains a minister. He, together with the ministers from the House of Assembly, would meet as a cabinet under the Premier's chairmanship and, in fact, make all executive decisions except those still retained by law in the hands of the full executive body, the Governor-in-Executive Council. These powers, in the exercise of which the permanent officials would still have a voice, include the passage of subsidiary legislation, hearing appeals and making certain appointments. The Chief Secretary retains his seat in the Legislative Council but no longer has the responsibility of representing the government in the introduction of bills and their defence in debate. The anomaly of a permanent official required to behave as if he were one of the elected ministers has thus been eliminated.

Legislative Councillors have been chosen, for the most part, on the basis of their representation of important, private, economic interests, notably sugar and commerce. But some are picked, as in the case of Sir John Saint, because they have expert knowledge of an important subject.[1] The Lord Bishop of Barbados (Anglican) is always a member, an obvious choice so long as the Church of England remains the established church of the colony. In certain respects, therefore, the Legislative Council resembles a miniature House of Lords. It was logical, in these circumstances, to permit the Premier to name a member of this body who would represent the elected, and now, more important part of the government of the day, as was done by Prime Ministers who advised the creation of Labour peers at Westminster. But the colour-class complex in Barbados has added a complicating factor to the bicameral system. The Legislative Council has been almost exclusively white in membership. There have been a few exceptions. In 1954 only two Legislative Councillors were coloured. In that same year only three members of the elected House of Assembly were white, and one of these was a 'maverick' white, a left-wing member of the Barbados Labour Party.

The debate in the Legislative Council on the eve of the introduction of the ministerial system reflected the attitude of the propertied white minority towards the acquisition of such power by coloured ministers dependent, in the final analysis, upon the support of a mass electorate. Obviously a racial argument could not be advanced openly.[2] The attack was focussed mainly upon the cost involved, with about half of the Labour Party's elected members now due to receive ministerial salaries. Die-hard conservative members in the Legislative Council asserted that universal suffrage had been granted prematurely and predicted grimly the financial collapse of the government, the breakdown of popular government and an eventual dictatorship.

The introduction of the ministerial system did nothing to obviate the possibility of conflict between the two chambers. The Legislative Council, however, had possessed only a one-year suspensory veto since 1947. Subsequently it tended to behave like the House

---

[1] Sir Sidney John Saint, Kt, CMG, OBE, MSc, etc., Director of the Sugar Technological Laboratory since 1949, General Chairman, International Society of Sugar Cane Technologists, 1950-53, formerly Director of Agriculture, Barbados.
[2] In the House of Assembly one of the new ministers, the Honourable R. G. Mapp, was more outspoken. He remarked: 'A lot of people are disappointed that Barbados isn't like BG . . . They want to see ministerial status collapse. . . . They want to say that the coloured boys cannot run anything. The Malans do not want to see the Nkrumahs come up by their side'.

of Lords, avoiding an all-out battle with the other chamber but trying to secure modifications in legislation it considered ill-advised. The most serious disagreement with the House following the establishment of ministerial government was over the Maude Bill, passed by the House in 1952, rejected by the Legislative Council and repassed by the House in 1953. This bill provided for universal adult suffrage in the election of local government bodies which formerly had been chosen by an electorate meeting a property requirement. This change, it was felt, would encourage extravagance on the part of vestries chosen mainly by ignorant field hands who paid no direct taxes. In this issue the Legislative Council raised a point of British constitutional usage, protesting against the resubmission of the bill without an intervening general election.[1]

The existence of a nominated second chamber has been attacked sometimes as a peculiarly colonial institution. This is not the case. A weak, revisionary chamber, not representative of the majority of the population, is a conservative device found in many countries with a parliamentary form of government. Good arguments can be advanced in favour of the existence of such a body.

But an obvious colonial limitation in Barbados is the retention by the officials of control of foreign affairs, police and security and the administrative establishment. Certain routine police administrative matters were turned over to the Premier but the control of police activities remained with the Chief Secretary, responsible to the Governor. This, together with control of the administrative establishment is a principal limitation, felt by the Colonial Office to be necessary at the intermediate stage of self-government.

THE LEEWARDS AND WINDWARDS

The small islands of these two groups are in general poor and over-populated. The vast majority of their inhabitants are wage-workers. Only in Grenada are there a considerable number of peasant-proprietors owning nutmeg and cocoa groves. Following the riots of the depression period the political pattern in all of them was substantially the same. The older, conservative, property-holding, middle-class politicians became less influential. They remained chiefly as nominated members and seldom secured election. Labour unions were organized, some of which were real unions and others little more than names. The organizers or leaders of these, usually of poor Negro origin, became the outstanding figures on the elected side of the legislature and loud in their demands for constitutional advance and social welfare projects.

[1] See *below*, pp. 191, 192.

The first intercolonial step towards a constitutional change was taken at a Windward Islands Conference of delegates from the island legislatures which met in Grenada in January, 1945, to discuss the conclusions of the Moyne Report. The conference requested a federal legislature for the Windwards to be elected by the island legislatures, a reduction in official voting power, an increase in the number of elected members and universal adult suffrage for literates. These suggestions were countered by the Secretary of State with a proposal to federate the entire Windward-Leeward group and give the federal legislature an unofficial but not an elected majority. The proposed federation would be highly centralized, the island governments being reduced to virtual county status. These proposals were then discussed at a conference which met at St Kitts and consisted of representatives of all the legislatures in both island chains. This conference, under the chairmanship of Sir Clement Malone, Chief Justice of the Windwards and Leewards, made elaborate and detailed counter-proposals for a federation of the two groups. As completed, the plan was acceptable to most of the island legislatures, either as it stood or with minor modifications. Relatively prosperous Grenada, however, objected strenuously to parting with its right to set and collect customs duties and income tax. The Secretary of State questioned several provisions of the plan, particularly its reduction of official voting power in the federal legislature to a simple casting vote in the hands of the Governor, especially as the legislature was to consist mainly of directly elected members. Had the island legislatures been unanimous in their demand for the scheme he might have sought to work out a compromise but Grenada's attitude gave him a good excuse to drop it.

In fact, no important constitutional changes resulted from these conferences. A few minor ones were made, such as giving Grenada an Administrator like the rest of the Windwards so that the Governor, normally resident there, should be free of his duty of presiding over the legislature and able more frequently to visit the other members of his governorship.

Gradually, however, there were some changes in practice and convention in the island legislatures. The Governor was not the sole source of policy as he had been. Nor were his policies pushed through the Executive and Legislative Councils by means of the automatic vote of the official bloc. More and more, he or his deputy, the Administrator, would accept policies originating with the elected membership and try to carry them out. This is not to imply that the official side was now out of the picture as to policy-making. The leading figure in each little parliament was its president, the Administrator. He still resembled a Prime Minister rather than an impartial Speaker in his control of time and business. The preparation and defence of the budget was still in the hands of another permanent official, the Financial Secretary, and he was more likely to be concerned about reducing the need for Treasury grants and achieving a balance than about the implementation of grandiose plans for social services. But the officials' policies were put across to the greatest possible extent by persuasion rather than official power and compromise was preferred to a rigid insistence upon the official view.

The next advance towards self-government came with the offer to the Windwards in July, 1950, of a plan to give all four legislatures in the group the same composition. They would consist of fourteen members: the Administrator as president with a casting vote only, two other officials, ex-officio, with voting power (the Financial Secretary and the Attorney General), three nominees of the Governor, eight members elected by universal suffrage with no literacy test. Candidates for election would require no property to qualify but would have to put up a substantial election deposit (£120) to be forfeited if they failed to obtain a specified proportion of the vote. The elected members would choose three of their own number to sit in the Executive Council and would also elect a Deputy President to preside over meetings of the Legislative Council in the absence of the Administrator. The members elected to Executive Council could be removed by a two-thirds vote of the Legislative Council. The Governor would also pick one of the nominated members to sit in Executive Council.

A similar system was also offered to the Leewards for the Presidency legislatures. The two larger ones (St Kitts-Nevis-Anguilla and Antigua) would have legislatures identical with those in the Windwards. Little Montserrat would have a smaller one of nine members: two ex-officio, two nominated and five elected.

There were few strenuous objections to the Secretary of State's offer in the Windwards. In St Kitts the new labour leader, Bradshaw, took violent exception to provisions which he thought might deprive him and his party from the total control of the elected side of the Presidency Legislative Council. Formerly the island voted as a single constituency and Labour swept all before it. The new plan called for single-member constituencies. Bradshaw also wanted the legislative quorum to be set at seven so that he and his colleagues could, at will, walk out and stop business. He threatened that he and his party would win all the elected seats and then refuse to serve. Nevertheless the plan was put through in St Kitts by use of the Governor's reserved powers and in Antigua by the Administrator's casting vote.

In the ensuing elections the labour-based parties won readily. In Antigua, Bird and his associates won all eight seats, four without contest owing to a boycott by the conservatives. In the Windwards, Labour victories were also general. In Dominica, five of the eight members were 'Labour' at least nominally. In St Lucia the Labour Party divided the victory with Garnet Gordon's moderate People's Progress Party. Labour candidates won in St Vincent and in Grenada the nascent People's Party led by the founder of the Mental and Manual Workers' Union, Eric Gairy, won six of the eight seats. That these 'parties' were sometimes more in the nature of a temporary election alliance of independents was demonstrated in several cases, but far more significant was the nearly universal tendency to discard the older, middle-class, moderate politicians for new men of the labour-leader-demagogue sort. Approximately five out of six of the elected members were novices and most of these pretended to represent the landless labourer. It is a tribute to the political skill of the Governors and Administrators that they were able to 'work' the constitution under these circumstances with a minimum of discord and trouble. The only serious public disturbances occurred in Grenada where adherents of Gairy's union attempted to recruit new members by threats and violence including house-burning, animal-killing and riots. Here the Governor was compelled to supplement his local police with troops from Trinidad to restore and preserve order.

A further step towards self-government was taken by the introduction of the committee system. This familiarized the elected members of the Executive Council with the work of the departments of administration. In 1956 the ministerial system was introduced in the Leeward Presidencies, now separate colonies following the repeal of the Leewards Islands Act, 1871. The elected members of Executive Council were placed in charge of groups of departments as ministers. They now constituted a majority of the Executive Council so that, subject to intervention in emergencies by the Governor or Administrator, they would now control policies in their assigned fields. Police, security, external affairs, and other less important matters remain in the hands of the Administrator. A similar system was introduced in the Windwards except for Dominica.

The tiny Virgin Islands Presidency had a measure of representative government restored to it. The Virgin Islands Constitutional Act, 1950, authorized a Legislative Council presided over by the Commissioner and consisting of two nominated officials, two nominated unofficials and four members, meeting a property qualification, elected by literate adults. This restored a partly-elected legislature to the Virgins for the first time since 1902.

CHAPTER V

CONSTITUTIONAL AND POLITICAL DEVELOPMENTS IN THE MAINLAND COLONIES

BRITISH HONDURAS

THE large but sparsely inhabited Central American colony was first settled by English buccaneers from Jamaica who set up a permanent camp on one of the islets or cays near the mouth of the Belize River in the early seventeenth century. Between piratical adventures they began to cut and ship logwood to Europe for the manufacture of dye-stuffs. Later, other adventurers from Jamaica joined them to participate in this profitable industry and slaves were imported to work in the forests. About six hundred slaves were sent to the colony after Tacky's Rebellion in 1760, the most serious of the slave insurrections up to that time.

While all this was going on, Central America remained legally Spanish territory and although the British authorities did not forbid the settlers to go there, there was no official disposition to challenge Spanish sovereignty on their behalf. The settlers, unsupported by His Majesty's forces, had to defend themselves as best they could against sporadic Spanish attempts to oust them. When the budding colony moved to the mainland about 1786 and founded the town of Belize on the mud-flats at the river mouth, the settlement was almost immediately destroyed by the Spanish and the survivors deported. The name of the this town, incidentally, is cited by Guatemalans as proof of the Spanish origin of the community. It is true that the Spanish word for buoy is *baliza* and buoys certainly were used at the moorings in the roadstead off the river mouth, but the British claim is that the name represents a corruption of the name of one of the buccaneer founders, Captain Peter Wallace.

The destruction of Belize did not finish the infant colony. The deportees and others returned and in 1789 Spain agreed by treaty to their presence there for lumbering purposes but not for permanent colonization. After this only one other Spanish attack took place. The battle of St George's Cay on September 10, 1798, was the final encounter in which a Spanish armada of thirty-one vessels was repulsed. Thereafter the 'Baymen', as they called themselves, were

G

left unmolested although Guatemala, and less frequently Mexico, as Spanish successor-states in that part of Central America, have challenged the British title from time to time.[1]

As a result of British reluctance to push colonial claims in Central America, the Baymen were left to their own devices as regards local government. The outcome was a system very much like that of the New England town meeting. In the case of Belize it was called the Public Meeting. Of course the colonists were British subjects and under no foreign jurisdiction. They were supposedly under the control of the Governor of Jamaica as the nearest Crown authority. But it was difficult for the Governor to keep a tight rein upon the little settlement. It is reported that the settlers rarely paid attention to any orders from the Jamaican officials. They preferred to run their affairs by means of a board of six or seven magistrates to hear any local court cases and to spend the public funds. These magistrates, one of whom was chosen Chief Magistrate or Superintendent (much like a First Selectman of a New England town), were elected at an annual meeting of the freemen of Belize. This meeting was of practical size for the freemen could not have numbered more than a few hundred at any time.

This form of government received informal recognition by Admiral Sir W. Burnaby who was sent to Belize by the Governor of Jamaica in 1765. Burnaby not only recognized the validity of the elected magistrate system but codified the laws which had been passed at successive public meetings. 'Burnaby's Code' became the basic law of the colony.

As time went on and the British authorities became more inclined to interest themselves in this self-made colony, a Crown-appointed Superintendent was sent from Jamaica to replace the elected one. Created in 1786, the office was left vacant between 1791 and 1797 but thereafter continued without a break until the creation of the Crown Colony of British Honduras.

Even with the Crown-appointed Superintendent the remainder of the governmental establishment long retained its early form. In time, the meeting of all freemen gave way to a more limited gathering still called the Public Meeting. Membership in this had a property restriction, the possession of £400 in cash, and a curious club-like requirement that a new member had to be proposed by an old one and receive at least twenty-six votes from old members. The Public Meeting had no precise size but varied from fifty to seventy at various times. Once elected, a member served for life.

This assembly met spontaneously, without summons, every four

[1] For the diplomatic history of this dispute, see M. W. Williams, *Anglo-American Isthmian Diplomacy* (Washington, 1916).

months and proposed and passed laws and financial measures on its own initiative. The elected magistracy continued to act as judges and public disbursement officials.

The Superintendent had the power of veto over acts of the Public Meeting but no way of enforcing any positive policies upon it or of controlling the Magistrates even if their actions were out of harmony with the Superintendent's instructions from Jamaica. The Superintendents therefore, one after another, tried to get the Crown to enlarge their powers at the expense of the elected Magistrates and the Public Meeting. This was done and eventually the Superintendent came to occupy a position similar to that of a Crown Colony Governor. He appointed the Magistrates; his pre-approval was required for the introduction of measures in the Public Meeting; he was given an Executive Council of the principal officials. In 1853 the Public Meeting voted to abolish itself in favour of a Legislative Assembly of three nominated members and eighteen members elected by voters with a small property qualification.

In 1862 the settlement of Belize became officially the Crown Colony of British Honduras with a Lieutenant-Governor replacing the Superintendent but still subordinate to the Governor of Jamaica. In 1884 British Honduras was separated administratively from Jamaica and its chief official raised to the rank of Governor.

But even the remnants of the representative system were finally destroyed. The Legislative Assembly had become the scene of a permanent conflict between the timber and the commercial interests in the colony. The electorate was still confined to citizens of Belize in spite of the gradual expansion of population in other districts. In 1856 there were only eighty-five registered and fifty-one actual voters electing eighteen members.[1] Tired of the legislative battle, it would seem, the Assembly voted in 1870 to abolish itself in favour of a purely nominated Legislative Council of officials and at least four nominated unofficial members. From a direct democracy of the old *folkmoot* kind, British Honduras had regressed through the Old Representative System back to a purely official autocracy with only a trace of representation in the limited number of nominated unofficials.

Then the tide turned. As time went on, more nominated unofficials were added to the Executive Council, the number of unofficial nominees in the Legislative Council was gradually increased, and there was occasional agitation in favour of a resumption of elections for the legislature. That there was not more and earlier demand for self-government possibly was due to the

[1] According to Report for 1869, Parliamentary Papers 1871, vol. xlvii, cited in Wrong, *op. cit.*, p. 106, footnote 1.

frontier nature of British Honduras society. Slavery and colour presented few problems. The slaves had been lumbermen for the most part. Abolition meant the introduction of wages and little more. The freedmen continued to work in the forest. The inhabitants of Belize were interested in shipping, the export business, the import and sale of food and manufactured articles and such commercial enterprise. Belize was the port and shopping centre of the hinterland. There were few whites, the small middle class being predominantly the usual West Indian Afro-British blend. The labouring class was chiefly Negro. In the back country near the Mexican and Guatemalan borders were many Spanish-speaking Mayan Indians and Spanish-Indian *mestizos,* as well as a few primitive Mayans. In Stann Creek were the remnants of a band of 'Black Caribs', of Afro-Carib descent who had been deported from St Vincent in 1796, and who remained a distinct people, retaining Carib as their first language. Most of these people outside of Belize were politically inert and Belize itself was a sluggish, frontier town which grew but slowly.[1]

Without the development of the colony agriculturally there was little need for growth and, indeed, it was to the immediate advantage of the powerful Belize Estate and Produce Company to restrain development which it was able to do by its influence upon the Crown Colony government.[2] This company had acquired timber rights to about one-fifth of the entire colony, some 1,200,000 acres, including most of the best mahogany forest. Its lumbermen felled the age-old mahogany trees and floated the logs downriver to Belize whence they were shipped abroad. It was more profitable to leave the cut-over land untouched and it is only recently that re-afforestation has been undertaken. A report on the colony's economy issued by the British Honduras Treasury in 1954 announced that timber had been overcut to an extent requiring thirty to fifty years for replacement so that there would have to be greater reliance upon agriculture and light industry. For long, too, the logs were shipped as they came from the forest and only recently has the company

[1] The population of Belize in 1911 was 10,478 and by 1927 had increased only to 12,600.
[2] It is difficult to cite concrete evidence for this influence which was exerted chiefly in informal ways upon the Governors, inducing them to use their powers to block suggestions for road-building, agricultural expansion and the sale of Crown lands to individual farmers. The author was informed by a former civil servant (without his having been able to confirm the statement) that a proposal by the British Honduras government to increase taxes on timber land by one-half-cent per acre in order to subsidize agricultural development was vetoed by the Secretary of State. At this time, Sir Samuel Hoare (later Lord Templewood) was a member of the ministry. At this time also, the Belize Estate and Produce Company was largely owned by the Hoare family.

established a sawmill at Belize for the manufacture of lumber. Company influence too was used to prevent the sale of timberlands to individuals who would clear them and establish farms. All of this meant that for centuries British Honduras was little more than a 'timber-mine' and has a good claim to the appelation 'most neglected' among the British Caribbean possessions. It was not until 1954 that an all-weather road, the Hummingbird Highway, was completed to link Belize and Stann Creek, the third town in the colony in point of size, and the centre of the citrus country.

For all these reasons, British Honduras long retained, and still retains to a considerable extent, the characteristics of a frontier society. The main product continues to be timber, with pine now of equal importance with mahogany. Chicle, the solidified sap of the wild sapodilla trees, is the second largest money-maker for the colony and citrus fruits are now approaching chicle in importance. There are also some experiments with cattle-breeding. Because it was not tied to the sugar-economy as were the islands, British Honduras has been self-sustaining throughout most of its history. Not only was it able to balance its own budget without Treasury aid but its products, mahogany and chicle, did not require preferential tariffs to hold their own in the world market.

Like the other colonies, British Honduras suffered economically in the depression of the 'thirties. A disastrous hurricane in 1931 occasioned such expenditure for rebuilding and relief that the local government had to turn to the British Treasury for aid. A Treasury loan of $3,000,000 was made but with the usual stipulation that the Governor be given the reserved power to legislate positively. These reserved powers were not used until after the devaluation of the pound Sterling and the decision to devalue the British Honduran dollar. The local currency had been tied, like that of Canada, to the US dollar and businessmen and firms in Belize with surplus funds had been able to purchase devalued pounds as a hedge against local devaluation. This was an additional cause of resentment, because it was believed that certain favoured persons had been able to secure advance information of the intention to devalue in time to buy Sterling and avoid devaluation of their personal fortunes. For a time there was much uncertainty as to British policy on this point but many British Hondurans believed, on the basis of speeches in the British Parliament, that the British Honduran dollar would be permitted to remain outside the Sterling bloc. The final decision of the Secretary of State, however, was to devalue the British Honduran dollar by thirty per cent and the Governor was instructed to force the measure through. This was done by the use of the reserve power to legislate against the unanimous vote of all unofficial legislative members, both nominated and elected. Resentment was widespread, not only among the propertied class. Because the necessities of life, including food and clothing as well as all kinds of manufactures are imported, there was a general price rise equivalent to the devaluation and everyone felt the inflationary pinch.

Previous to the devaluation controversy, the constitution of the colony had been modified in line with developments elsewhere and local demands for increased representation. From 1892 to 1935 the Legislative Council had had only official and unofficial nominated members. In 1935 elected members were re-introduced along with adult suffrage based upon a low income or property qualification. This gave the Legislative Council an unofficial majority, though not a majority of elected members. It was the combination of nominated and elected members that compelled the Governor to use his reserved power as noted above.

By 1954 the Executive Council had come to consist of three ex-officio members: the Colonial Secretary, Attorney General and Financial Secretary, and four nominated unofficials. The Legislative Council presided over by the Governor, consisted of the three top officials, ex-officio, four unofficials nominated by the Governor, and six members elected for a three-year term from five constituencies (Belize elected two members) by voters meeting a small property qualification and a literacy test.

Control of business rested with the Governor whose pre-approval was needed for the introduction of all measures. The Governor also had both an original and a casting vote as well as veto power. He possessed reserved powers to legislate positively as well as the power to reserve approval of a measure until 'the Crown's pleasure' could be ascertained. He was required so to reserve several categories of bills. The budget required the approval of the Secretary of State before enactment.

Basic liberties were limited by Ordinance number 43 of 1935 prohibiting any utterance, verbal or otherwise, even if true, if likely to lead to hatred or contempt of the Monarch, the Governor, or the Government. Unionization was not illegal but the strike weapon was limited by the ability of the government to declare an industry or business 'essential' which, by ordinance, made illegal any strike in that industry.

The result of the devaluation struggle was a widespread demand for more self-government and an upsurge of resentment against the British government amounting to something approaching a nearly universal sentiment of disloyalty to Great Britain. This found expression in various ways including the semi-boycott of all patriotic celebrations. Only about fourteen hundred spectators gathered to watch the military parade in honour of the coronation of Queen Elizabeth whereas about seven thousand had been expected. On National Day (November 25) 1953, Belize was a forest of empty flagpoles. Only two or three of the larger British-owned stores displayed the Union Jack. The two motion picture theatres discontinued the recorded playing of 'God Save the Queen' at the close of the showing because of the disorderly behaviour of the audiences and their truculent attitude towards the few persons who stood respectfully during the rendition of the national anthem. This disloyalty, however, was far short of revolutionary and included neither a civil disobedience movement nor any disposition to challenge the legal authority of the government.

The most significant result of the wave of anti-British feeling was that it enabled the creation of a coherent political party for the first time in the colony's history. The People's United Party, formed in 1950, offered a release in action of the frustrations and resentments, long smouldering, which devaluation had fanned into flame. The PUP leaders expressed in admired oratory the outraged feelings of the average British Honduran; they dared to say terrible things about the government and they promised many reforms. Previously the elected members of the Legislative Council and the Belize City Council had been elected as independents. They were mostly of the respectable middle class, typical of pre-depression West Indian politics. The PUP leadership included, to begin with, some men of this same category but the extremist nature of its anti-British position led to their withdrawal. This radical, anti-colonial attitude did not repel the working-class voter and the PUP succeeded in electing five of the seven members of the Belize City Council in November, 1950. Their opponents attributed PUP success to the fact that their opponents were disorganized and consisted of too many independents who split the vote among themselves.

In August, 1951, an attempt was made to form a moderate party to oppose the PUP. This was the National Party, favouring gradual development of self-government within the Commonwealth and federation with the West Indies. It was led by several of the former independents, but lacked organization and enthusiasm. Local businessmen who did not care for the quasi-socialism of the PUP were still unwilling to back this feeble opposition party. Several prominent independents were either nominal in their support of the National Party or refused to join it, preferring to remain independent candidates. No united front against the PUP could be constructed. The National Party, however, enjoyed a modest success in the Belize City Council elections of 1952, electing four of the nine members under the old limited franchise. This gave them control because they were joined by an independent, John A. Smith, a former PUP leader. The PUP had three seats and the support of another independent. This Council replaced a purely nominated one which the Governor had appointed to supersede the PUP-controlled Council of 1950. The 1950 Council had been dismissed from office by the Governor for refusing to permit the royal portraits (Queen Elizabeth and Prince Philip) to be hung in the Council chamber.

The British response to this political ferment was to proceed in April, 1954, with constitutional advances to a pre-ministerial system. The electorate was greatly expanded by the introduction of universal adult suffrage, the only requirement other than age being the ability of the voter to write his name. This reform enlarged the electorate from 1,737 to about 21,000. The requirement that the voter be able to sign his or her name enabled the PUP to attack the reform as incomplete and discriminatory against the illiterate Amerindians. Why this limitation was written into the law remains obscure. It served to disfranchise very few of the urban Negro population who provided the main support of the PUP and it cannot be defended by the common-sense argument usually given in defence of a literacy test. Indeed, PUP volunteers worked hard at the job of training illiterates to trace a copy of their names until able to write the name without assistance. The end result may have been to win friends and votes for the PUP among the otherwise politically indifferent *mestizos* and Mayan Indians.

The Legislative Council elected in 1954 consisted of the three top officials ex-officio, three unofficial nominees and nine elected members from single-member constituencies. The Governor appointed a speaker from outside the Assembly. The elected members chose four of their number to sit in Executive Council along with two of the nominated members of the Legislative Council and the three top officials. Three of these elected members were given the responsibility of representing groups of departments in the legislature and raising questions about them in Executive Council. Three other members of the Legislative Council were named to assist the quasi-ministers. Internal order, justice and external affairs along with finance and the administrative establishment remained in the hands of the permanent officials.

The elections of 1954 saw a sweeping victory for the PUP which won a 'little slam', eight of the nine elected seats, giving the party a majority of one over the combined vote of all others. Over two-thirds of the registered voters cast ballots. This victory was made possible by the energy and enthusiasm of the PUP leaders, their organizing ability, and the close association with the General

Workers' Union. Even though the General Workers' Union had but 3,500 or so members in Belize and a scattering elsewhere (its claim of a total of 9,000 was almost certainly exaggerated), it provided the nucleus for a real campaign at the voter's level, something the National Party and the independents were quite unable to match. The tie between party and union was close. A union plebiscite was held in September, 1953 to vote on the question of whether or not the union should have political aims (those of the PUP). The union officers announced that of the 1,361 votes cast all but four were in favour of political action. Possibly most of the non-voters were indifferent rather than hostile. In selecting candidates care was taken to have both the party and the union represented by their leaders.

The vigorous and near-seditious language used by PUP leaders in the election campaign,[1] the belief that they were in receipt of monetary aid from Guatemala, then ruled by the Communist-dominated Arbenz government, had led some observers to fear another British Guiana incident. In fact, however, the PUP 'ministers' and their colleagues in the Legislative Council worked within the restrictions of the new constitution in proper, parliamentary fashion as they had promised to do before the elections. Despite constant trade deficits (over $BH 4,000,000 in 1954) indicating that exports pay for something less than two-thirds of imports, British Honduras has avoided Treasury aid along with Treasury controls in recent years because of CD & W grants. Hence the quasi-ministers were able to look forward to an increase in power and responsibility with the achievement of real ministerial government in the not-distant future.

The PUP leadership suffered from internal disagreements after the elections as to the attitude to be taken towards the continuation of the British connection. Leigh Richardson, Belize journalist, who shared top leadership of the party with George Price, came to favour the Commonwealth connection and upon the occasion of the welcome to the new Governor, C. H. Thornley, in January, 1956, spoke of . . . 'our unalterable determination to remain British now and forever.'[2] Richardson had attended West Indian federation talks as an observer for his colony and seemed to take a more

[1] Leigh Richardson, a PUP leader, and Philip Goldson of the General Workers' Union had been given eight-month prison terms in 1950 under the 'Subversive Control' Ordinance of 1935. This was the only use of this ordinance until the arrest of George Price in 1958.
[2] See Reuters despatch from Belize in Trinidad *Sunday Guardian*, dated January 17, 1956.
In 1954 Richardson had been made Member for Natural Resources, Philip Goldson (Asst. Secretary. PUP) Member for Social Services, and Herman Jex (GWU leader) Member for Public Utilities. Price was Associate Member for Natural Resources.

favourable attitude towards federation than that of his party. This led to a break with the bitterly anti-British and anti-West Indian Price. The disagreements broke into the open in 1956 in connection with a dispute between leaders of the General Workers' Union. This resulted in the expulsion of Richardson, Jex and Goldson from the PUP and the formation by Richardson of a new party, the Honduran Independence Party. But in the general elections of March, 1957, Price's PUP won all nine elected seats, its chief campaign appeal being a pledge to keep British Honduras out of the West Indies federation. In December, 1957, Price was dismissed from the Executive Council by the Governor, on the charge that he had broken faith with the government in trying to conceal private conversations he had had with the Guatemalan Minister in London concerning the possible annexation of British Honduras by the Central American republic.

On January 17, 1959, the Legislative Assembly voted eight to six in favour of a resolution affirming the colony's loyalty to the Queen and rejecting the old Guatemalan claim to the territory. The six negative votes were cast by PUP members but all six, as well as another who abstained from voting, insisted that they were not disloyal to the Queen but could not accept the resolution as it stood. George Price, as leader of the PUP, introduced an amendment asserting the demand for immediate self-government either within or without the British Commonwealth. This amendment was defeated. Evidently Price's semi-concealed stand in favour of the union of British Honduras with Guatemala has some popular support but others fear that it may create an obstacle to British acceptance of further constitutional advance. Some who favour the rapid advance to full self-government are highly sceptical of any advantage to be gained by a merger with a 'banana' republic.

BRITISH GUIANA

This, by far the largest in area of any of the British Caribbean possessions, has had the stormiest recent political history. It is unnecessary here to give the details of the old Dutch institutions which were inherited when the British in 1803 made the final conquest of three Dutch river colonies of Essequibo, Berbice and Demerara. In securing the capitulation of the colonies the British agreed that 'the Laws and Usages of the Colony shall remain in force and be respected, the mode of Taxation now in use be adhered to.[1] Accord-

---

[1] Quoted in Wrong, *op. cit.*, p. 116. Wrong, pp. 113 ff., gives a brief account of constitutional history in these colonies under the Dutch. A much fuller treatment is that of Sir Cecil Clementi, *A Constitutional History of British Guiana* (London, 1937).

ingly, the British Governor presided over a Court of Policy (the legislature) of four officials and four representatives of the planters, the latter elected for an eight-year term by a College of Kiezers (electors) who were chosen for life by colonists owning twenty-five or more slaves. In addition there were six Financial Representatives, also indirectly elected to sit with the Court of Policy whenever it was considering financial measures.

In 1831 the three Dutch colonies were merged to become the colony of British Guiana. Thereafter there was a prolonged dispute over the precise legislative powers of the Court of Policy and the financial powers of the Combined Court (the Court of Policy plus the Financial Representatives). The colonists claimed complete power for these bodies in their respective fields, as guaranteed by the articles of capitulation. The Governors admitted the binding force of the guarantees given in 1803 but denied that the Court of Policy and the other institutions had ever had such powers as were now claimed for them.

The planters of British Guiana were hard hit by emancipation and the tariff policies of Great Britain. To an even greater extent than in the islands they suffered from both a severe labour scarcity and low prices for their product. The planters expressed their feelings of outrage against the British through their representatives in the Combined Court who refused in 1840 and 1848 to pass any revenue measure at all. This did not affect the routine business of government because the Civil List had been passed for a term of seven years. The end result of the struggle was a more precise definition of the powers of the Combined Court. It was agreed that this body might decide upon the nature of the taxes to be used to pay for the estimates presented by the Governor, and that it might, after passing the Civil List in a form satisfactory to the Crown, discuss the estimates and even reduce or strike out items not included in the civil list or required to meet legal obligations. It might not add to expenditure in any way.[1]

Down to 1891 the colony continued to be governed under a system frozen in the old pattern, a Dutch version of the Old Representative System modified by a large element of officialdom. The legislature for non-financial matters was the Court of Policy, half officials and half unofficials. This same body served as the Governor's executive council. The unofficials, however, were not directly chosen by the colonists but by the College of Kiezers whose members were elected for life. A slight element of direct repre-

[1] The right to decide upon the nature of the taxes to be levied rested upon the terms of the capitulation of 1803, the others upon a succession of Orders in Council, the first of which was issued in 1842. See Wrong, *op. cit.,* p. 119.

110 THE BRITISH WEST INDIES

sentation (of course, of the property-holders only) occurred in the
biennial election of the Financial Representatives who sat with the
Court of Policy to form the Combined Court.

The nineteenth century witnessed a number of abortive reform
proposals by various groups. The Governors were almost always at
loggerheads with the elected part of government which represented
only the plutocracy. In general, the Governors favoured an extension of Crown powers, rather than a widening of the suffrage in
view of the fact that the freeholders of the colony were predominantly Negro and illiterate. In the upshot, nothing came of the
reform proposals until near the end of the century.

The event which led to reform was occasioned by a report, issued
in 1887, by the colony's Medical Inspector. In this he described the
living conditions of estate labourers. His description outraged the
planters and the elected members of the Court of Policy asked the
Governor to suppress the report.[1] He refused to do so and all elected
members of the Court of Policy withdrew. By ancient constitutional
custom the Court of Policy did not do business without the presence
of at least one elected member so legislation came to a standstill.
A local reform group, the Political Reform Club, secured over four
thousand signatures to a petition requesting a reform in representation to permit some voice to groups outside of the plantocracy. This
went to the Secretary of State along with the Governor's suggestions.

After three more years of delay a reformed constitution was
granted. The Court of Policy was increased by three appointed
officials and three elected members. The unofficials in the Court of
Policy were to be elected directly from constituencies, the College
of Kiezers being abolished. The franchise was granted to all with an
income of $480 per annum. The Governor could dissolve the Court
of Policy which, in any case, should not serve more than five years.
Dissolution would be followed by a general election of the Court
of Policy and the Financial Representatives. The Court of Policy
also lost its executive powers, these being transferred to an
Executive Council, created by Letters Patent in 1891, consisting of
the Governor, two ex-officio members (Colonial Secretary and
Attorney General), two appointed officials (usually the Colonial
Treasurer and Agent General for Immigration) and three nominated
unofficials. The Governor was required in most matters to consult
his Executive Council but was not bound by its advice. If he decided
to act in opposition to it he had to report to the Secretary of State.

The first election under this constitution was held in January,
1892. As usually happens, there was no immediate change in the
type of member elected by the enlarged electorate. Indeed, about

[1] See Clementi, *op. cit.*, Chap xvi.

half of the former members were returned and the proportion of white to coloured members was unchanged, roughly six white to one coloured.

The Court of Policy was still under the control of the Governor who presided. There were eight elected members and only seven officials (four ex-officio and three appointed) but the Governor had both an original and a casting vote so the official side could outvote the entire elected bloc. In addition, the Governor had veto power and the exclusive right to originate ordinances. The Court of Policy, therefore, resembled other Crown Colony legislatures. The peculiar feature of the British Guiana constitution, however, was the Combined Court which consisted of the Court of Policy *plus* the six elected Financial Representatives. This body, therefore, had an unofficial majority. It had considerable power over the taxation system of the colony. As noted above, the elected members of the Combined Court could not originate any proposal to initiate or increase spending but it could decrease or strike out items. The Combined Court, therefore, was in a position to prevent a taxation system of a 'progressive' type and to prevent any Governor from spending money to develop the colony along lines not profitable to the plantocracy.

Bad times in the 'twenties resulted in a budget deficit every year except one, from 1920 to 1927. The 'twenties also saw the rise of a political party led by a journalist, A. R. F. Webber. Webber had come to British Guiana from Tobago as a young man. He had been much influenced by Marryshow of Grenada and Cipriani of Trinidad. His Popular Party was interested mainly in the development of the Guianese hinterland and was strongly in favour of reaching an agreement with Henry Ford who had made a tentative offer to build a road from Georgetown to the Brazilian frontier in order to connect with a road to his new rubber plantation on the Amazon. This was an exciting prospect to Webber and his party but a gloomy one to the sugar interests who foresaw backcountry developments draining off their supply of cheap labour. The plantocracy was alarmed when the Popular Party swept the polls. This was in the background of the memorial addressed to the Colonial Secretary by the Court of Policy resulting in the investigation commission of 1926 which issued a report suggested the abolition of the Combined Court and its replacement by a Legislative Council with nominated unofficial members chosen to represent classes and interests otherwise unrepresented.[1] The Governor then appointed a local commission to recommend constitutional reforms. The end

[1] Cmd. 2841, 5 April, 1927.

result of these various suggestions was an Act of Parliament[1] which abolished the Combined Court and created a Legislative Council composed of the Governor as president with a casting vote only, two ex-officio members (Colonial Secretary and Attorney General), eight nominated officials, five unofficials and fourteen elected members. Candidacy was still confined to males but the franchise was extended to women. The Act contained the usual safeguards; the Governor alone could initiate money votes and he had the reserve power to legislate contrary to the majority of the Legislative Council.[2] The Act reserved full powers to the Privy Council to legislate for the colony and the Crown reserved the right to revoke and amend the constitution by Order in Council.

These reforms placed British Guiana in the Crown Colony system without the anomalous institution of the Combined Court. According to some observers, including Sir Cecil Clementi, who had been Colonial Secretary and several times the acting administrator of the colony, this was a step forward, removing British Guiana from a cul-de-sac in which there was no hope for any significant political or economic advance.[3]

By 1943 the Legislative Council had an elected majority and unofficials formed a majority of the Executive Council. The Legislative Council consisted of the Governor, the three top officials, seven nominated and fourteen elected members, sitting for a five-year term unless sooner dissolved.[4] The Executive Council included the Governor, the three top officials and five members of the Legislative Council appointed by the Governor.[5] The pre-ministerial advisory committee system was also instituted in 1943. Several members of the Legislative Council formed a committee to sit with the official heading a department and become familiar with its administration. In 1950 there were five of these committees concerned with Agriculture and Fisheries, Communications and Interior, Education, Public Works, and Public Health.

In 1945 also the property requirements for the franchise and for election to the Legislative Council were lowered. The vote was now given to all adult literates owning or occupying three acres worth $150 or renting property worth $45 per annum or with an annual income of $120. Members of Legislative Council had to have an income of $1,200 per annum, own real estate worth $1,000 or lease

[1] 18 George V., Ch. 5, 28 March, 1928.
[2] Letters Patent of 1928 amended 1943.
[3] Clementi, *op. cit.* For the objectives by local reformers who considered the 1928 changes a step backward, see Cmd. 3047, 1928.
[4] Order in Council of 1928, amended 1943.
[5] Royal Instructions of 1928, amended 1943. in 1951, of the five Legislative Council members in Executive Council, four were elected members and one a nominated member.

property worth $300 per annum. They had to be literate in English. An election deposit of $240 was required, to be returned unless the candidate polled under fifteen per cent of the votes cast.

It was obvious that a further advance should follow as soon as practicable. In order to receive advice on this point the Secretary of State appointed a Royal Commission in November, 1950, to investigate and recommend constitutional changes. This commission consisted of Sir John Waddington, a former Colonial Officer, Professor Harlow and Dr Rita Hinden, both of whom are academicians interested in colonial problems and members of the Labour Party. The Commission's report advocated changes designed to bring British Guiana up to political parity with the more advanced West Indian colonies.[1] The Commissioners advocated universal adult suffrage with no property or literacy requirement. The absence of a literacy test was defended on the ground that such a test would operate to disfranchise many East Indians. The Commissioners differed as to the check to be placed upon full responsible government. Sir John Waddington favoured the retention of a unicameral legislature to contain both nominated and elected members. The other two commissioners advocated a bicameral legislature like that of Barbados, with one house of elected members only and the other of nominated members. They recommended also that the Executive Council have a majority of elected members, chosen by the elected house of the legislature, to perform ministerial functions and be responsible to the legislature. Only the areas of law and order, personnel administration, foreign affairs, defence and information would remain in official hands.

This advance, placing British Guiana in the final stage of Crown Colony government, was justified by the Commission on the ground that '. . . many . . . of the present unwholesome tendencies have been fostered by a sense of inferiority springing from inadequate opportunities for responsible political expression', and '. . . irresponsibility is bred if responsibility is too long withheld.'[2]

The new constitution went into effect in April, 1953.[3] The Executive Council was to consist of the Governor, the three top officials, ex-officio, and seven ministers, one from the State Council as Minister Without Portfolio and six elected by the House of Assembly. These six then were to choose one of their number to be Leader of the House. The Governor was to assign portfolios to

[1] *Report of the Constitutional Commission* 1950-51 (Col. No. 280).
[2] Col. No. 280, pp. 17, 25.
[3] By the British Guiana (Constitution) Order in Council 1953, under authority of the British Guiana Act (1928) empowering H.M. in Council to create and amend legislative powers in British Guiana.

the elected ministers who could be removed from office by the Governor only with approval of the Executive Council or by a two-thirds absolute majority of the House. The Governor was also empowered to appoint under-secretaries from the House membership to assist both the ministers and the top officials.

The legislature was bicameral, the nominated members (as in Barbados) being segrated in a second chamber, the State Council. This body had nine members, six appointed at discretion by the Governor, but not to include individuals defeated at the previous election. Two were to be appointed by the Governor on the recommendations of the ministers and one other consulting with the independent or opposition members in the House. The State Council, therefore, was ingeniously designed to represent in miniature a primitive Crown Colony legislature, largely of the old-fashioned sort containing nominated non-party independents representing various interests but with some representation, indirectly, of the elected side. The only qualifications were British nationality, age thirty-five or over, domicile or two years residence in the colony and non-membership in the House of Assembly. The State Council elected its own president and one of its members to sit as a minister in the Executive Council. If the State Council rejected a bill the Governor, at his discretion, might within six months summon a joint session of the two chambers to reconsider the matter.

The House of Assembly consisted of the Speaker appointed by the Governor from outside the House membership, the three top officials, ex-officio, and twenty-four elected members. The members, elected by universal adult suffrage from single-member constituencies, had to have the nationality and residence requirement as in the case of the State Councillors, age twenty-one or older and be literate in English.

The limitations on self-government in this constitution were those customary in Crown Colonies. The vital matters of security, civil service and foreign affairs remained with the officials. No money bill could be introduced without the Governor's approval. The Governor also had the usual reserved powers to veto bills, reserve them to ascertain the 'pleasure' of the Crown (certain types had to be so reserved) and to legislate directly in the case of bills that had failed of passage, after consultation with his Executive Council. The Secretary of State also had a veto on measures approved by the Governor.

Why did this constitution fail to work as intended and why was it considered necessary to suspend it after a few months? The answer, of course, is political and not constitutional. There would appear to have been no sound reason for assuming, in advance of the event, that the political evolution in British Guiana would take a turn unlike that of any other West Indian colony. As in many other places, political party development had been embryonic. Elections had always been dominated by independents, in recent years coming mainly from the educated middle class. With the organization of several labour unions it might be assumed that a new class of politician could emerge from the union leadership. As in Trinidad, the East Indians would certainly make their appearance in the legislature in increased numbers. But the House of Assembly of 1953 was no carbon copy of the Trinidadian House of 1946, with its small Butlerite opposition group and a dominating government bloc of officials and independents. Instead, the People's Progressive Party swept the polls, winning eighteen of the twenty-four elected places, enough to guarantee victory in a joint session with the State Council. It is easy to explain the party's success. Like most successful West Indian political movements it stressed local nationalism and the rapid achievement of complete independence. It went further than many in condemnation of imperialism, colonial institutions and monopoly capitalism. Its arguments were effective because based upon what seemed self-evident facts to the poor people of the colony. This alone would not have been enough. But the difference between the PPP and its opponents was chiefly a question of organization and pre-campaign techniques which had never before been used in the colony.

The party was founded by Dr Cheddi B. Jagan, Chicago-educated dentist and son of an East Indian sugar estate driver. When in the United States he married Janet Rosenberg, American-born of poor immigrant stock. She had attended the University of Detroit, Wayne University and Michigan State University and took part of a nursing course at Cook County School of Nursing. Mrs Jagan is said to have been a Young Communist during her student days and when she joined her husband in British Guiana saw the chance to use the local miseries and the neglect under which the labouring class of the colony had long suffered to establish the ascendancy of a party which might be able to transform British Guiana into a 'people's democracy'.[1]

[1] Mrs Jagan has denied membership in the Young Communist League. It has been charged, on the other hand, that the entire plan was drawn up in Moscow and represented an actual Stalinist conspiracy to create a South American beachhead useful for the infiltration of other, more important countries, particularly Brazil, which shares a frontier with British Guiana. This charge was made by Serofino Romualdi, Assistant Secretary of ORIT (the Western Hemisphere organization of the ICFTU). Romualdi made the accusation at the second annual conference of the National Workers Union in Jamaica (see the *Gleaner,* issue of November 2, 1953). He charged that the plan was to send arms shipments through British Guiana to Communist insurgents in Brazil.

H

Dr Jagan, having acquired his dental degree from Northwestern University returned to Georgetown in 1943 and brought his bride with him. Their social and political agitation activities began at once. Mrs Jagan identified herself as well as she could with the East Indian community, often appearing in a sari. The first association she founded was the Women's Political and Economic Organization which participated in May Day parades in 1946 and 1947. In 1946 she, her husband and others formed a Political Affairs Committee and organized a co-operative to publish a labour paper called the *People's Free Press.*[1] Just before the election of 1947, this group founded the Labour Party. It ran several candidates but only one, Dr Jagan, secured election despite the increase in the East Indian electorate.[2] The Labour Party was disbanded but organization efforts were redoubled and in January, 1950, the People's Progressive Party was formally launched. It emphasized the rights of labour against the bosses but even more emphatically the need for the rapid achievement of full self-government. Several of the old Political Affairs Committee were active in the new party including the respected secretary of the waterfront and dock labour union, Ashton Chase. A noted barrister, Linden Forbes Burnham, who was president of the waterfront union and other prominent Negroes also joined and the party was able to appeal both to the urban Negro and the rural East Indian smallholder and estate labourer.

The PPP organizing drive had started as early as 1948 with the activities of field representatives throughout the colony. These were volunteer enthusiasts who sold pamphlets for a penny and were reimbursed for their efforts by the money raised in this way. They were also paid a commission on the fees of new party members they recruited. Members paid an annual subscription of sixty cents and received free the party paper *Thunder* edited by Mrs Jagan.[3] In every district a chief organizer was appointed and he organized working committees which convened regularly to discuss plans and agree upon a co-ordinated drive. Dr Lachhmansingh, owner of a chain of drugstores and head of the Guiana Industrial Workers' Union, became a member and was able to contribute the efforts of his union organizers to the party campaign. When the PPP was

[1] According to *Thunder,* issue of February, 1953, other founding members were Ramkarrab, Sidney King, Ashton Chase. Note that this was an interracial group.
[2] The 1945 decrease in income qualification for voting, noted above, enabled some 17,755 East Indians to qualify out of a total electorate of 59,384.
[3] Some help from foreign Communist sources was forthcoming. It is known that when Sidney King returned from Vienna in March, 1953, he brought with him a considerable sum in United States dollars.

founded officially in 1950 it was already far more than a paper organization.

In every district, roughly corresponding to the police districts, each including one considerable village, a district committee was set up. The committee has a chairman, treasurer and secretary. The chairman is often a local notable and sometimes does little but lend the prestige of his name. The driving force is usually the secretary, chosen for his ability and enthusiasm. He is constantly in touch not only with all local party activities but also with the Secretary-General, Mrs Jagan, who keeps him informed of the directives issued by the high command. In 1950-53 this consisted of five leaders: the Jagans, Burnham, Chase and another Negro, Sidney King. The party chairmanship was held in turn by each of these leaders.[1] The party is controlled by a General Council of twenty-two members. Fifteen of these are the representatives of the annual Party Congress, consisting of one delegate for every twelve members. The fifteen persons elected each year by the Congress are joined by the seven members of the Party Executive to form the General Council. The Executive consists of the party officers: Chairman, two Vice-Chairmen, General Secretary, Assistant Secretary, Treasurer, and the Leader of the Parliamentary Group. There is also an Executive Committee consisting of the officers and five persons elected by the General Council.

In the usual Communist pattern, auxiliary organizations were also formed to appeal to young people of pre-voting age and others not party members. These included the Pioneer Youth League, the Demerara Youth Rally and the British Guiana Peace Committee. All were used as gatherings for party indoctrination alternated with entertainment and the members were induced to contribute volunteer work as distributors of party literature, canvassers for signatures to petitions and so forth. The Pioneer Youth League became affiliated with the Communist-controlled World Federation of Democratic Youth. The PYL was the key organization intended to direct and control all other youth groups.[2]

In the pre-election period the leaders campaigned with the tireless enthusiasm of West Indian politicians. Burnham, Chase and some of the other leaders concentrated on the Georgetown Negro districts. The Jagans, and others campaigned chiefly in East Indian

[1] Because of the unexpectedly complete victory in 1953 no plans had been made for ministerial posts and Burnham happened to be chairman at the time. This led to a short conflict between Burnham and Dr Jagan for the position of Leader of the House.
[2] All these organizations were proscribed and dissolved by the Governor following the suspension of the Constitution as was the Union of Progressive Youth formed by the officers of the abolished PYL.

villages. The Jagans employed a 'grass-roots' technique never before used in British Guiana. They not only went to the villages and spoke to the people but visited with them, ate and slept in their cabins and demonstrated convincingly their self-identification with the poor estate-labourers. Dr Jagan also set up dental clinics in various places and did much dental work free of charge. He flirted with various union leaders as to acceptance of union posts and became president of the Sawmill Workers' Union. He was also to command considerable union support in any case because of the adherence of Lachhmansingh and Chase, among others.

The Mahasabah, much the larger of the two Hindu lay societies, is a very conservative body and its leaders at no time supported the PPP. The Arya Samaj, a smaller and more liberal organization, at first supported the PPP. After the suspension of the constitution the Arya Samaj pandits took a neutral stand but hardly dared openly to oppose the party. Neither organization, as such, had any influence upon party policies or leadership or much, if any, effect upon its fortunes.

No serious attempt was made to indoctrinate the masses with the theories of Marx-Lenin-Stalinism. But the party faithful were familiarized with Communist symbols and with Communist phraseology used in speeches and in the columns of *Thunder,* the little party newspaper. The poverty and wretched living conditions of the majority of the population was sufficient to render attractive appeals based on dislike and jealousy of the small propertied class, the colonial officials and the alleged exploitation of labour and natural resources by the sugar kings and bauxite barons. The war boom had collapsed. This boom had been caused chiefly by the construction of a large American air base at Atkinson Field, near Georgetown and the exploitation of bauxite deposits. This had come in 1941 at a time when the colony was severely depressed largely because the German submarine menace had made it nearly impossible to ship sugar. Many Negro smallholders had sold their land to East Indians and joined the 'gold rush' to Atkinson Field. Then, when the air base was decommissioned they had to swell the ranks of the underemployed in Georgetown. Dr Jagan made good use of their frustrations. At a Bourda Green meeting in 1949 he told them that they had been underpaid by the Air Force under orders from 'Wall Street capitalist brigands' acting in collusion with the sugar interests (translation: the Air Force had paid only somewhat more than the 'going wage' in the area) and that he, Jagan, would get their back pay for them. At once he gained popularity with Georgetown Negroes, ordinarily anti-East Indian. Under these circumstances it was easy to secure credence for the claim that the colony's poverty was due to white malevolence and selfishness and to create faith that great things would come from the nationalization of bauxite and sugar and political independence. Independence in particular had a strong appeal to people suffering from the inferiority feelings of a coloured colonial society in which they felt themselves doomed to a position of permanent subordination to the handful of whites and upper class coloured families who control the economic and social life of the colony.[1]

The first election to be held in British Guiana under universal adult suffrage took place on April 27, 1953. There were one hundred and thirty candidates for the twenty-four seats. The PPP ran candidates in twenty-two constituencies. Other parties sponsored twenty-nine and there were seventy-nine independents. Approximately 150,000 of the 208,939 names on the roll were those of new voters. Of these, perhaps 40,000 were illiterate and special voting arrangements were made for their benefit.[2]

About seventy-five per cent of the registered electorate actually voted and of these, fifty-one per cent voted for PPP candidates. Had the poll been represented precisely in the candidates elected, the PPP could have been outvoted by the rest with the support of the three ex-officio members. However, the PPP won eighteen of the twenty-four elected seats and was thus enabled, so long as party discipline was maintained, to name the six elected ministers and be certain of outvoting the rest even in a joint session of the two chambers, with twenty out of thirty-six votes.

The other political parties were able to offer but a feeble contest. Many of the older politicians were too much associated with 'government' to be acceptable to the newly enfranchised voters. The appeals addressed to the electorate by the various parties paralleled that of the PPP in general terms as regards welfare objectives but these parties were poorly organized and represented in many instances the usual hasty pre-election, temporary alliance of independents. They lacked adequate machines at the 'grass-roots' level. In many constituencies there were a number of independents who split the vote and ensured a plurality for the PPP candidate. Seven of the victorious PPP members were elected by less than a

---

[1] As a well-paid Negro employee remarked to the British Guiana Constitutional Commission: 'It is not enough to be able to afford to get drunk every evening'. *Report of the British Guiana Constitution Commission*, 1954 (Cmd. 9274) p. 17.
[2] Each candidate was assigned a ballot box of his own, bearing not only his name but his photograph and an assigned pictorial symbol. The illiterate voter cast a numbered but blank ballot in the box of his choice. Illiteracy was greatest among the Amerindians in remote areas. The percentage of voting among the Amerindians was much lower on the average than among other groups.

majority varying from 48.2% of the poll for Janet Jagan in West Essequibo to 29.2% for C. S. Persaud in Mahaica-Mahaicony where eight candidates contested the election. The number of candidates in each constituency varied from three to eleven, averaging over five.[1]

The new Governor, Sir Alfred Savage, had no choice but to accept the ministers named by the PPP executive. These were four of the five 'Politburo' members plus Dr Lachhmansingh and Jai Narine Singh. Mrs. Jagan was not given a ministerial post but instead was elected Deputy Speaker of the House. This was a position of potential importance because of the considerable age of the nominated Speaker, Sir Eustace Woolford, who might be expected to be absent from time to time. His absences would give Mrs Jagan the opportunity to admit resolutions sponsored by her party which the Speaker would have disallowed.

From the beginning the new ministers retained the attitude of an opposition rather than a government *vis-a-vis* the officials. In his initial speech in reply to the Governor's address, Dr Jagan attacked the constitution, the officials and the State Council. In their months of office the ministers did relatively little to tackle the immediate problems of the Colony but rather sought to obtain, first of all, absolute party control of all independent boards and commissions and of the civil service. Their view of democracy was the Communist one: that a party allegedly representing the proletariat should admit of no checks whatever upon its policies and would be justified in using any means to destroy all effective opposition.

In the House, Dr Jagan and others spent much time in attempting to show that the constitution was fraudulent in that, despite their electoral victory, the PPP was prevented from implementing its programme because of the power still held by the Governor and other officials and the veto power of the State Council. They were especially resentful of their legal inability to purge the civil service and install their own supporters and of the fact that the police were under the Chief Secretary, a permanent colonial official.

The first controversy arose over a motion, introduced by the opposition, to accept Jamaica's invitation to send two representatives to that island to participate in the welcome to the Queen on the occasion of her visit. This was rejected by the votes of all but one of the PPP delegation. The second controversy arose over a bill to repeal the Undesirable Publications (Prohibition of Importation) Ordinance which had been passed in February, 1953, because of the quantity of Communist literature imported and distributed by the PPP. The bill as a whole had little opposition ex-

[1] From the report of the Registration Officer.

cept as regards a clause removing the immunity given the Comptroller of Customs by the original measure for his action in con-
fiscating literature imported by Dr Jagan on the ground that it had
not been declared to the customs. The controversy over this clause
led to a dispute between the Attorney General and Mr Burnham
and to the amendment of the bill in the State Council.

But the two measures which aroused most apprehension on the
part of the opposition were the Rice Farmers (Security of Tenure)
(Amendment) Bill and the Labour Relations Bill. The former gave
extraordinary powers to the Minister (Dr Jagan) through his District
Commissioners to require work by the landlord which, if not done
immediately, could be done by the Commissioner and the cost
assessed against the landlord by a summary action based on the old
Roman-Dutch law which would have amounted to a forced sale of
the property. If abused, this power could have been employed to
confiscate property rights with no recourse to the owner. This bill
was rejected by the State Council. The Labour Relations Bill was
allegedly based on the Wagner Act and its declared intention was
to permit the free formation of labour unions. It was introduced at
a time when the Lachhmansingh union, the Guiana Industrial
Workers' Union, had once again failed in an attempted strike to
secure recognition as the sole representative of the sugar workers.
The Sugar Producers' Association had recognized the Man Power
Citizen's Association as the sugar workers' union long before the
formation of the GWIU in 1948. However, there seemed to be a
chance for a compromise settlement between the GWIU and the
MPCA with the approval of the SPA. There is some evidence that the
party extremists feared a settlement of this dispute and moved to
bring about an immediate strike which could be exploited politically.[1] A strike was called on the sugar estates by the GWIU and
received the blessing and active support of the PPP ministers, who
informed the sugar workers that this was a 'government' strike and
must be supported in order to back the PPP. They attempted also to
bring about sympathy strikes which might spread into a colony-
wide general strike. In fact, although sugar production was halted
for twenty-three days there were no other results and at the end of
that time work was resumed. The Minister of Labour, Ashton Chase,
then introduced his labour ordinance and requested leave to move
suspension of the rules so the measure could be put through all
stages in a single day. The Speaker denied the request on the
ground that a matter of such importance required full considera-

[1] See *Report of the British Guiana Constitutional Commission* 1954 cmd.
9274, p. 61. This document gives a reasonably complete and fair account
of the events leading to the suspension of the constitution.

tion. Upon this ruling almost the entire PPP membership in the
House rose and left the chamber tumultuously accompanied by their
gallery. The bill subsequently was passed by the House of Assembly
but never considered in the State Council because the legislature
was prorogued the day after its passage. The chief objection to this
ordinance was the dictatorial powers it conferred upon the Minister
of Labour who could hold enquiries, with or without a committee
appointed by himself, decide whether an industry should be represented by one or several unions, decide who should be permitted
to vote in a union recognition election, decide how often a vote
should be taken and so forth. In short, there was no guarantee of
employer representation, no attempt at creating an impartial labour
relations board and in effect, the minister would have been given
the power to create and destroy unions.

Although this ordinance was passed on the eve of the suspension
of the constitution it was not this or any other specific bill or policy
that convinced the Governor that he should take this drastic step.
There were several factors in the situation which combined to determine the Governor's decision. Firstly, the PPP leaders seemed to
believe that their majority justified them in attempting to control
all the non-political boards and commissions. They had moved to
control the secondary educational system, largely private and
denominational, by subventions given at the price of controlling
the curriculum. They attempted, by studied insults, to provoke the
resignation of the top civil servants in several ministries. They used
the government radio for party propaganda. They threatened the
Press with newsprint control. Their whole conception of 'democracy'
was one-party rule without compromise.

Secondly, they did not operate in the Executive Council as had
been intended. The six PPP ministers met before Executive Council
meetings and there reached agreement among themselves as to all
matters on the agenda. They then formed a united front at the
Executive Council meeting and presented the Governor and the ex-
officio ministers with the decision of the 'Council of People's
Ministers', sometimes with little or no discussion.[1]

Thirdly, they encouraged an atmosphere of permanent crisis and
near revolution among their followers. The limited space for visitors
in the House of Assembly was crowded at every session with PPP
members. Some of these seats are very close to the chairs occupied
by members and there was constant heckling of opposition members

[1] At first they called themselves the 'Council of Ministers'. The Governor
objected to this because their group did not include the ex-officio ministers
or the minister without portfolio from the State Council. They then in-
serted 'People's' in the title.

by the public during debates. Others packed the galleries outside the chamber whence they could see and hear through open door- ways and join in the cheering and booing of the crowd inside. It was the custom at the conclusion of each session for the PPP ministers accompanied by their crowd to go to Bourda Green, the Georgetown cricket grounds, and there continue to make inflamma- tory speeches. This species of permanent mass meeting was reminiscent in some ways of the Petrograd Soviet of Soldiers' and Workers' Deputies in the early stages of the Russian Revolution when the Soviet was able to threaten and sometimes control the actions of the Provisional Government. Opposition members were threatened with physical violence, there was some tyre-slashing, and as time went by there was no diminution of these disturbances. There is no record of any attempt by the PPP leaders to curb the near-riotous behaviour of their supporters. Indeed, the situation was deteriorating; Opposition speakers did not dare to hold public meetings and there was some fear that the police might prove to be unreliable in the event of an actual riot. There is no substantial evidence that any police officers had actually been subverted, but there is no doubt that the ranks included many PPP supporters and that some would have been afraid to act vigorously against a PPP mob because of possible relaliation. The PPP had proposed the creation of an auxilliary police force to be under the control of the local government authorities rather than the Colonial Secretary. They had also proposed a local government ordinance which would have ensured their control of most local governments.[1]

Under these circumstances the Governor had to choose between suspending the constitution and setting up a temporary official autocracy or permitting the PPP leaders to continue to legislate and agitate, compelling the Governor to rely upon the State Council and his own powers of veto and certification. This latter course would have allowed the PPP to continue to use the House of Assembly as a platform, make further inflammatory speeches and quite possibly produce a situation in which it would have been impossible to maintain law and order without the use of troops. In fact, British military units were brought in just before the suspension but there was no disorder and it was not necessary to quell any riots. If the

[1] For additional details see the White Paper, *British Guiana: Suspension of the Constitution*, Cmd. 8980, October 20, 1953; *Report of the British Guiana Constitutional Commission 1954*, Cmd. 9274; issues of *The Daily Chronicle* (Georgetown, B.G.) October, November, 1953; *Guiana Times News Magazine* (Georgetown), vols. 4 and 5, 1953, 1954; *The Daily Argosy* (Georgetown) issue of November 21, 1953. The PPP version of these events is given in a pamphlet by Ashton Chase, '133 Days Towards Freedom in Guiana', Georgetown, B.G., n.d. (March, 1954.)

military had been brought in and the PPP left in control of the legislature there is more than an even chance that bloodshed might have resulted.

It is easy to be wise after the event. Some Guianese criticized Sir Alfred for not adopting a firmer tone to begin with and some thought that a police force strengthened by men borrowed from other colonies could have kept order even though the PPP remained in control of the Assembly and the Governor had been compelled to use his reserved powers. But it seemed perfectly clear to Sir Alfred Savage by this time that the PPP leaders had no intention of working within the spirit of the constitution, that their aim was total domination of all aspects of the colony's life and the destruction of all opposition. To have relied upon the reserved powers would merely have provided further excuse for agitation and might in time have brought about a situation which could only have resulted in something approaching civil war.

Of course the constitutional collapse of 1953 had its roots in the long history of neglect during which the colony had been governed as if it were nothing more than a complex, large-scale enterprise with almost no attention paid to the well-being, physical or social, of its inhabitants and no attempt to advance their political education. The result of the long domination by the indifferent rather than malevolent autocracy of the sugar and commercial interests was grinding poverty for the many and a galling sense of frustration among a number of the educated few. The political advances and projects for economic development came too late to forestall the results of accumulated grievances. It was the colony's misfortune that the opportunity to use these grievances to acquire electoral power was seized by a Communist-led party. It is perhaps not so much a matter for astonishment that this was the outcome in British Guiana as that it happened in no other British Caribbean colony. Once it has become clear that the PPP ministers would not work within the spirit and limits of the constitution there was really little choice but to suspend it and institute a 'crash' programme of economic development in the hope that an appreciable improvement in living standards might soon follow and encouraged people might turn away from extremist leaders and Communist panaceas. At the same time there was a widely held belief that the suspension order was in part due to United States pressure and this was resented. There would seem to be no tangible evidence for this belief but its existence indicates the general tendency to be suspicious of United States power and influence in Central and South America.

The Governor had communicated his fears to the Secretary of State in September and asked for troops to strengthen local security forces. On October 8th, five hundred Royal Welsh Fusiliers landed in Georgetown, having been sent hastily from Jamaica. Governor Savage then declared a state of emergency and dismissed the 'People's Ministers' from office and prorogued the legislature.[1] On October 9th the announcement was made that the constitution would be suspended and that a Commission of Inquiry would be formed to investigate and recommend constitutional revision. The suspension was debated in the Commons on October 22nd and in the Lords on October 28th, and approved by Parliament.[2]

Governor Savage took the necessary steps to order the dissolution of the subversive organizations set up by the PPP and to restrict the movements of the party leaders. In December he established an entirely nominated single-chamber legislature and an Executive Council of the three top officials plus seven nominees. Two of the latter were given ministerial portfolios. The nominees were chosen to represent various interests and sections of the community and included the opposition members of the previous House of Assembly and State Council. It was recognized that this was a purely stop-gap arrangement to last only until a measure of elected government could be restored safely. Simultaneously with the establishment of the temporary nominated legislature the Governor embarked upon a five-year development plan costing about $66 millions, three-quarters to be spent for economic development and one-quarter for social services[3] This programme was to be financed by local revenues, a long-term loan and CD & W. grants.

The PPP was taken by surprise when the constitution was suspended. They had hoped and expected, by cutting the police appropriation drastically, to force the Governor to use his reserved power to legislate. This would have given them a constitutional issue. Their reply to suspension was to continue party organization activities as well as possible, occasionally disobeying the orders restricting their movements and acquiring a measure of political martyrdom by gaol sentences.

Other parties began to proliferate. Would-be leaders who had not been associated with the PPP thought that the limitations imposed

---

[1] The Governor was empowered legally to take these steps by the British Guiana (Constitution) (Amendment) Order in Council, 1953 (Oct. 4, 1953), additional instructions signed Oct. 4, 1953 amending the Royal Instructions of April 1, 1953, and given wide emergency powers similar to those of the war period by the British Guiana (Emergency) Order in Council. (Oct. 10, 1953).

[2] For the Commons debates see *Hansard*, vol. 518, No. 156 (Thursday), October 22, 1953).

[3] In 1956 the plan was revised and the amount increased for the ensuing five years to $91 millions, $57 millions of which was earmarked for economic development (mainly drainage, irrigation and transport).

upon Jagan, Burnham and the rest offered a splendid opportunity to advance their own political fortunes. For the most part these 'leaders' were such in their own eyes only. They lacked loyal supporters and had no general appeal. Their 'parties' were little more than names attached to their own small, personal following.[1] The abler conservative politicians had no hope whatever of attracting a mass following. The nearest approach to a genuine opposition party was the United Democratic Party led by John Carter. This is a middle-road, social welfare party and included several politicians of experience. One of these, Lionel Luckhoo, president of the MPCA sugar union, left the UDP before the 1957 elections to form a new party, the National Labour Front. Luckhoo made overtures for a election alliance with the UDP but was rebuffed. The UDP tried to secure an arrangement with the Burnham faction of the PPP but was rejected. The result was, as in 1953, a failure at anything like a united front against the PPP.

The split between the Jagan and Burnham factions of the PPP, long predicted, came in 1955. As noted by the Robertson Commission, the discipline and unanimity of the PPP in public, particularly remarkable for a West Indian party, did not prevent rumours and reports of differences of opinion among the leaders. The Commission reported that the Jagans appeared to be the leaders of the extremist Communist faction whereas Burnham and Chase seemed to be left-wing socialist.[2] At the party conference held on February 13, 1955, the Burnham faction had sufficient voting strength to reduce Dr Jagan to the position of First Vice-Chairman and Mrs Jagan to Treasurer after passing a vote of no confidence in the old executive. Burnham was elected Leader of the Legislative Group, Dr Lachhmansingh, Interim Chairman, Jai Narine Singh, General Secretary. Westmaas and Martin Carter were removed from the Executive Committee. The Jagans and about forty of their followers walked out of the meeting and promptly held a conference of their own, expelling Burnham and his group. Thereafter there were two parties both claiming the name People's Progressive Party and both publishing a paper called *Thunder*. Burnham's paper was distinguished as PPP-*Thunder*.

[1] Examples of these parties: The Guiana Labour Party, founded in 1954 by Charles A. Carter of the Bauxite union; Robert Adams's New Independent Party, announced in March, 1956; the Guiana National Party led by W. H. Pilgrim.
[2] *Report of the British Guiana Constitutional Commissioners* 1954 (Cmd. 9274) pp. 36-38. The Commission reckoned that the Jagans, R. Westmaas (Junior Vice Chairman), Sydney King (Assistant Secretary), B. H. Benn (Member, Executive Committee) and Martin Carter (Secretary, Pioneer Youth League) were Communists while Burnham, Chase and Clinton Wong (Senior Vice Chairman) appeared rather to be socialists.

At this point the Governor, Sir Patrick Renison, who had worked successfully with the People's United Party in British Honduras, believed the time ripe to readmit a measure of elected government. He announced in April, 1956, the imminent restoration of a Legislative Council of twenty-four members, twelve of whom would be elected. The others would consist of four officials and not more than eight nominees. The Executive Council would be nominated by the Governor. At the same time (April 25, 1956) Sir Patrick removed the restrictions on the movements of Burnham and Jai Narine Singh, who previously had been confined to Georgetown under the Emergency Regulations.

The Renison constitution was less 'advanced' than that in force before the Waddington constitution and was at once roundly denounced by all leading politicians. Both Jagan and Burnham called it a 'farce'. John Carter of the UDP said it was 'too limited'. Subsequently Governor Renison proposed an increase in the elected side to fourteen and a corresponding increase of two seats on the non-elected side. This met with no more enthusiasm than the previous suggestion and was condemned by an all-party conference in October, 1956.

The elections under the Renison constitution were held on August 12, 1957. There was a greater element of racial communalism involved than in the 1953 elections. The three main parties, Jagan's PPP, Burnham's PPP and the UDP, all attempted to cut across communal lines and all presented both Negro and East Indian candidates. Nevertheless both the Burnhamites and the UDP were pre-eminently Negro parties whereas the Jaganites were strongest among the East Indian sugar workers and rice farmers. Dr Jagan, indeed, had been elected vice-chairman of the BG Rice Marketing Board and had effective control of the Rice Producer's Association.

The Jagan faction of the PPP won nine of the fourteen elected seats. The Burnham faction won all three seats in predominantly Negro Georgetown. Kendall (UDP) retained his New Amsterdam seat, as he had in 1953, and so did Campbell (NLF) in the predominantly Amerindian North Western District, where only 1,570 votes were cast. Altogether there were fifty-four candidates for the fourteen places. The proportion of the total vote polled by the Jaganite faction was considerably below that achieved by the united PPP in 1953, amounting to a fraction over forty-five per cent. But as is often the case in single-member-district elections, this was enough to give Jagan and his colleagues sixty-four per cent of the elected seats.

Perhaps because the Jaganites had won only nine seats, the

Governor chose not to use his power of nomination to its full extent. He named only six additional members to the Legislative Council, giving it nine non-elected (three officials and six unofficial nominees) to fourteen elected members.

Governor Renison also refrained from adding to the Executive Council the two nominated unofficials permitted by law. He invited Dr Jagan and four other PPP elected members, including Mrs Jagan, to occupy the five ministerial posts which he assigned. The rest of the Executive Council consisted of the Governor and the three other principal officials.

In April, 1960, the British government accepted the principle of eventual independence for British Guiana.[1] In August, 1961, the colony will be given a new constitution providing for complete internal self-government but with transitional safeguards concerning the police and civil service and with defence and external affairs remaining under British control. Two years or more after the first election held under this constitution there will be another conference to decide upon the next advance. This conference may be held sooner if the West Indies Federation attains complete independence in the meantime. The caution implied in these arrangements is due, of course, to the politics of the colony in 1953 and the fact that the Jaganite PPP remains British Guiana's biggest party.

---

[1] *British Guiana Constitutional Conference,* Cmnd. 998, April 8, 1960.

CHAPTER VI

BRITISH COLONIAL POLICIES AND THEIR IMPLEMENTATION

W H E N the expansion of Europe began in the late Fifteenth Century there were no colonial theories although colonies of settlement are probably as old as mankind. No doubt population pressure, with or without inter-tribal warfare, was the principal reason for the migrations that brought the prehistoric Asiatic peoples into Europe, that led to the Greek colonies in Sicily, the barbarian invasions of a decaying Roman Empire, the Norse raids upon France and Britain, and so forth. These incursions often resulted in colonies of settlement, the indigines being killed, pushed out, or absorbed by the newcomers. The significant difference between these ancient colonial adventures and those of the Renaissance world was that the new, vigorous nation-states of Western Europe did not simply despatch or expel bands of emigrants but retained control of these emigrants and claimed legal sovereignty over the lands they settled or conquered. A variety of motives might impel the individual to become a colonist: poverty, love of adventure, the hope of profit and many more. But the metropolitan governments always thought of their colonies in terms of benefits to the home country, economic, military, or both. The only other reason for the sponsoring of colonizing efforts by the powers was the missionary motive, especially strong in the case of the Roman Catholic countries as it had been earlier among the Moslems. The Protestant states, Great Britain and Holland, were rather less concerned with spreading Christianity among the heathen and took a more 'practical' view of colonies. But Spain and Britain were both in agreement upon the proposition that colonial efforts were justified only as they were profitable in one way or another to the metropolitan power.

The British merchant adventurers of Elizabeth's time could not hope to oust the Spanish from their rich American possessions and the early British efforts in the New World, therefore, had to be devoted to the Caribbean islands and to the temperate zone in North America. No store of gold and jewels awaiting plunder existed in these places. The western colonies, therefore, were of use only for two purposes: as a source of raw materials and tropical products and a convenient dumping-ground for unwanted persons, criminals, paupers or political dissidents. That the colonies, even those settled and inhabited entirely by British subjects, might eventually develop along lines of their own without regard to imperial interests, was regarded as an aberration to be avoided at all costs. Almost on the eve of the American war of Independence it was possible for an Englishman to write as follows: 'The Colonies were acquired with no other view than to be of convenience to us, and therefore it can never be imagined that we are to consult their interests preferably to our own.'[1] As Miss Hinden observes, this was the guiding principle of the First British Empire. Because of current economic theory, this principle was applied by using mercantilist trading methods. Every effort was made to export to the colonies, to confine all colonial trade to metropolitan shipping and to have the home country serve as an entrepôt for the sale of colonial goods to foreign buyers. To little Britain, colonies were of particular importance because only by the establishment of a colonial trade monopoly could Britain hope to have that mercantilist desideratum, a 'favourable balance of trade.' With this it might be possible to maintain great power status alongside the larger and richer European kingdoms.

The American troubles did not leave all observers as unmoved as Mr Richardson. Parliament heard eloquent appeals by Pitt, Burke and Fox for a new attitude in which the colonial viewpoint might receive some consideration. In one of his more famous speeches Burke even foreshadowed the Commonwealth concept.[2] But these appeals did not serve to change British policy in time to avert the War of Independence. Perhaps more important than Whig eloquence in affecting colonial policy was the revolution in economic thinking brought about by Adam Smith's *Wealth of Nations*. Smith attacked mercantilism at its foundations by holding that the buyer profited as well as the seller and that international trade was not a fixed quantity to be monopolized or shared between the trading nations. Free trade, he believed, would cause a rapid expansion in the exchange of goods and a general rise in prosperity. But free trade would mean the doom of the existing colonial system and really remove any reason at all for having colonies. That British trade could still flourish with America even after the thirteen

[1] Robert Richardson in *The London Chronicle*, 1764. Quoted in Rita Hinden, *Empire and After* (London, Essential Books, 1949) p. 16.
[2] Speech on Conciliation with the Colonies: 'My hold of the Colonies is in the close affection which grows from common names, from kindred blood, from similar privileges and equal protection. These are ties which, though light as air, are as strong as links of iron. Let the Colonies always keep the idea of their civil rights associated with your government; they will cling and grapple to you; and no force under heaven will be of power to tear them from their allegiance'.

colonies had achieved independence seemed to go far to prove his point.

When the industrial revolution enabled British factories to multiply production, Smith's theories began to appeal to many. Free Trade was demanded by an ever-increasing and important middle class of merchants and factory-owners. The protection of colonial goods in the home market was now of little advantage to any but the planters themselves. The Radicals, James Mill, Cobbett and others attacked the whole colonial system as providing wealth for a tiny class only and actually worse than useless to the majority of the British people. Radical attacks were also based upon humanitarian arguments, the moral importance of the individual human being, and these arguments were reinforced by the contemporary upsurge of evangelical Protestantism.

One of the most important practical results of the Radical approach was the Durham Report which advocated a measure of colonial self-government hitherto considered impossible to harmonize with colonial status. Responsible government, advocated in the Report and effectively introduced by Lord Elgin in Canada shortly afterwards, was the key to the development of Dominion status and the subsequent Commonwealth.

The Radical view was consistent with the eventual friendly disintegration of the Empire, advocated by many from Adam Smith to Disraeli. It was in 1852 that Disraeli made his famous remark: 'These wretched colonies will all be independent in a few years, and they are a millstone round out necks.' As late as 1870 the same idea in politer language was expressed by Gladstone who held the loss of the colonies to be inevitable and advocated that it be accomplished in a friendly spirit. But a totally different viewpoint was taken by the men who founded the Colonial Reform Society in 1850. The Reformers attacked the Colonial Office as inefficient, understaffed and utterly inadequate to its task. It was also charged with being the pawn of pressure groups.[1] That Wakefield's theories of colonization were based upon faulty premises was proved in Australia but that colonies might be more than a waste-basket for human rubbish and that the Colonial Office was not up to its job was brought to public attention by Wakefield, Butler and Molesworth.

Exactly twenty years after the remark quoted above, Benjamin Disraeli did a complete about-turn in his attitude towards the colonies. The Liberals were still clinging stubbornly to free trade

[1] See Charles Buller, *Mr Mothercountry, of the Colonial Office* (London 1849) and Edward Gibbon Wakefield, *A View of the Art of Colonization* (London, 1849).

I

and resigned to the eventual disintegration of the Empire. But times had changed; Britain was no longer the uncontested manufacturer to the world. British farmers were being undersold in the home market by imported wheat and beef. European factories already were turning out goods at competitive prices and many countries were erecting tariff walls against British imports. In his Crystal Palace speech of 1872 Disraeli now urged that increases in colonial self-government could and should be combined with . . . 'a great policy of Imperial consolidation.'

Miss Hinden has expressed the changing attitude towards the colonies by a vivid analogy.[1] Colonies, she observes, had been treated as Cinderellas—drudges to serve the mother country. As they outgrew their infancy they began to act like obstreperous adolescents of more trouble than comfort to their parents so that the latter could hardly wait for them to grow up and get out on their own. But now the new imperialism began to look upon them as adults but still permanent members of the family, managing most of their own affairs in their own households to be sure, but behaving as loyal members of the family and acting together especially in relation to outsiders under the general direction of the family's hereditary head. It is interesting to observe that this view has much in common with the French concept of empire throughout the Third and Fourth Republics.

Disraeli's imperialism was accompanied by a new pride in the Empire which contained elements of racism and amounted to a sort of imperialist religion. It reached its peak of popularity in the 1890's and Rudyard Kipling was its poet laureate.[2] Kipling's poetry as well as Joseph Chamberlain's colonial ideas were strongly suffused with *noblesse oblige*. This made them an easy target for the cynic who saw in such expressions a mealy-mouthed hypocrisy, a cover for the same eternal profit-motive which had been stated with blunt honesty by Mr Richardson in the eighteenth century.

Nevertheless, English colonial policies and administration, sometimes at any rate, were in fact motivated by considerations other than mere profit. Research into colonial problems was commenced. In 1870 the Royal Colonial Institute was founded. The colonial viewpoint was given a hearing at the series of Colonial conferences begun in 1887. Naturally this kind of deference was paid chiefly to the colonies of white settlement. In the African, West Indian and Asiatic colonies discipline of a military nature might need to be applied sometimes to preserve the *Pax Britannica*. It was, as Kipling thought, sufficient justification that a courthouse now stood

[1] Hinden, *op. cit.*, p. 67.
[2] See in particular Kipling's 'Song of the English', 'The White Man's Burden' and 'The Recessional'.

where the regiment had camped and the river ran clear where once it had been red with blood.

But soon critics of the new imperialism in its application to tropical colonies began to appear. Some persons who knew such colonies at first hand were not satisfied with their treatment by the Colonial Office. It seemed to these critics that while profit might be a good reason for colonial agriculture, mining and the like, there was no moral justification for colonial exploitation unless it were accompanied by advances for the colonial people as well. The most devastating attack upon the colonial system was contained in J. A. Hobson's *Imperialism,* first published in 1902. Hobson was influenced by Marx and in his turn, influenced Lenin's writings. The England of Marx and Hobson was the classical Marxist example of a country where capital accumulated faster than it could be invested at home because the poverty of the labouring class prevented an expanding home market. This surplus capital was compelled to find investment abroad and preferably in colonies where the investor could count upon a friendly and protective government. Hobson echoed the old 'Little England' argument in part. He held that the colonies were useful not to the English people but only to the investors and a few others who were dependent upon their enterprise.

The guiding principles of British colonial policy in the nineteenth century were: 'firstly, the maintenance of conditions of internal security so as to give economic enterprise a permanent right of way and assured elbow room; secondly, the avoidance of expenditure which might lead to demands on the British taxpayer.'[1] Colonial officials, whether in the Colonial Office or serving overseas, were rarely economists or much interested in colonial economic development. They tended to rely upon traditional colonial taxation systems which leaned heavily upon customs duties. . . . 'It does seem fair to say, that until 1939 the Gladstonian principles of "leaving money to fructify in the pockets of the people" and "keeping your charge within your income" still reigned supreme, even if not completely unchallenged.'[2]

The British Labour Party from its inception had accepted in principle the Marx-Hobson view of imperialism but had combined this with a sentimental attachment to the Empire, a desire therefore to preserve some imperial connections along with the humanitarian objective of advancing colonial welfare and self government and inducing the colonies to accept the blessings of socialism. In 1933 the Labour Policy Report announced that 'Labour's object

[1] *Principles and Methods of Colonial Administration. Colston Papers* (London, Butterworth's Scientific Publications, 1950), p. 13.
[2] A. R. Prest, 'A Fiscal Survey of the British Caribbean', Colonial Office, *Colonial Research Studies, No.* 23 (London, 1957), p. 9.

will be to develop the Empire into a Commonwealth of self-governing Socialist units.' With the passage of time and the general acceptance of the idea that the British government bore considerable responsibility for the development and welfare of the colonies, the Conservative view of the colonial problem came to correspond closely with the Labour view except, of course, as to the spread of socialism. The inevitability of constitutional reforms in the colonies and the desirability of a flexible and receptive attitude on the part of the imperial authorities towards such reforms was expressed by Major Wood (Lord Halifax) as early as 1922 when he wrote: 'We shall be wise if we avoid the mistake of endeavouring to withhold a concession ultimately inevitable until it has robbed by delay of most of its usefulness and all of its grace.' (Wood Report, Cmd. 1679, p. 7.) When the depression riots had drawn the attention of the English people to the West Indies, even the Conservative *Daily Telegraph* admitted that British 'sins of omission and commission' had produced 'revolting conditions' in the colonies.[1]

The key word now became 'trusteeship'. The colonies were to be looked upon as a moral trust, to be helped towards self-sufficiency and self government within the British Commonwealth. Paternal benevolence alone is never enough to forestall the growth of independent nationalism in a colony, as both the Dutch and Belgians discovered in the Netherlands East Indies and in the Congo, unless accompanied by political and constitutional advances. As regards some British colonies, the trusteeship policy may have been adopted tardily. At any rate, this attitude of rather complacent benevolence received a jolt during World War II when so many Asian colonials proved to be woefully lacking in gratitude and even in loyalty.

Not long after the fall of Singapore Lord Hailey suggested that 'trusteeship' with its paternalistic implications be replaced by the concept of 'partnership', certain to be less offensive to colonial sensibilities. Lord Hailey's suggestion was echoed by Harold Macmillan, then Under-Secretary of State for the Colonies. It was later seconded by Oliver Stanley, the Secretary of State.[2] As already

---

[1] *Daily Telegraph*, editorial, issue of June 3, 1938.
[2] See House of Lords *Hansard*, 20 May, 1942, and House of Commons *Hansard*, 24 June, 1942, and July 13, 1943. On the later date Stanley said: . . . 'some of us feel now that the word "trustee" is rather too static in its connotations and that we should prefer to combine with the status of trustee the position also of partner'. That 'partnership' would scarcely differ from 'trusteeship' would seem to be indicated by subsequent statements issued by the Colonial Office. *The Colonial Empire* 1947-1948 (Cmd. 7433) contained the following: 'The central purpose of British colonial policy is simple. It is to guide the colonial territories to responsible self-government within the Commonwealth in conditions that assure to the people concerned both a fair standard of living and freedom from oppression from any quarter' . . . The subsequent number of this periodical substituted the word

observed, the war situation tended to freeze political arrangements temporarily, but even so some advances were made and plans were formulated for the spending of money allotted to the West Indies under the 1940 Colonial Development and Welfare Act.

It has been suggested that American influence was employed subtly during and after World War II to 'liberalize' British colonial policy. It is hard to see how this policy could have been other than it was, quite apart from any suggestions from Washington. It appears to be true that President F. D. Roosevelt took some personal interest in West Indian developments, possibly because of the destroyer-bases exchange which would naturally draw his attention to the locations in which the bases were to be established. He appears to have had some direct discussions with the British regarding West Indian political arrangements.[1] Subsequently the establishment of the Anglo-American Caribbean Commission in March, 1942, to which the American government appointed Puerto Ricans, may have influenced the appointment of colonials as well as British officials to later West Indian conferences. The President discussed Caribbean affairs, including political reforms, with both the British and American members of the Commission.[2]

More influential on local political developments, particarly in Jamaica, were the ideas and financial contributions of West Indians in the United States. The pre-party Jamaican nationalist movement had important roots in the United States and' substantial monetary support has been given, year after year by former Jamaicans, now American residents, to Manley's People National Party.[3]

When the Labour Party won its victory at the close of World War II the colonies waited anxiously for the application of Labour principles. In Asia the larger colonies were, indeed, permitted to assume Dominion status at once and one of them, Burma, chose to emulate Eire and cut all, or nearly all, connections with the Commonwealth. Malaya, less advanced politically, remained for the time being a Crown Colony. As regards the West Indies no drastic reforms were instituted and the Colonial Office went on

'territories' for 'Empire': *The Colonial Territories* 1949-50 (Cmd. 7958). This issue repeated the earlier statement of policy and also a caution to the effect that self-government requires energy and enterprise, economic self-sufficiency and honest, skilful administration.
[1] See *West India Committee Circular, LVII,* (November, 1942), 186.
[2] Bernard L. Poole, *The Caribbean Commission: Background of Cooperation in the West Indies* (Univ. of South Carolina, 1951) and despatch to the *New York Times,* headed 'President Weighs Caribbean Problem', issue of October 28, 1942.
[3] It is estimated that as of 1945 there were about 32,000 West Indians permanently resident in the United States. About 28,000 of these were from Jamaica. See *West India Committee Circular,* LX, 1173 (Sept., 1945) 163. See *below,* p. 216.

much as before to apply a 'benevolent imperialism'.[1] It seemed to the Labour government that reform would necessarily continue to be gradual and to include not only political advance in the shape of more local representation in the colonial governments but also such British aid as might enable the colonies to attain a minimum of social welfare and a sound economic advance. As Miss Hinden notes, the logic of Britain's post-war economic crisis required as rapid development as possible if the entire Sterling area and the growth of a market within that area in which British goods might be defended against foreign competition—the new mercantilism!

Whether or not the new mercantilism is more profitable to Great Britain or the colonies is a question that could be answered only by careful analysis. In any case the British government had little choice in the matter. It was unthinkable that the poorer colonies should suddenly be cast adrift and to retain them meant the contribution of considerable sums of Treasury money. Under these circumstances and because of the dollar shortage it was imperative that the colonies remain within the Sterling area with their currencies tied firmly to the devalued pound, painful though this might be to some of them.[2] Possibly the colonies with more or less permanently unbalanced budgets profited by this arrangement. It would seem that in some of the small islands, tariff preferences on colonial produce, Treasury subventions and CD & W spending more than counterbalance profits on British investments. The economic study needed to establish this point definitely has not been made. British and Commonwealth exporters enjoy a virtual monopoly of the colonial market as do British and Dominion banks and the colonies remain a field for the profitable investment of modest amounts of British capital. The relatively high degree of control over the local budget and government generally which the colonies now enjoy has not prevented the Secretary of State from acting against their wishes in the restraint of foreign competition with British investments. For example, in April, 1956, the British government refused to permit Barbados to license Pan American Airways to operate a service to Barbados although the House of Assembly had addressed a formal request to the Secretary of State asking that an American airline be licensed because of the probable benefit to the tourist industry. Barbados had been served only by the British West Indian Airways, a subsidiary of the government-owned BOAC. On the other hand there are signs of relaxation in the policy of British economic

[1] Hinden, *op. cit.*, p. 151.
[2] The outstanding case was British Honduras. See p. 103. The Netherlands, on the other hand, was able to allow the relatively rich Netherlands Antilles to remain within the dollar area and trade freely with the USA.

monopoly. The permission to Pan American, refused in 1956 was granted in 1957 and in September, 1957, for the first time in ninety years the British government turned down a concession application of the Belize Estate and Produce Company in British Honduras for additional timber lands and awarded it instead to a new American-financed firm, the British American Pulp and Paper Company.

It is the contention of the West Indian economist, Professor W. A. Lewis, that the foreign investors in the area, largely British, have made few attempts to train colonials in the techniques of business and finance and have tended to keep them in subordinate positions. Dr Lewis also agrees that the widely-held belief of colonial reformers that outside firms have made unduly high profits and have 'milked' the colonies of irreplaceable resources has also been true in certain times and places. As to the value to the colonies of imperial preferential tariffs, Dr. Lewis writes:

'Before 1939 the United Kingdom extended valuable preferences to a few commodities. The system was limited at first by a refusal to extend it to raw materials, and secondly by the fact that it could benefit only those commodities of which Empire production exceeded Empire demand. Only the sugar and tobacco producers made substantial gains. What the United Kingdom took in return for its limited preferences were the preferences that all colonies were asked in 1920 to grant to British manufactures, and the still larger and more widespread preferences imposed upon them, against bitter protest, in 1932 and after. It is difficult to believe that there is much future for these arrangements.'[1]

Despite the advantage to British investors, and to the Treasury through the income tax, of the continued British economic domination of the colonies, the self-government movement is now too powerfully under way to be stopped without explosive results in the colonies and politically dangerous reactions at home and abroad. Both British parties are committed to colonial advance, political and other. It is their hope that this can be accomplished with so little friction and so much good will that when complete independence is achieved, British economic interests will not suffer severely and by means of their 'ground-floor' advantage and long-accumulated knowledge of the area may be able to retain a large measure of the quasi-monopoly they have enjoyed in the past.

[1] W. A. Lewis, 'Colonial Development', *The Colonial Review,* IV, 2, (June, 1949), 37-41.
For a survey of tariff policies in relation to sugar, see W. E. Gordon, 'Mercantilist Tariff Policy in a British Colony: Jamaica', *Kyklos,* Separatum, Fasc. 2, 1956.

THE COLONIAL OFFICE AND THE COLONIAL SERVICE

The policies outlined above have always been carried out at the field level by the Colonial Service, responsible to the Secretary of State for the Colonies, who, as a temporary political figure, has had to rely for many of his decisions upon the advice tendered him by the permanent officials of the Colonial Office.

The Colonial Office is a product of the early Nineteenth Century, following the creation of a new Secretary of State 'for the War and Colonial Department' in 1801.[1] In 1854 the War Office was given a separate Secretary of State. From this time to the establishment of the Dominions Office in 1925, the Colonial Office dealt with a wide variety of territories in all degrees of self-government and subjection. Since 1925 it has had to deal only with non-self-governing territories: colonies proper, protectorates, protected states and trust territories.

The Colonial Office has the duty of representing the colonies and their interests as they may be affected by the policies of Commonwealth countries, the various departments of the British government, other countries and international bodies. This is done by information and suggestions given to the Secretary of State for the Colonies who will then make the proper representations in Cabinet meetings. The other aspect of Colonial Office responsibility is seen in the general oversight of the Colonial governments to ensure that the policies of the British government are duly carried out by the Colonial Service.

For a long time the Colonial Office confined itself chiefly to seeing that the detailed Colonial Regulations were strictly adhered to. These 'Col. Regs.' have been in existence since 1832 and covered such matters as the rules regarding colonial finance and administration. The Colonial Office was always much concerned about the colonial budgets, whether or not the colony was in receipt of Treasury assistance, and the principle which determined its approval or disapproval of a budget was that of the balancing of estimated income and expenditure rather than the urgency of local needs.

Until 1925 the Colonial Office was organized chiefly into geographical departments, each under an Assistant Secretary of State. Subsequently, and especially since the first of the CD & W Acts in 1940, the subject-matter method of organization has been used increasingly. The General Department has grown and there are several

[1] Sir Charles Jeffries, *The Colonial Office* (London, Allen & Unwin, 1955). Its predecessors were the Committee of the Privy Council for Plantations (1660-1782) and the Home Office (1782-1801).

departments concerned with special problems as advisers on agriculture, fisheries, education and so forth who visit the colonies and report to the area departments. Inevitably the functional approach was required by the growing importance and difficulty of technical problems and the need to see that development funds were wisely apportioned and spent.

The Colonial Office is headed by the Secretary of State for the Colonies. This personage may be a politician of no colonial experience but often he is chosen because of his background as a Colonial Official. Not infrequently he is a peer, because retired Governors have often been elevated to the peerage.[1] If this is the case, his Parliamentary Under Secretary is usually a member of the House of Commons. Since 1948 the Secretary of State has had another parliamentary assistant, the Minister of State for Colonial Affairs who, like the Under Secretary, represents the Secretary in Parliament, and may perform other duties as assigned by the Secretary of State. All three reply to questions in Parliament and defend the actions and policies of the Colonial Office. The Secretary of State must handle a great deal of business. Not only does he have the responsibility of formulating broad policies and defending them in Cabinet meetings and subsequently in Parliament, but he must hear a variety of appeals from Governors' decisions, decide upon the advisability of legislation reserved for the Crown's pleasure, and make a large number of principal appointments in all the colonies. In doing all this he must rely heavily upon the career civil servants in the Colonial Office. These are headed by the Permanent Under Secretary of State, his Deputy, several Assistant Under Secretaries (one for each department) the special advisers on law, agriculture, and so forth, and the staff of something over five hundred.

The chief civil servants, all those with any policy-making functions, belong to the administrative grade. Formerly these were exclusively male (women were not appointed until recently) and nearly all were graduates of Oxford or Cambridge. Labour Party spokesmen used to complain that they included too few experts and that there was too little in-service training. The same critics alleged that in making appointments sheer merit and brains were sacrificed to secure recruits of the right background and breeding. As Harold Laski wrote in 1938:

---

[1] Since 1884, forty-eight individuals have held office of Secretary of State for the Colonies, some of them more than once. Of these, thirty-one have been members of the House of Commons and seventeen have been peers. Of the Commoners, except for some Labour Party members, the great majority either inherited peerages or later were created peers.

'The administrative service is drawn from too narrow a source. Broadly it represents the 'public school' mind. It has been trained, therefore, to the acceptance of the historic assumptions of empire. It is a mind capable of efficiency and the team-spirit within the limits those assumptions impose. It is rarely a mind which questions them, or looks to innovation in fundamentals.'[1]

Certainly, this method of recruitment virtually eliminated the likelihood of a colonial securing an administrative grade appointment. Critics have held that a Colonial Office, so constituted, has tended to remain provincial in its outlook, too remote from the world and from the colonies over whose destiny it presides.

Formerly the Colonial Service, known now as Her Majesty's Overseas Civil Service, was recruited entirely by patronage handled by the Secretary of State's Private Secretaries. The governorships were very lucrative and much in demand. As a result they went very often to utterly incompetent and unworthy persons who had the necessary connections or money to acquire them. The present appointment system was established in 1930 when a Personnel Division was created, with one section dealing with recruitment and training and another with promotion, transfer, pensions and so forth. All appointments to the unified Overseas Service are made with the approval of the Secretary of State and even those in the local services with a salary of £600 or more per annum. In fact, the Secretary of State depends usually upon the advice of the Colonial Service Appointments Board consisting of the First Civil Service Commissioner, two active members of the Colonial Service and an unofficial person named by the Secretary of State. The board, in turn, may take advice from the Appointments Department of the Colonial Office. Promotions are handled by the Promotions Committee of the Colonial Office.

There is a period of one year's training given to all prospective administrators: 'Overseas Services Course A' at Oxford or Cambridge. Some also take an additional 'Course B'.[2] All appointments, whether administrative or specialist, are made in response to requests from the Governor of a colony. The Governor may

---

[1] *Political Quarterly* (Oct.-Dec., 1938) IX, 4, 546. Laski was writing actually about the overseas service but the same strictures apply to the Colonial Office itself. See also Fabian Society pamphlet, *Downing Street and the Colonies* (London, 1942). Sir Charles Jeffries mentions the club-like atmosphere of the old Colonial Office in which a new recruit would be taken around and introduced to the entire staff. See Jeffries, *op. cit.*, p. 7.
[2] In an average year (1953) 1,227 new appointments were made by the Secretary of State, the great majority were natives of the United Kingdom, a few from other Commonwealth Countries and some from Eire. One hundred and eight were administrators, the rest specialists of various kinds. Jeffries, *op. cit.*, p. 141.

recommend a specific person but there is no assurance that his advice will be accepted.

At one time, all of the administrative grade posts were filled by Britons. This has altered radically, especially since World War II. Not only the lower posts are recruited within the colony but many of the top positions in the colonial hierarchy are filled by West Indians. On one occasion at least, the Secretary of State was induced by local reaction to withdraw an appointment already made to the post of Financial Secretary in an important colony and fill the office with a local man. It is not now unheard of for the Governor only among the top officials to have been born in the British Isles. Usually, however, the Colonial Secretary is also an Englishman. In the principal colonies he is normally in line for a next appointment as Governor. The judiciary in the West Indies now consists almost entirely of local men, all, of course, English trained.

What control does Parliament have over the policies and behaviour of the Colonial Office and the Overseas Service? Legally, of course, Parliament is supreme but in fact, except occasionally, there is little interest in the affairs of remote and unimportant dots on the map. There may be a debate in the House of Commons following the issuance of a White Paper, the report of a Royal Commission or a bill of importance such as the Colonial Development and Welfare Act or when serious local disturbances occur. There may be one or two Members who delight in bothering the Secretary of State with questions. But not even every year is there a Supply Day devoted to a discussion of the Colonial Office. Colonial affairs in general are left, except at rare intervals, to the management of the Secretary of State and the Colonial Office. The House of Lords, containing as it does, a number of ex-Governors and ex-Secretaries of State, and with its greater freedom and time for debate, is often the scene of more thorough and better-informed discussion of colonial affairs than is the Commons.

THE GOVERNOR

His Excellency, the Governor, is very much the monarch of his little kingdom, even if he now tends to refrain from the overt dictation of policies. In the words of Hewan Craig, he is . . . 'at the same time the King's representative, prime minister, agent of the imperial power and guardian of the welfare of the local community and also the head of the community and the symbol of its precarious unity'.[1] A somewhat earlier description emphasized his

[1] Hewan Craig, *The Legislative Council of Trinidad and Tobago*, (London, Faber, 1952) p. 132.

autocratic powers. Colonial Governors were said to be . . . 'a succession of carefully chosen and experienced autocrats, watchful and considerate of local public opinion but not responsive to it, and controlled from a common centre by a high Officer of State'.[1] In the principal colonies the Governor is usually a man with previous experience in the office. In the minor units he is often a former Colonial Secretary who has had the task of administering the civil service in a colony and probably has also been Acting Governor at times. His previous tours of duty may have included West Indian posts but often will have been in Africa or Asia. He may have had military experience but not necessarily. Almost always he comes from within the career Overseas Service. Formerly he was always born and educated in the British Isles.[2]

Some years ago the Labour Government decided to try the experiment of appointing a few governors from among inexperienced politicians who would, presumably, be well equipped to discuss colonial affairs after their tour of duty, and who could hold their own against the numerous Conservatives who had retired from the Colonial Service. The first choice fell upon Lord Baldwin, a Labour peer who was the son of the former Conservative prime minister. Lord Baldwin, a brilliant but eccentric man, soon managed to throw his colony (the Leeward Islands) into social and political confusion. He was recalled before the completion of his term and the experiment was not repeated.[3]

Formerly governors were their own prime ministers, not only presiding over and directing the business of Executive Council meetings where policies were decided, but subsequently acting as both speaker and prime minister in the Legislative Council, introducing and defending the measures embodying these policies. They

[1] Henry L. Hall, *The Colonial Office* (London, Longmans, 1937), pp. 113, 114.
[2] But note the designation in 1959 as Governor of Trinidad of Sir Solomon Hochoy, the first native-born West Indian Governor of non-European descent.
[3] The West Indian Governors, as of 1957, with their previous colonial experience (that in the West Indies italicized) were:
Jamaica: Sir Hugh Mackintosh Foot, KCMG, KCVO, OBE (Palestine, Trans-Jordan, Cyrenaica, Cyrprus, Nigeria).
Sir Kenneth Blackburne, KCMG, OBE (Nigeria, Palestine, Gambia, *CD&WWI, Leewards*).
British Guiana: Sir Patrick Renison, KCMG (Ceylon, India, *Trinidad, British Honduras*).
Barbados: Brig. Sir Robert Arundell, KCMG, OBE (Tanganyika, Uganda, *Caribbean Commission, Windwards*).
Windwards: Sir Colville Deverell, KCMG, CVO, OBE (Kenya, Jamaica).
Leewards: A. T. Williams, CMG, MBE (Northern Rhodesia).
British Honduras: C. H. Thornley, CMG, CVO (now Sir Colin Thornley, KCMG (Tanganyika, Kenya, Uganda).
Trinidad and Tobago: Sir Edward Betham Beetham, KCMG, CVO, OBE (Kenya, Swaziland, Bechuanaland, *Windwards*).

could always be certain of having their policies accepted in Executive Council because it would consist entirely or largely of subordinate officials. In the early stages of Crown Colony government they could be certain of a legislative victory as well.

Even though much of the Governor's function as real executive head of the government has now passed in the more advanced colonies to the Premier or Chief Minister, he still retains certain genuine executive powers. In addition he remains, as always, a Chief of State in miniature. As the Sovereign's representative he has a number of ceremonial functions to perform and a great deal of official entertaining to do. He and his lady occupy the summit of the colony's social pyramid, a conspicuous and important position in class-conscious colonial society. He presides over what is essentially a viceregal court. He may also, of course, be the target at times of ill-mannered and undeserved verbal abuse from politicians whose appeal is to the poor labourer for whom the Governor is a living symbol of hated colonialism. If he is politically sophisticated the Governor will recognize the fact that part of his job as chief of state at one stage of the colony's political and social development is to serve as a scapegoat for colonial resentments based on wrongs, real or imaginary, that can be blamed upon the imperial connection.

With the coming of universal suffrage, the rise of labour parties and the replacement of official and nominated by elected majorities in the legislature, the Governor's political role has altered considerably. He has had to become more the diplomat and less the autocrat. Along with these changes the Colonial Office has deemed it wise to add to his powers of emergency action. Accordingly, together with the gift of an elected majority in the legislature went the Governor's reserved power to certify bills in Executive Council after the bill had been rejected by the legislature. This power was given in British Guiana as part of the 1928 constitution which was the first to provide an unofficial majority in a mixed legislative Council. The reserved power was conditioned only by the requirement that any action taken in accordance with it be referred to the Secretary of State for final approval or reversal. Similar powers were given to the Governors of the Leeward Islands and the Windward Islands in 1936 and to the Governor of Trinidad in 1941 and of Jamaica in 1944. It is obvious that the reserved power to certify bills must ordinarily be kept in reserve. It cannot be used to turn the government into an executive dictatorship without subverting the constitution.

This power has had its most frequent use in the small islands in which the elected members have composed a solid labour party delegation. They have not had to be employed very often—only nine times altogether since their first use in Montserrat in 1943. This first case came about because the Presidency legislature refused to pass the appropriation for the police force. Indeed, their principal use has been to overcome legislative attempts to strike out appropriation items. In 1952 Governor Arundell in the Windwards used the power in Grenada, St Vincent and St Lucia to restore the provision of a salary for an Assistant Administrator in each of the three islands, a new office regarded by the legislators as extravagant and unnecessary. Also in 1952 the power was used in the St Kitts-Nevis-Anguilla Presidency of the Leewards to pass an ordinance providing for several single-member constituencies instead of the colony-wide multi-member constituency favoured by the labour party because it assured them a complete electoral sweep. In the same Presidency it was used in 1954 to certify the entire appropriation ordinance after the elected members had declared a 'general strike' against the government. In 1950 the certifying power was used in Jamaica to provide for an immediate payment of money to Jamaica Utilities Limited. Without question, the instance of the use of the certifying power which led to the loudest popular outcry and did most damage to British-colony relations was its employment in British Honduras, as mentioned earlier, to devalue the local dollar and bring it into line with the Pound Sterling. Naturally, every use of this power has inspired vigorous protests by the elected members but it has not produced prolonged political crises nor a refusal to work the constitution on the part of the legislatures.

The Governor's veto power and his power to reserve bills for approval or disallowance by the Secretary of State rarely need to be employed. They are used only in the event of an attempt by a legislature to legislate in a field denied to it by law, such as the amendment of the colony's constitution.[1]

Governors try to avoid the use of their reserved powers and prefer to rely upon their persuasive ability in Executive Council meetings and upon the debating skill of their officials (where these are still present) in the legislature. The fact that the powers exist may give the Governors some leverage in debate except when it is the object of the elected members to force the Governor to certify a bill over their objections as dramatic evidence of colonial subjection.

[1] According to a communication from the Colonial Office, of June, 1958, 'Our experts can recall no cases of reservation or refusal of assent in British Guiana, British Honduras or Bahamas since about 1954; in Jamaica, the "Attestation of Instruments (Further Facilities) Law, 1956", was reserved but passed into law as No. 24 of 1957; in Trinidad, the Leewards and Windwards reserve powers have not been used in the past two years'.

The successful modern Governor, therefore, must be a skilful politician. The fact that he no longer rules his colony like an ancient monarch does not mean that he requires less ability than his predecessors. On the contrary, he must be able to get along with local political leaders who may be suspicious of his motives, inclined to distrust him, and who, sometimes, are at least subconsciously resentful of his position and prestige of office. He must resist attempts to open the civil service to political patronage although the immediate pressure in this case may fall upon his Colonial (or Chief) Secretary. He must be friendly with opposing leaders and ready to co-operate with the winners of the latest election. In striving to advance the colony socially, economically and politically he must work through the local political leaders and at the same time must avoid the appearance of identifying himself with any group or party. However impartial his behaviour he may have to submit to severe criticism for a failure to oppose his will to that of the elected government and these attacks may come not only from conservatives but from a nationalist opposition.

An editorial in *Public Opinion,* the organ of the Jamacian PNP (issue of November 7, 1953) entitled 'How's That, Umpire?', made a vigorous attack upon the Governor, Sir Hugh Foot, for having 'forced' the 1953 constitutional advances without first having a general election; for having consented to the irregular appointment of two civil servants (the Governor gave in to ministerial pressure in this case and the two men were later convicted of abuse of authority);[1] and finally, for not having intervened as 'umpire' when the Speaker of the House of Representatives rejected a motion with a long and argumentative preamble tabled by Mr Manley, calling for an inquiry into ministerial corruption. The editorial demanded that the Governor face the Bustamante ministry with the alternative of proceeding with the inquiry demanded by Manley or an immediate dissolution and general election. One is reminded of the abuse heaped upon Lord Elgin for his refusal to veto the Rebellion Losses Bill in Canada, a refusal prompted by his determination to introduce responsible government.

To be a great Governor requires tireless industry and immense political skill. It is remarkable that so many West Indian Governors have measured up with outstanding success to the exacting requirements of their office. Both Sir Hugh Foot in Jamaica and Sir Kenneth Blackburne in the Leewards are recent exemplifications of

[1] The Governor is rumoured to have given way to a demand by Bustamante that he confirm these appointments and override the Public Service Commission, under threat of a boycott by Bustamante (who was then Chief Minister) of the imminent royal visit to Jamaica.

this statement. Sir Kenneth was appointed to the Leewards in 1950 at a time when the colony was suffering from the effects of a hurricane and the social and political turmoil created by the preceding Governor, the unpredictable Lord Baldwin. He inherited a hostile attitude on the part of the labour leaders and politicians and a general disposition to regard the Governor with distruct. But by 1954, in the words of a West Indian journalist:

'To Sir Kenneth's administrative ability, embodying astuteness and firmness coupled with good humour, the people of Antigua, at least, attribute a large measure of their social and economic revival.

So they wish him to remain as Governor of the Leeward Islands for another five years. And, encouraged by the very Labour politicians with whom it was feared Sir Kenneth would have the most trouble, they are affixing thousands of signatures to a Labour-sponsored petition.'[1]

It is most unusual for a Secretary of State to extend a Governor's term beyond the normal five years but in this case Sir Kenneth was reappointed for one additional year, to September 16, 1956. Subsequently he succeeded Sir Hugh Foot in Jamaica when the latter was appointed to Cyprus.

Governor Blackburne's success is attributable to his ability to gain and keep the confidence of the elected members and ministers by his obvious devotion to the welfare of the colony and his willingness to help these inexperienced labour politicians and work with them in hammering out legislation embodying their policies, within the colony's capacities. So completely had he won general admiration and friendship that the colonial officials were no longer the targets of verbal abuse as a matter of course at political street meetings. Instead, the local conservative opposition as represented by the nominated members of the legislature became the target of labour's resentments.

Sir Hugh Foot in Jamaica had an equally difficult task in guiding constitutional reform and in seeing that the new ministerial system worked well and smoothly with Alexander Bustamante as the First Chief Minister. Sir Hugh had to deal with two of the most astute and experienced politicians in the West Indies, Bustamante and Manley, both of whom were anxious to display independence in their relations with the official side.

A Governor may be tempted to influence elections to the extent of letting his views be known publicly as to the kind of legislature he prefers and even as to the individual politicians he hopes to see

[1] David J. Nelson, in the *Trinidad Guardian*, issue of May 16, 1954.

elected. This is a risky course and may backfire if it offends many voters who resent such pressures and are suspicious of politicians who receive official approbation. If the Governor's electioneering is unsuccessful he may find himself compelled to deal with politicians whom he has alienated. Further, such activity is incompatible with the Governor's position as Chief of State within the colony. For these reasons few Governors have indulged in anything approaching active electioneering. The few examples that might be cited occurred in colonies without a party system.

A recent example of official interference in local politics occurred in British Honduras. Before the 1954 elections in that colony the government-issued periodical was highly critical of the principal political party, the People's United Party, and its leaders who were accused of disloyalty and sedition. Although the newspaper was paid for by government funds and edited by a colonial official, the Public Relations Officer, the Governor himself, Mr (now Sir Patrick) Renison, refrained from any personal expression of these views and was able to work successfully with the PUP leaders following their victory at the polls.

There is no evidence that modern Governors have employed corruption or what might be called Tudor tactics in an attempt to secure a pliable legislature. However, there is an interesting example of the Governor in politics alleged to have taken place in Jamaica during the governorship of Sir Arthur Richards, now Lord Milverton. It is impossible to find proof for the widely held belief that the Governor, who had been holding Alexander Bustamante in detention under the Emergency Regulations, released him on the understanding that he would at once form a new political party in opposition to Manley's People's National Party, despite the fact that hitherto Manley and Bustamante had been working together. It is conceivable that the Governor took this step, if he did, because he was convinced that Bustamante's radicalism was confined to trades union objectives whereas he feared the extremist nationalism and avowed socialism of the PNP and thought a political sweep by this party might be disastrous to the British connection and the colony's economy. A PNP victory would have been certain had Bustamante and Manley continued their previous collaboration.

The prominence of the Governor's position, his symbolical headship of the colony and his function until recently as genuine chief executive have made it difficult for the ordinary colonial citizen to think of their ministers as anything more than the Governor's subordinates. Despite publicity as to where responsibility now lies the tendency remains for members of the public to appeal to the Governor rather than to the ministers.

K

It should be noted that, *legally* speaking, sovereignty remains located in the King-in-Parliament, no matter how much self-government the colony has acquired nor how long it has enjoyed this degree of self-rule. From the viewpoint of the Crown all colonial powers are considered delegated rather than inherent and are legally removable by Act of Parliament if not by simple Order in Council.[1] The loyalty of the Governor is totally to the Crown and his instructions and Letters Patent are to be obeyed in spirit as well as letter. His immediate superior is the Secretary of State for the Colonies and the Secretary of State has unlimited authority to recall the Governor at any time, and in any difference of opinion as to policies the Secretary of State's decision is final.

Most Governors remain in one colony for a five-year tour of duty and are then re-assigned elsewhere. If a Governor has been particularly successful he may expect to go to a more important colony at a higher salary. The salary differences have resulted, the poorer colonies say, in their getting the worst governors. Certainly they must expect to get men at the start of their career in this office rather than the more experienced administrators. Some critics have criticized also the shortness of the tour of duty. A Governor barely has time, they say, to become well acquainted with a colony and its problems before he is taken away and this happens just at the time when he should be best able to contribute to the welfare of the area and see the fruition of his policies.[2] This criticism has less cogency today with the Governor tending to become a nominal executive and policy determination tending to be the business of the elected ministers.

THE COLONIAL SECRETARY

Next to the Governor, the most important official in the Colony is the Colonial Secretary or Chief Secretary as he is called in colonies with a ministerial system and semi-responsible government. His duties are numerous and exacting. He is invariably the head of the civil service with a general oversight of all departments and personnel administration. He is in charge of security and police administration. He must be ready to undertake any special assignment given him by the Governor and when the latter is absent from the colony, he becomes His Excellency, the Acting Governor. As the Governors retired from active political leadership in the legis-

[1] Jeffries, *op. cit.*, p. 29.
[2] Fabian Society, *Downing Street and the Colonies* (London, 1942) Ch. III. . . . . "he generally spends the fifth year of his tour in regretting the mistakes he made in the first four."—Sir George Maxwell in *The Crown Colonist*, July, 1945. 451.

lature, this function was taken on by the 'Col. Sec.' who became, in some colonies, a kind of prime minister. In colonies with unicameral legislatures the Colonial Secretary or the Administrator remains the principal official member. Of course, with the ministerial system becoming universal, the Colonial Secretary has tended to retire into a purely administrative role. In Barbados he remained until 1958 the principal representative of the government in the second chamber, the Legislative Council, and had the task of introducing and defending in debate the measures of the Executive Council which was dominated by the elected ministers. The Colonial Secretary is always a member of the Executive Council (except in Jamaica), although his importance in this body tends to become that of an administrative expert rather than a policy-maker as the latter function is taken over by the elected ministers. Nevertheless, he remains second in importance only to the Governor and he requires all the skill and diplomacy he can bring to the office, particularly in the early stages of the ministerial system. The smooth working or otherwise of the departments as they come under inexperienced ministers must depend to a considerable extent upon the ability of the Chief Secretary, as he is now called, to educate the new ministers tactfully in the administrative side of their work as it is the Governor's job to educate them in the conduct of Executive Council business. The Chief Secretary must serve also as a buffer between the ministers and the civil service, preventing politely but firmly ministerial attempts to introduce a personal or party spoils system.

THE ADMINISTRATOR

In the small islands of the Windward and Leeward groups, the legislature of each colony is presided over by the Governor's deputy, the Administrator.[1] As his title suggests he is in general charge of administration, performing a function like that of the Colonial Secretary in the larger colonies. He is also the local substitute for the Governor, the formulator of official policy and its spokesman in both Executive and Legislative Councils. Indeed he is essentially a Governor of the pre-ministerial period in his relation to policy and the legislature. Naturally, too, as the ministerial system is

[1] The Windward Islands Governorship includes the colonies of: Grenada, including the principal islets of the Grenadine chain, St. Vincent, including the rest of the Grenadines, St Lucia, and Dominica.

The Leeward Island colonies, formerly the Presidencies of the Federation of the Leeward Islands, consist of: Antigua, including the little island of Barbuda, St Kitts, Nevis and Anguilla, Montserrat, and the British Virgin Islands.

applied, even in the smaller islands, his function becomes more that of an impartial chairman and influential adviser in both legislature and Executive Council. He is immediately responsible to the Governor and ultimately to the Secretary of State.

COLONIAL REACTION TO BRITISH OFFICIALS

Subsequent to the adoption of the 'partnership' policy by successive British governments, there was in general an easing of tensions between colonial nationalists and the official side. But despite the wide popularity of this policy and a disposition to accept as sincere the declarations of successive Secretaries of State that self-government will be advanced as rapidly as prudence permits, there is still a tendency for West Indians to find fault with British officials.

The complaints are various. The fact that governors and minor officials often come to the West Indies with a background of African training and experience has been offensive to West Indian pride. This objection was more frequently heard a few years ago when West Indians considered African society to be uncivilized and before the achievement of self-government in West Africa.

The fact that newly-arrived British officials have to be taught the details of their work by West Indian subordinates makes it hard for the latter to understand why they have not been promoted to the higher post. It would seem that the Overseas Service tends to attract a type rather different from the young men who prefer the home service, the most brilliant of whom usually enter the Treasury. The overseas candidates are likely to be less scholarly and more adventurous. They probably include a greater proportion of what English undergraduates used to call 'hearties'. There can be no doubt that many Britons of the Overseas Service are admirably suited to their duties, but at the same time, West Indian civil servants may be justified sometimes in believing that British birth and education may be a more important factor than brains or sheer ability in securing high positions in the service. Insofar as there is any admission that British birth and ancestry and the right sort of educational background may be more important than intellect, this bias can be defended on the ground that it provides the Secretary of State and the Colonial Office with subordinates in the key posts who 'speak the same language' and whose probity and loyalty to the British connection are above suspicion. As late as 1939, in fact, the Colonial Office Recruiting Circular specified that recruits to the unified branches of the service be of European descent.

Another complaint is that the elected ministers sometimes encounter inexcusable delays in securing the execution of their approved policies within the departments, either because the officials are lazy and disinclined to change their ways or because they dislike the new policy and take a 'poor view' of the minister. The automatic loyalty of departmental subordinates to the minister in power, regardless of party or personality, cannot always be assured when the subordinates are protected by law from interference by the government and when they soon may be continuing their careers in other colonies.

Within the civil service, on the other hand, junior civil servants sometimes prefer a British to a West Indian superior because the former is unlikely to play favourites, whereas the West Indian is only too likely to have his own coterie whose careers he will try to advance at the expense of the rest.

But more and more the service is being West Indianized. By 1953 two-thirds of the departmental secretaries in Jamaica were West Indians. Whites of British birth and education long monopolized the top offices of the Overseas Service but a few years after the ban on non-Europeans had been lifted, some non-whites had achieved promotion to the posts of Attorney General, Financial Secretary and even Chief Secretary, and finally, in the case of Sir Solomon Hochoy, to the Governorship.

The standard of honesty among officials of the Overseas Service is high, but there have been instances of corruption among them. In Trinidad in March, 1953, strong criticism of the government was voiced in the legislature and the Press, following the publication of a report by Mr Justice Gomes on the Caura Dam project. This laid bare a scandalous misuse of public funds and pointed the fingure of suspicion at some permanent officials as well as one of the elected members of the Executive Council. By this time, however, all the officials who were implicated had been transferred out of the colony or had retired and nothing was done about their alleged misdeeds. This method of 'punishing' official dishonesty by simple transfer to another post is believed in the colonies to be standard Colonial Office practice due to official solidarity and a disposition to conceal official misconduct if possible and never to admit publicly that a British official has been guilty of a crime. Such cases are rare but when they occur they cause resentment and at least temporary loss of prestige by the Colonial Office in the colony concerned. In the Caura Dam case the official explanation was that the waste of funds was due to inefficiency and lack of proper supervision rather than to corruption.

The complaint of rule by British officials is rapidly becoming historic as federation gets under way. No doubt in the future the civil service will be staffed at both federal and unit levels entirely by West Indians except when it is still necessary to use outsiders with specialist skills. Some of these may be needed for some time to come largely because professionally-educated West Indians have shown an overwhelming predilection for law and medicine. There are very few West Indian economists, architects, engineers, and so forth. No doubt this situation will change as there is greater industrialization and diversification of the West Indian economy and as the federation provides opportunities for wider careers.

COLONIAL LOYALTY

A principal objective of the Overseas Service in these days of rapid growth of self-government in the colonies is the fostering of loyalty to the British connection. It is of considerable importance to the British economy that the political advances should be associated with a feeling of good will towards Great Britain. The Overseas Service, therefore, has a public relations task to perform as well as administrative duties.

In some respects this task is easy because of the long history of British connection and the fact that there is a negligible amount of any other culture among the West Indians except that of British derivation. Insofar as West Indians feel any strong loyalty beyond their home colony, it is British. British loyalty is strongest, naturally, among the middle and upper classes many of whom have had some British education. The majority of West Indian physicians and surgeons and all West Indian lawyers and judges have been British trained. A British university degree has the highest prestige—an American degree much less. Some scholarships are available through the British Council and the CD & W organization. West Indian education is on the British model and secondary schools emphasize British history and literature so that even an education confined to the West Indies has its accultural aspects.

On the other hand, the actual and alleged neglect of local welfare by the British officials for long periods and the attitude of white superiority assumed by some officials and many white creoles have led to antagonism or indifference towards the British connection on the part of many of the poorer colonials. It should be noted that colonial loyalty to the Mother Country, whether or not racial differences are involved, is likely to be a fluctuating emotion and subject to abrupt diminution if the colonials believe themselves to be abused or neglected by the home government. A number of British Canadians for a time favoured annexation of Canada by the United States following the repeal of the Corn Laws and even the most

British of all overseas peoples, the New Zealanders, displayed an anti-British attitude in 1870 because imperial troops were withdrawn and a military loan refused by Great Britain despite the danger from still unsubdued Maori warriors. A recent example is the resolution of the Maltese legislature, passed in December, 1957, favouring separation from Great Britain because of the threat of reduction in force at the naval dockyards. The upsurge of anti-British feeling in British Honduras after devaluation of the dollar and in British Guiana after the collapse of the war boom are entirely characteristic of colonial loyalty swings.

As noted earlier, the system of rewards and honours has long been used to emphasize the British identification of leading colonials in all fields. Without exact proof of this, it may be hazarded that the disposition to scorn and ridicule such imperial gew-gaws, which characterized the early stages of the colonial nationalist movements, has now softened somewhat. Politicians who were once considered less than enthusiastic supporters of the British connection have accepted honours in recent years and apparently without sacrificing their political appeal to the voters.

The 'social lobby' to use an American term is an integral part of the colonial system. The bottom rung of the ladder is achieved with an invitation to a Government House function. The higher stages involve decorations, usually the MBE or OBE, and eventually a successful career in the judiciary, a profession or politics may be recognized by the award of a knighthood. It is part of the Governor's duty to see that these honours are properly assigned and to make the necessary recommendations to the Crown. Hughes quotes a Bermudian legislator as defining the Executive Council as a machine for receiving rugged individualists at one end and grinding out CBE's at the other.[1]

The royal symbol remains of great importance. It would seem that for people brought up in the tradition of reverence for an hereditary monarch nothing can replace this human symbol of national or empire unity. Certainly the royal visits to the West Indies were highly successful in stimulating a feeling of British identification among classes hitherto seemingly indifferent. Queen Elizabeth and the Duke of Edinburgh visited the West Indies in 1953 and Princess Margaret made a West Indian visit in 1955. It was observed that after the royal visit to Jamaica, the poor people occupying the 'pit' in the moving picture theatres who had formerly walked out during the playing of 'God Save the Queen', now stood and cheered. Evidently Queen Elizabeth was now 'their Queen' in a personal sense after they had themselves seen her and heard her

[1] Colin A. Hughes, op. cit., MS p. 298.

speak. It is evident that one of the most effective public relations devices at the disposal of the British government is the royal institution, especially as it is personified in a charming young Queen.

Another of the most effective 'links of Empire' is cricket. American enthusiasm for baseball as a universal sport cannot compare with the West Indian devotion to cricket. And cricket is a British game. Only in India, Pakistan and the West Indies is cricket played by people of non-British origin. The international test matches between crack British and Australian and West Indian teams are so important to West Indians that when one is taking place in a West Indian island all business is suspended there during the playing period. Shops and offices are closed and government employees are released to attend the match. The West Indian equivalent of a sand-lot baseball team is the village cricket eleven of small boys who have whittled bats out of the stems of coconut leaves and who dream that some day they may play for the West Indies. It has been suggested that this universal enthusiasm provides one of the most significant sources of West Indian national feeling as a necessary psychological support for federation.

The Colonial Development and Welfare organization has operated since its establishment to assist the colonies in a variety of ways. Many of its projects are quiet and unspectacular and are of importance in the long run rather than immediately. As well as providing considerable sums for welfare activities and development projects it will undertake to train a colonial in a skill urgently needed in his colony. As a British-financed and largely British-staffed agency it has been accumulating good will in the West Indies since its inception. Certainly it has the general approval of West Indians familiar with its work.

The Colonial Development Corporation has been less effective in building good will. Established to provide the needed capital and skills to undertake projects intended to be self-liquidating, the CDC representatives have been roundly criticized in the West Indies for a failure to take local advice and a disposition to waste money, sometimes on projects chosen hastily and inadvisedly and with supervision too much centralized in London. Even when the project was urgently needed, as in the case of rebuilding the town of Castries, St Lucia, following a disastrous fire, the costs have been so great that they have been impossible to repay despite the writing off of half the actual investment.

Finally, the work of the British Council may be mentioned. In some respects the British Council performs a task similar to that of the British Information Service in foreign countries. But it does a great deal more than provide an information centre. It has sponsored libraries and spent Carnegie funds on these. It also provides the rooms and instructors for a variety of adult education courses in everything from art and music to public administration. It has a few scholarships to award to colonial students most of which are for training at the sub-professional level, often in purely cultural subjects. The British Council, performs its task well, within its limitations of funds and personnel and plays its part in preserving and furthering British acculturation and stimulating intellectual activities in the colonies, not always without arousing the resentment of local nationalists.[1]

COLONIAL TUTELAGE

The tendency in societies recently uprooted from a traditional authority-system or in which the old political and social myths have lost their magic, is for a political vacuum to result, only to be filled at once by rival contenders for power. Power nuclei may form within existing associations, religious, economic or other. They may be dominated by leaders who are able to transfer prestige acquired as pastor, labour leader or whatever into the arena of political competition. In the early stages of this competition, before a stable pattern of superior-subordinate relationships has been established, there may be rapid shifts in the relative importance of the contenders for power and the simultaneous existence of a number of them. Such an 'unstable pluralism' may bring about a series of governments unable to find a broad consensus and consequently unable to formulate satisfactory solutions to urgent social problems. The inability of the government to solve its problems will produce general political cynicism and disillusion with existing constitutional forms, which, in turn, may well further the rise to power of a charismatic leader and the release of social tensions in the acceptance of an autocracy. This may happen, indeed, even when the autocrat did not intend in the beginning to establish a dictatorship. He may be compelled by the intransigent and disorderly nature of the opposition and the lack of firmly established democratic procedures, either to give way or ensure the continuance of his rule by force and fear.

The over-all task of the Secretaries of State acting through the Colonial Office and the Overseas Service has been to organize and guide the development of self-government in such a manner as to avoid disorder and the emergence of despotism. West Indian nationalists, of course, have been impatient with what seemed to

[1] See Lloyd Braithwaite 'The Problem of Cultural Integration in Trinidad' *Social and Economic Studies* 3, 1, June, 1954, 83-85.

them to be the crawling pace of the advance. On the other hand, conservatives in both Great Britain and the colonies have criticized the officials for their unseemly haste in executing what might be called 'Operation Exeunt Omnes'.[1] Many were more than dubious of the wisdom of granting universal adult suffrage without literacy or other qualifications. They have been scornful too of the panoply of ministerial institutions in little islands which would hardly amount to a county in England. They have complained of the cost of this top-heavy government as beyond the means of such poverty-stricken colonies. All this elaborate and expensive governmental machinery, they observe, merely to decide a few simple problems, virtually those of a local government unit.[2] Such views have been confined to a minority of the colonial population. It should be remembered that these colonies have had a long history as separate and complete governments, never as local subdivisions of a larger whole.[3] Because the parliamentary system is universal, self government means ministerial government and for the great majority this is a goal demanded by national pride.

The question remains: have the Secretaries of State and their officials indeed moved too fast in conferring powers of government upon West Indians not yet trained to use them properly? Have the reforms been granted prematurely, almost as soon as they were demanded by local politicians and before the general population was interested in them? To answer the second question first, it may well be that the conservatives underestimate the depth of the latent desire for self government among the people at large. In any case the important issue is rather the question of the ability of the West Indian voters to operate the institutions of democracy.

To answer this question involves first delineating the criteria of successful self-rule. The writer would offer the following list as including the indispensable factors:

1. Sufficient concensus as to the composition of the state and the ends of government to enable the whole (or nearly the whole) community to operate as a political unit without serious stresses.
2. Sufficient comprehension of the problems the government must solve on the part of both politicians and public to permit the former to formulate practical policies and the latter to understand them and choose between them.

[1] The phrase of a former colonial officer, Harold Cooper of the Johns Hopkins University, which he coined in reference to West Africa.
[2] The French have turned their former West Indian colonies into local government units: *départements*.
[3] Except in the case of the (psychologically) unsuccessful Leeward Federation.

3. The necessary mechanisms of popular government: broad suffrage, freely elected representatives, an executive responsible to the electorate either directly or by means of responsibility to the elected legislature.

4. On the negative side, these conditions must not be distorted by so much terror, force or fraud as to render them a mere simulacrum of democracy concealing what is essentially an autocracy.[1]

It is customary also to list as a necessary ingredient of genuine self-government a high degree of economic independence so that the political unit is not dominated economically by another state or states. This factor is perhaps less important in today's world than in the heyday of imperialism. The degree of international economic interdependence is now so high and the lack of self-sufficiency on the part of many countries that have acquired independence since World War II is so obvious and the growth of international aid mechanisms through the United Nations and otherwise is so considerable, that the economic viability of a given state must be understood in less than absolute terms and in relation to the international assistance it is receiving or will receive as well as its own economic growth potential. The contention that complete economic self-sufficiency must precede political independence has been attacked time and again by West Indian nationalists, particularly N. W. Manley. Speaking in the Jamaica House of Representatives in 1951, Manley said:

'Outside of the United States and the countries in the other half of the world, which of the countries of the world is standing on its own financial legs? How many countries in receipt of financial aid are now asked to surrender their independence? The fact is, this is a colonial idea, carefully given to us by our colonial masters, and to be totally repudiated by us.'[2]

Another criterion often advanced, especially in connection with parliamentary systems, is the existence of political parties so that the government of the moment can be confident of consistent support over a period long enough to enact and administer its policies, and so that at all times there is an alternative government ready to take over should the government fall from power.

[1] For a list by a West Indian political scientist, see Eric George James, *A Presentation and Critical Analysis of Criteria for Self-Determination with Special Reference to Jamaica*, unpublished MPA thesis, New York University (June, 1948).
[2] Jamaica Hansard, House of Representatives Proceedings, August, 1951; II 317.

How well do the West Indian territories measure up to these criteria?

The first mentioned requirement in the above list is found throughout the area. Everywhere there is sufficient agreement as to the ends of state action. The distinction between 'socialist' and non-socialist parties and politicians is not wide or deep enough to render intolerable to one side the victory of the other. All agree in the promotion of welfare activities, in the need for capital investment and so on. All agree in promoting the advance to complete self-rule, differing only in matters of degree and timing.

It is in connection with item two: the comprehension of actual problems, that conservatives would assert their lack of confidence in West Indian ability to meet the demands of self-government.

It must admitted that the degree of illiteracy, highest in Jamaica and also high in some of the small islands, does indeed prevent a good part of the electorate from gaining much idea of the world in general or any significant knowledge beyond that gained by personal experience. But there are mitigating factors. The small size of the units makes it possible for the interested voter to hear and see contending politicians in person at the street meetings. The sedulous attender of these will be exposed to a great deal of political argument covering virtually every possible subject of political debate. He will, in fact, get a much more complete exposure to the arguments of the parties than if he depended upon the limited coverage of these meetings given by the local press. His understanding of the issues may be limited as a result of his illiteracy but he will be able nevertheless to judge performance as against promise. It is sometimes a mistake made by literates to assume that illiterates are necessarily stupid. Certainly the inability to read is less important in the West Indies than it would be in large, industrial states. Altogether illiteracy is probably less of a hindrance to intelligent voting than literates are accustomed to think. Unquestionably mere literacy, on the other hand, is no guarantee of political intelligence. And the questions that the West Indian governments are called upon to decide are, so far at least, unconcerned directly with issues that reach far beyond the ken of the average voter. They concern local taxes, the upkeep of local governmental services, the undertaking of social services, the adoption of fiscal policies calculated to help the local economy. While the average voter may be unable to discuss such problems with much depth of perception he is able broadly to judge the impact, as he feels it, of the policies actually adopted. He knows whether or not he and his neighbours are better off than they were, whether or not the public services are being maintained, whether or not he is enjoying any 'psychic gains' from his government in a feeling of improved status, economic and social. And he is free to vote according to his judgement as to the success or failure of the politicians in meeting his needs.

But conservatives point to the inability and ignorance of many politicians chosen by the inexperienced electorate, to the corruption of some, to the dangerous and irresponsible demagoguery of a few. They point also to the electoral success in many places of the purely emotional appeal based upon prejudice, past wrongs and hatred of such abstractions as 'colonialism', and showing no evidence of coming to grips with real and urgent problems. They note that the followers of such leaders sometimes display mob reactions, a disposition to deify the leader and to use violence against his opponents. They claim that a high degree of illiteracy in most units prevents the voter from making an intelligent choice because his knowledge of the world and even of his own little society is too limited to allow him to choose except in terms of his own ignorance and prejudices and narrow experience. The conservatives also point to the frequent use of abusive, unparliamentary language in the legislatures, to the puerility of many debates, to the selfishness and corruption of the legislators. In sum, they call attention to a general lack on the part of leaders and followers alike not only of political capacity but also of the altruism and civic virtue which Machiavelli long ago pointed out as the basic necessity of a democracy.

But lack of wisdom on the part of many voters is not peculiar to the West Indies. The significant question is whether or not the electorate contains enough thoughtful, uncommitted voters to swing the elections and produce a change of leadership if the old government seems to be unsatisfactory. The independent voter who makes a cool appraisal of governmental actions and votes according to his estimate of the total situation is predominantly a middle-class phenomenon. It is the proportionately small numbers of the educated middle class in most West Indian units that is the chief obstacle to the growth of truly responsible, secular leadership. In some of the islands there is a sufficiently numerous and politically concerned middle class to hold at times the political balance of power. It may be assumed that economic development will lead to the enlargement of the middle class in all the units and this, together with lengthened experience of elected governments will result in the proportionate increase of the politically sophisticated element of the electorate.

As regards item three: the mechanisms of democratic government, these now exist universally or nearly so. Except in some small units there would seem to be a sufficient development of political leadership associated with parties to provide the voter with the guidance he needs to enable him to make a meaningful political choice between policies. The only way to learn how to operate a representative democracy, after all, is by experience. The new constitutions provide the opportunity to gain this experience and British officials and others have worked hard to help the legislators and ministers to learn their jobs. While the officers of the Overseas Service have borne the heaviest 'teaching load' in this educational process, West Indians also have been given a chance to visit England and study the Mother of Parliaments at first hand. For example, members and clerks of the legislatures of Trinidad, Barbados, Pakistan and the Gold Coast attended a three-weeks course in parliamentary procedure and practice held in London in the autumn of 1953. They were addressed by the Speaker and the Clerk of the House of Commons, the Whips of both major parties and other experienced parliamentarians. Again, in January, February and March, 1956, representatives of the legislatures of the Windwards, Trinidad, British Honduras and British Guiana attended a course of lectures given by D. W. S. Lidderdale, Fourth Clerk of the Table in the House of Commons.

The British Trades Union Council has helped in the organization of unions and the training of union leaders who are in many cases an integral part of the political life of the colony. Aid in this respect has been given also by the Caribbean Division of ORIT, the regional organization of the International Confederation of Free Trades Unions. The British Labour Party has given moral encouragement and even financial aid to some of the local labour parties. It is safe to say that no imperial power has ever provided more assistance in both formal and informal ways, through governmental and private instrumentalities, in the training of colonial peoples in the techniques of self-government.

The final basic requirement is that the voter be free and unintimidated, that the government be chosen by an electorate not under the political domination of the police and military or any private organization using the instruments of fear and force. Both the threat and the actuality of mob violence employed for political purposes has existed in the West Indies at certain times and places. And in former times the police power was used occasionally to suppress political agitation even when peaceful in nature and legal in motive. This is no longer the case. In British Guiana the return to office of the Jagans under the Renison constitution is proof enough that the Guianese voter is neither intimidated nor influenced by official disapproval. The police power has indeed been employed in recent years to maintain order and to restrain riotous political movements which threatened the democratic process. The monopoly of weapons and disciplined force in the hands of the Governor has prevented any West Indian equivalent of Arbenz or Perón from proceeding beyond the initial steps of his march to power. Without such restraint it is possible that the Bustamante movement in Jamaica might have eventuated in a dictatorship in view of the extreme language employed by Bustamante and the constant use of force against the People's National Party before there was any police intervention. It is obvious that the People's Progressive Party in British Guiana was taking steps to eliminate or intimidate all opposition and gain control of the civil service and independent agencies when the Governor took preventive action. In many other colonies there have been instances of force and fraud in elections and the electoral success of irresponsible demagogues. All of this may be regarded as exemplifying the childhood diseases of democracy, prevented from becoming endemic or fatal by constitutional limitations upon the control of police and security forces, to be released to the elected authorities only when a sufficient degree of political stability and maturity has been attained.

In the final analysis any judgment as to the correctness or otherwise of the speed of constitutional advance must be largely subjective. The pace actually adopted has operated well, on the whole, in synchronizing advances in self-government with the growth of orderly democratic procedures. Without question it has minimized the violence and prevented the despotisms that so often result when political power is transferred from traditional autocratic institutions to the representatives of an inexperienced public. The evidence of its success is in the smooth working of the constitutions, the easy transition from official to ministerial administration and the emergence of a stable party system in one unit after another.

CHAPTER VII

WEST INDIAN LEGISLATURES AND EXECUTIVE COUNCILS

As the historical sections of this study have indicated, the Crown Colony legislature was typically a single chamber presided over by the Governor or his representative and consisting principally of officials, some sitting ex-officio, others nominated by the Governor. It might also include a few unofficial nominees of the Governor, chosen to represent the propertied class of the colony. This type of legislature was capable of infinite variations as to the precise proportion of the official to the unofficial element and still more permutations were possible with the introduction of members elected by the public. The most significant changes took place with the increase in the unofficial representation to the point where it could outvote the officials and secondly, with the increase of the elected members to the point where they could outvote both the officials and nominated unofficials. Subsequent advances amounted to the removal one by one of the officials and the reduction in nominated unofficials.

Generally speaking West Indian legislatures have remained unicameral throughout their development from a totally official to an almost totally elected body. An exception is Jamaica which has an entirely elected House of Representatives and a Legislative Council of nominees and (as of 1957) one ex-officio member. Barbados too, has a nominated and ex-officio second chamber, the Legislative Council, and an entirely elected primary chamber, the House of Assembly. During the short-lived 1953 constitution, British Guiana had a similar arrangement.

Both second chambers have become revisionary bodies only and seem bound to decrease in importance. The Jamacan Legislative Council has not acted to obstruct the policies of the House of Representatives which ever party was in control in that chamber. The Barbadian Legislative Council, representing as it does the propertied class, has made one or two half-hearted attempts to slow down the rate of constitutional change but without daring to engage in any real trial of strength with the elected Assembly.[1]

The important legislative chamber, whether unicameral with

[1] See *above*, pp. 92-94.

some official and nominated members or a primary, totally elected body in a bicameral legislature, is organized substantially like a miniature House of Commons. In appearance, these assemblies vary considerably. Antiphonal seating as in the House of Commons is found but several employ a casual, roughly amphitheatrical arrangement more characteristic of European chambers. No doubt this is a legacy from the pre-party period when the Legislative Council was mainly a group of officials facing the presiding Governor. In the Jamaican House of Representatives the benches are grouped in a semi-circular arrangement, the members facing the Speaker. But the Chief Minister sits at the extreme right of the Speaker and when addressing the House faces towards the Leader of the Opposition who sits at the extreme left. In Barbados the seats are placed in a similar semi-circle bisected by an aisle leading to the Speaker's chair. For some reason the Premier chooses to sit at the foot of the aisle and to the Speaker's left while the Opposition members occupy seats near the Speaker and at his right where one would expect the ministers to sit.

The legislatures are housed generally in old buildings sometimes dating from the eighteenth century which have considerable architectural charm and dignity although frequently as regards office arrangements they are not convenient.

The level of debate in these assemblies varies enormously. The small size of the body makes informality possible and backbenchers need not be silent. Debates are never held according to a formal list of speakers and anybody can get into the argument. There is fairly constant back-chat and exchange of remarks. Some of the party leaders are excellent speakers. Manley would be at home in any parliamentary body in the world. Bustamante tends to speak to the gallery, glancing about him to observe the effect of his sallies. He conducts most arguments on an emotional plane and prefers to ridicule the assertions of the opposition. Adams is a good if rather prosy speaker. Williams is erudite and academic but effective. Gomes is highly effective in debate. Butler is rambling and almost incoherent with a generous insertion of biblical references and imagery. Some of the less educated members employ a vocabulary that is more extensive than their understanding of the words they use. A few are remarkably bad speakers and are confined to the use of a dialect that is nearly incomprehensible to non-West Indians.

THE SPEAKER

The degree of advance from the Crown Colony stage is evidenced and symbolized by the nature of the presiding officer. Advanced

L

legislatures have elected speakers chosen from the elected membership or from outside the chamber. Speakers, despite the tropical heat (air conditioned chambers are now being considered in some colonies), wear the black gown and full-bottomed wig of British tradition and the formalities of the mace are observed.

Five of the West Indian colonies now have speakers. Barbados, never having been a true Crown Colony, has always had an elected speaker. Both Jamaica and Trinidad now have elected speakers as well. British Guiana and British Honduras have appointed speakers but the small island legislatures of the Windwards and Leewards are still presided over by their Administrators who serve not merely as presidents but also to some extent as prime ministers, steering government business through the chamber with the assistance of the other officials present. With the achievement of ministerial status in the Leeward presidencies the Administrators will tend, no doubt, to confine their participation to that of a chairman.

Appointed speakers have been chosen by the Governors from among ex-judges or barristers. They have therefore had some experience and background for the position and have sometimes taken additional training. Speaker Savary of Trinidad, an ex-judge, spent several months at Westminster in 1950 observing the procedure of the House of Commons and drafting Standing Orders for the Trinidad Legislative Council. Elected speakers have been labour party back-benchers as a rule and not well qualified for this position. The first elected speaker in Jamaica handed down a number of extremely partisan rulings favouring the Jamaica Labour Party. This led to such vigorous attacks upon him in both the legislature and the Press that he then began to lean backwards and rule unfairly against the JLP. Subsequently he was expelled from the party and his re-election prevented by Bustamante. His successor was also charged with partisan rulings. The Barbados speaker is an official of the Labour Party's Barbados Workers' Union.

West Indian speakers seem prone to inject remarks into debates and at times almost to enter the debate themselves. They exchange badinage with members and indulge in argument. In general they do not keep very good order. Loud conversations during debates are permitted and a degree of laxity in speech which would not be tolerated in the House of Commons. It must be remembered that neither speaker nor members have been trained in the traditions of parliamentary behaviour, nor are they as familiar as they might be with the Standing Orders or the British precedents. The rough language of the hustings is likely to be echoed in the legislature in moments of stress and the exchange of personal insults sometimes goes far beyond anything that would be permitted at Westminster[1] The West Indian speaker has, in some ways, a more difficult job than his English counterpart. He must be ready to intervene much more often than is necessary in the House of Commons and usually he is not well prepared to handle difficult situations.

PROCEDURE

In all West Indian legislatures the procedure is basically that of the House of Commons. Notice must be given of debate on pending bills. An agenda is printed. Bills have three readings, with general debate at the second reading followed by the committee stage. This may be either in Committee of the Whole or a Select Committee. It is quite usual, however, to move suspension of the Standing Orders so that all three stages may be completed at a single meeting. British formalities are observed when the chamber goes into Committee of the Whole. The Speaker is replaced by a Chairman and the mace removed.

Formerly motions were made almost exclusively by officials. With the introduction of the ministerial system the ministers began to share this duty and with the disappearance of the officials, to monopolize it.

The small size of the legislatures and the relatively simple nature of the business before them (simple, that is, in comparison with national legislatures harried by foreign affairs problems and those of the industrialized welfare state), has made extensive use of legislative committees unnecessary. The Committee of the Whole is sufficient for much legislation. Of course, select committees are used for some bills and the Finance Committee is often of great importance. It is chiefly in contacts between officials and elected members in meetings of the Finance Committee and select committees that the officials are able to influence legislation.

OFFICIAL MEMBERS

The extension of the elected principle in West Indian legislatures has been accompanied by a corresponding shrinkage of the official element. The first officials to be removed were the nominated ones,

[1] A particularly obstreperous independent member of the Jamaican opposition to the JLP, F.L.B. 'Slave Boy' Evans, on one occasion refused to leave the chamber and had to be carried out by the police. Upon another occasion he seized the mace and walked out of the chamber with it. On December 16, 1953, he referred to Bustamante and his ministers as 'damned thieves and grafters', and refusing to apologize, relapsed into creole dialect, 'Hunnu, t'ief hunnu. Sellin' de country . . . Damned criminals'. For this he was suspended for the remainder of the day.

appointed by the Governor as he pleased. There remain now certain ex-officio officials in some of the legislatures, usually only the Colonial Secretary, the Attorney General and the Financial Secretary. Where these officials are still present they introduce government measures relating to their official speciality, the Colonial Secretary often acting as the government's leader of the house. With the rapid extension of a complete ministerial system in most of the colonies the officials are dropping out of the legislatures and functioning as civil servants only.

Formerly, the question of the official's freedom to vote as he pleased was the occasion of a struggle between the Governor and his official subordinates at times. In Jamaica in 1881, a decision by the Governor, Sir John Musgrave, led to the resignation from the legislature not only of all the unofficial nominees but also of two nominated officials, the Auditor General and the Solicitor General. This action led to a change in the rules whereby the officials were required to vote as instructed by the Governor or resign not only the from the legislature but from office as well. In Barbados it had been customary for the Attorney General to seek election to the House of Assembly and so to have a dual position as official and as elected member. This led, upon one occasion, to the introduction of a bill by the Attorney General in accordance with the Governor's instructions followed by a vigorous attack upon the measure by the Attorney General himself. In this case the Attorney General was a native Barbadian. In Trinidad as well, a native Trinidadian, Sir Errol Dos Santos, had attained high official positions as Colonial Treasurer in 1933, Financial Secretary in 1941 and in 1947, Colonial Secretary. He did not hesitate at times to differ publicly with the official policy position.

The members of the nominated official bloc could hardly have been happy in their legislative duties, compelled as they were sometimes to support government proposals they did not agree with. This may be part of the explanation of their inactivity and obvious boredom. They were present merely to ensure an automatic majority for the Governor's policies. At times they were placed in the humiliating position of having to vote against their own expressed views. Craig mentions a 1927 case in Trinidad in which a committee, composed partly of officials, presented a report only to have it described by the Colonial Secretary as 'deeply disappointing'. Having accepted the rebuke in silence, the official members of the committee were then required to vote with the Colonial Secretary against the recommendations of their own report.[1]

[1] Hewan Craig. *The Legislative Council of Trinidad and Tobago* (London, 1952) Ch. III.

These criticisms apply with much less force to the presence of the three top officials, sitting ex-officio. They have consistently taken an active part in legislative business, acting essentially as ministers in the introduction of bills, and their defence in debate. With the introduction of the ministerial system they have remained as a part, rather than the whole of the governmental leadership in the legislature, co-operating with the elected ministers.[1] There can be no doubt that in the early stages of the ministerial system the presence and guidance of the officials in the legislature has been educative and has paved the way for a relatively smooth transition from the wholly official domination of legislative time and business to its complete control by elected ministers, as in Jamaica and Barbados, with the officials totally withdrawn from the chamber.

Officials with ex-officio seats in the legislature have remained part of the government team even though the government is now in the hands of elected ministers. As members of the Executive Council these officials are in the Chief Minister's 'cabinet' and the principle of cabinet solidarity applies to their behaviour in the legislature in normal situations. That is, once a decision has been made in the Executive Council, even if the officials are not personally in favour of it, they will not oppose it in the Legislative Council and will vote with the government side.

Another convention that has developed recently in connection with the legislative activity of officials is their voluntary abstention from debating and voting on purely constitutional questions. While this rule has not been followed invariably, it has come to be recognized that changes in a colony's constitution should be left to the decision of the elected and nominated colonials without participation by officials at the legislative stage of the reform.

UNOFFICIAL NOMINATED MEMBERS

All legislatures serve as instruments for the registration and transmission of pressures from special interests, economic and social. Sometimes these interests operate by means of 'lobbying', to use the American term. Sometimes the interest is shared by a sector of

---

[1] The continued importance of the officials following the introduction of the ministerial system in Trinidad is indicated by the Legislative Council agenda of 26th February, 1954. A printed question was to be asked of the Colonial Secretary by an elected member. The Minister of Agriculture and Lands was to make a motion to be seconded by the Colonial Secretary. A second reading was to be moved by the Minister of Health and Local Government to be seconded by the Attorney General. A bill was to be moved by the Financial Secretary and seconded by the Colonial Secretary and another bill reported by the Attorney General. Still another bill was to be presented by a minister.

the population large enough (such as the agricultural interest) to justify the organization of political parties devoted primarily to this interest although claiming, as a rule, broad devotion to the general welfare. Labour parties are of this sort and in the case of the British Parliamentary Labour Party, its trades union members sometimes bear a relation to their unions much like that of a pocket borough MP to his aristocratic patron in the unreformed House of Commons.[1]

When elected members began to appear in Crown Colony legislature, unofficial nominated members were retained and their retention justified on the ground that they were needed to give balance to the legislature, to ensure that a single interest did not monopolize the body and that all important interests and minorities would be represented whatever the results of a particular election.

Nominated members are chosen by the Governor and formerly there were no limitations upon his choice. Most tried to pick eminent persons who were considered to be good representatives of a class or interest. In some cases they might be chosen because of personal merit and statesmanlike qualities. Sometimes the nominating power was used frankly to strengthen the official side. As noted previously it was for a time the practice of Jamaican governors to keep several nominated places vacant until opposition to official policies made it advisable to fill them with nominees certain to support the officials. This use of the nominating power has been disapproved by recent Secretaries of State. Nowadays governors try to nominate individuals of prominence in various fields, mainly economic, of importance in the life of the colony. In this way the planter, financial, mercantile and similar interests which at one time were the only ones represented in the legislature are assured of a voice even though the elected majority is no longer theirs.

In Trinidad, for example, since 1930, there has always been a representative of the oil industry as well as the Chamber of Commerce. Agriculture is also represented as a rule. Of course, in most tropical colonies, a single entrepreneur is likely to have a variety of commercial and agricultural interests. One of the recent nominated members in Grenada owned an hotel, a general store, a garage, a stock farm, a salt-manufacturing industry and was the exclusive import agent for certain foreign manufactures.

Naturally the elected members have had little good to say of the institution of nominated membership. The latter have been attacked as a mere extension of the official group and a bulwark of the old

[1] See Samuel H. Beer, 'The Representation of Interests in British Government: Historical Background,' *American Political Science Review* LI, 3 (September, 1957) 613 ff.

official autocracy.[1] Possibly the contrary has been generally more accurate. That is, the officials have been influenced by the nominated members. It may be observed that in point of education, class background and social intimacy the nominated members more often have fallen into the same category as the principal officials than have the elected members. The views of the nominated members as to the economic advantages or otherwise of current proposals are likely to receive careful attention in official quarters especially as the nominated members can advance arguments based upon a thorough knowledge of their particular industry or business. They are likely, therefore, to be able to present convincing arguments and to exert influence upon policies receiving the support of the official side. In appearing to accept the official view they may actually be supporting policies which they have induced the officials to espouse.

That nominated members have invariably acted as an extension of the official delegation is not true. During the period of pure Crown Colony government when legislatures were composed entirely of officials and nominated unofficials, the latter tended to become the opposition to the official-dominated government. In the case of Jamaica, the nominated members were so opposed to a particular policy of the Governor, Sir John Musgrave, in 1881 that they resigned in a body and the government was carried on without any unofficial nominated members until 1884. In recent times, unofficial nominated members, especially in colonies without a well-developed party system, have sometimes taken the lead in opposing official policies. Sometimes they have been the most outstanding personalities in a legislature composed, except for officials, of inexperienced elected members. In British Honduras they joined unanimously with the elected members in opposing devaluation of the local dollar.

It has been observed that with the growth of parties, the nominated members in most legislatures have tended to take a less active part in debate, often confining their participation to discussion of matters related to their special area of interest.

Craig has analyzed the voting record of nominated unofficials in the Trinidad legislature and found that while they did display some tendency to agree on issues, they were by no means always unanimous. In sixty-one divisions between the years 1929 and 1934 they voted together about one-third of the time, but only upon one

[1] For example, the attack upon the nominated principle in the Trinidad legislature by Ranjit Kumar who repeated the charge that nominated members always voted with the government but in the same debate asserted that Mr. Hannays, a nominated member, was guilty of 'representing nobody but himself'. See Trinidad *Sunday Guardian*, May 20, 1956.

occasion did they stand united with the official side against the elected members.[1] Canon Farquhar, a Trinidadian clergyman and columnist, wrote in defence of the nominated members as recently as 1955, citing instances of courageous independence and devotion to public welfare on the part of such nominated members as Sir Lennox O'Reilly and Dr A. H. McShine.[2]

There is no doubt that some, at least, of the nominated members have been good exemplars of the 'virtual representation' ideal of Burke and Disraeli. They have been genuinely independent, public spirited and intelligent with a measure of the civic virtue by no means always evident in the behaviour of some West Indian politicians.

Since 1941 Governors have been directed by the Secretary of State to reappoint nominated members not more than once save in very exceptional circumstances, presumably the non-availability of any other qualified person. The idea behind this rule would seem to be the prevention of one man acquiring an unduly influential position through permanent hold upon a legislative seat as the representative of a special interest. It is true that the nominated members in some legislatures came to consist of old men who may have grown out of touch with the life of the colony. On the other hand this rule operates to terminate the services of a particularly valuable nominated member after two terms regardless of his qualities.

New principles have been employed in two recent constitutions. In the suspended British Guiana constitution of 1953 it was provided that the second chamber, the State Council, consisting entirely of nominated members, should contain in addition to nine members chosen by the Governor at his discretion, two members named by the elected ministers as well as one to be chosen by the Governor after consulting the independent and opposition side of the House of Assembly. This device was intended to ensure that both sides of the House should have representation in the debates of the State Council. It would seem to have been of little significance during the short life of this constitution. The State Council could hardly avoid being aware of the views expressed in the House of Assembly and it could be argued that it needed these additional members no more than the House of Lords needs a delegation from the House of Commons to repeat the arguments previously advanced in that chamber. Of course the House of Lords does contain spokesmen of all parties and the authors of the British Guiana constitution

[1] Craig, op. cit., Chapter IV.
[2] M. E. Farquhar, 'Candid Comments', Trinidad Sunday Guardian, May 22, 1955.

evidently feared that the points of view of the elected members might find no champions at all in a purely nominated body. It will be remembered that this had happened in Barbados and for this reason the Colonial Secretary had been compelled to introduce and defend government proposals in the Legislative Council, which measures were really those of the elected ministers.[1]

The nominated principle was retained in the 1956 Trinidad constitution but the number of nominees was reduced from six to five. The interesting change, however, was the agreement of the Secretary of State to allow the Chief Minister to suggest two of the nominees. Until after the elections, the Governor, faithful to his existing instructions, had announced that the nominations would be nonpartisan. But while the PNM won a majority of the elected seats, thirteen out of twenty-four, it lacked a clear over-all majority in the chamber. Accordingly the Secretary of State, Lennox-Boyd, countermanded the previous instructions and wrote to the Governor as follows:

"I desire you, therefore, to take such steps by way of nominating suitable persons to the Legislative Council after consultation with the Leader of the majority party, as will provide a reasonable working majority for the party."[2]

This gave the PNM two additional votes in addition to those earned at the polls. Dr Williams could count also upon the votes of the two ex-officio members to give him a normal voting strength of seventeen to fourteen.

The Secretary of State evidently did not contemplate creating a binding precedent by his transfer of nominating power to the Chief Minister. It was alleged that at constitutional discussions in London in September, 1958, the PNM delegates suggested that this be done.[3] Although before his election Dr Eric Williams approved of the nominated principle as giving a necessary representation to important economic interests otherwise unlikely to have any spokesman in the legislature, his post-election attitude was less favourable to the continued existence of nominated members, possibly because there was no guarantee that in the future he would be allowed to control any nominations. The conservative *Sunday Guardian* at once sprang to the defence of nominated legislators, justifying them in these words: 'Like Wordsworth's perfect woman

---

[1] See above, p. 92.
[2] Quoted in Trinidad *Sunday Guardian*, October 21, 1956. The PNM nominees were Wilfred Alexander, a barrister and a vice president of the party, and C. A. Murray, a director of a large shipping and general business firm. The Governor's nominees were Sir Harold Robinson (sugar), Patrick Hobson (oil), and H. N. Fahey, a planter.
[3] See editorial, Trinidad *Sunday Guardian*, issue of Sept. 28, 1958.

nobly planned, their function should be to warn and comfort though not to command . . .'[1]

It would seem that a principal objection to nominated members is that their very existence is indicative of colonial status, at least if they are members of a mixed, unicameral legislature. There is less objection to their membership in a separate, second chamber so long as this body is revisionary and without permanent veto power. It has been contended also that the presence of nominated members retards the growth of a sense of responsibility. By voting together with a minority of the elected members they may be able to turn this minority into the dominant group. Thus they militate against the development of party government for the nominees are usually independents and are not beholden to the parties for their seats. Upon the assumption that party government is a necessity in a parliamentary democracy, nominated members in an other-wise elected chamber must be regarded as a hindrance to progress.[2] This, no doubt, was the underlying reason for Lennox-Boyd's action, mentioned above.

The nominated principle has been retained for the federal Senate of the West Indies. The first appointments to this body in 1958 were made by the Governor General on the advice of the unit Governors who received suggestions from their elected ministries. Of the nine-teen senators, nine, or approximately one-half had had previous experience as unofficial nominated members of a legislature.

The steady diminution, year after year, in one colony after another of the number or proportion of nominated members would seem to foreshadow the imminent disappearance of this category in the units with unicameral legislatures. It will remain for the land-owning, planter, commercial and financial interests, hitherto given direct legislative representation, to rely, more than they have had to do in the past, upon indirect representation and pressure group tactics as they do in connection with the British Parliament and the American Congress. In some territories only the organized labour interest can count with certainty upon adequate representa-tion by elected members.

ELECTED MEMBERS

During the early stages of elected membership in the legislature the elected members tended not to differ substantially in class or economic status from the nominated unofficial members. The high

---

[1] See editorial, Trinidad *Sunday Guardian*, issue of November 23, 1958.
[2] These arguments were presented by Dr. Hinden and Professor Harlow in the Waddington Report, Col. No. 280, pp. 46-53.

property qualifications set by law ensured the election only of persons of far above average income.[1] In general such members tended to take a conservative position on taxation and spending policies which harmonized with the traditional Colonial Office position and its application by the colonial officials. Their differences with the officials were likely to occur over policies affecting special interests, as in the case of the nominated unofficials. There were a few exceptions to this pattern. An outstanding one was Captain Cipriani of Trinidad who represented a Port-of-Spain constituency for a number of years until his death in 1945. As noted previously, he was a 'labour' spokesman who preceded the emergence of union leaders in the 'thirties. In espousing welfare schemes he found himself in constant opposition to government policies although he had a measure of success.[2]

With the rapid organization of trades and general labour unions that resulted from the depression of the 'thirties and the general lowering of property qualifications for legislators together with universal suffrage, it became possible for the new union leaders to acquire legislative places. Soon the legislatures throughout the area reflected this change. The older, conservative, propertied members were to be found only among the nominated unofficials and the elected delegation consisted of new men. The new type of member was often a Negro and frequently of little formal education. Although often unskilled in debate he was likely not to be inhibited in the use of rough and rude tactics and abusive language. The parliamentary tradition was unknown to him. In general he felt it needful to strike a pose of permanent opposition to the government which was still in the hands of white colonial officials. Changes in the direction of West Indianization of the colonial service made little difference to this attitude and even when the new leaders found themselves in the Executive Council there remained a tendency to resent official leadership. The nominated members were also a target of attacks by the elected members. Their presence was resented as was their representation of upper-class and property interests.

The official hope was that the new type of elected member would fit smoothly into the legislative 'team'. This ideal was expressed in 1944 by the Administrator of Dominica in these words:[3]

[1] For example, in Trinidad, an income of £400 and real property worth £2,500.
[2] He was partly responsible for the Labour (Minimum Wage) Ordinance of 1935 and the Old Age Pensions Ordinance of 1939.
[3] Dominica Legislative Council Debates, 24 October, 1944, quoted in Hughes, *op. cit.*, MS p. 357.

'Will you allow me to use a homely metaphor to illustrate my view of the present constitutional situation? It seems to me that the official and unofficial members of the Council work in this House as a team, whose duty it is to kick the ball of the common weal in the same direction, not taking it away from each other's feet, but passing it to each other as the good of the game demands. The forwards of this team are, or as I think should be, the Elected Members, wary and fleet-footed, the shooters of goals. The half-backs are the Nominated Members, feeding the forward line and speeding its progress toward the goal. The backs are the Hon. Treasurer and the Hon. Crown Attorney, doughty champions of the home base; and the Administrator is the ultimate defender of the goal who occasionally roars words of encouragement to the team in front of him. Then, if you will, you may regard the Governor as the coach of this glorious team, whose business it is to see that the players do not play against each other but collaborate in carrying the ball forward for the honour and the victory of Dominica.'

This delightful 'public school' view of a colonial legislature had little possibility of realization in action, especially as the 'goal-keeper' might be bound at times to prevent his own 'forwards' from scoring. In such a case it would not seem to the latter that they were playing on the same team as the Administrator. They were more likely to maintain a pose of rather irresponsible opposition to a government which they could not hope to control. Future developments which were to give a positive rather than a merely negative function to the elected members were their entry into the Executive Council and the formation of genuine political parties.

Trinidad presents an increasing picture of the shift in the role of the elected member in relation to the government. Before World War II the nominated and official members tended to agree on policies and the elected members to form an ineffective opposition. After the introduction of universal adult suffrage in 1946 the elected members split between those who secured places in the Executive Council with the help of official and nominated members' votes, and who now identified themselves with the government, and the rest of the elected members who tended to remain in opposition. Subsequently the ministerial system confirmed the identification of the ministers with the government. Perhaps because of the in-effectual leadership of Butler in the legislature, the opposition broke up. In the end the 'Opposition Bloc' came to consist only of Butler himself and two or three faithful members of his party. The rest of the non-ministerial members took an independent position. Then the PNM victory of 1956 and the establishment of the office of Chief

Minister led to a solid party ministry with some of the characteristics of a cabinet and its safe majority support in the Legislative Council. All other elected members composed the opposition, although united in opposition only and not yet organized as an alternative government.

The rise of the party system has meant a rapid reduction in the proportion of elected members without party affiliation. But only in Jamaica, for reasons peculiar to that island, two strong parties developed almost simultaneously which were able between them virtually to monopolize the elected seats. The rare independents in the Jamaica House of Representatives are usually in fact firmly associated with one party or the other. A more usual pattern is for a legislature to contain a majority of members belonging to the local labour party and a minority of independents who may or may not be loosely associated with an opposition party or parties. The trend is unmistakable. The independent member, even if he is a local celebrity, is finding it more and more difficult to win against candidates backed by a party organization. This is now the case even in Trinidad with its history of many ephemeral parties and ministers, before 1956, who in reality were independents. In Grenada, after the elections of September, 1957, there were no independents left in the legislature among the elected members. Even T. A. Marryshow, the island's 'Grand Old Man', had chosen to join the People's Democratic Movement. Of course independents are still to be found in some territorial legislatures. The St Vincent Legislative Council elected in September, 1957, exemplified the older pattern: a party majority (the People's Political Party) and an opposition of unorganized independents. But it is safe to assume that the independent member will become increasingly rare in West Indian legislatures as has been the case everywhere else in the history of representative systems.

The elected membership in a West Indian legislature nowadays represents a wide range in class and education. Whites, either immigrant or creole, are rare. In Trinidad a few, particularly those connected with labour, have been elected. In Barbados also elected white members did not vanish completely with the advent of universal suffrage. Many legislatures contain no elected whites. Antigua and St Kitts have had none since the introduction of the elected principle in 1936.

The ministerial group in a labour party is likely to contain some members of the professional middle class but may include also officers of the basic union who have little education but are chosen for their loyalty to the party and their popularity with the voters. Among the professionals lawyers predominate and an occasional physician is found. The teaching profession is represented as a rule among the back-benchers, especially in Jamaica, where there are usually a few elementary schoolteachers from rural constituencies. The average of education and income among elected members, as one would expect, is considerably above the average in the total population.[1]

THE EXECUTIVE POWER IN THE WEST INDIES

In discussing parliamentary systems it is impossible to consider the executive and legislative branches of government separately without distorting reality. Accordingly, in previous chapters the growth of elected power in both legislatures and executive bodies has been described. Nevertheless, it may be useful at this point to review and summarize the steps taken in the various colonies to advance from an executive consisting entirely of Crown officers to the final goal of a cabinet of elected political leaders.

The Old Representative System in the West Indian and North American colonies provided a sharp separation of executive and legislative powers leaving all executive matters to be dealt with by Crown officers. This led to an endless dispute between the Governors and their legislatures to be resolved finally only by the establishment of pure Crown Colony government vesting both executive and legislative authority in the Governor. With the reappearance of elected members in the legislature the old problem also reappeared. Elected legislators felt helpless and frustrated in their inability effectively to control executive policies and, as noted earlier, became essentially a permanent opposition to the government. All the struggles of the Old Representative period seemed bound to be repeated with the difference that now the legislatures represented a popular electorate. Potentially the situation had possibilities of producing a revolutionary temper among the politically active part of the population.

[1] For forty-nine of the individuals mentioned in the Trinidad *Sunday Guardian*, issues of Feb. 23 and March 2, 1958, as actual or potential candidates for federal legislative seats from Jamaica and Trinidad, the occupational breakdown was as follows:
18 had received a professional education. These included 6 barristers, 4 solicitors (one of whom was also a teacher and another a planter), 4 physicians, one college teacher, one clergyman, one engineer, one accountant. The 31 others included 5 professional politicians of various backgrounds (journalism, union activities, business, etc.), 5 farmers (one also a trades unionist and one also a contractor), 5 elementary schoolteachers, 4 businessmen, 2 planters or landed proprietors, 2 shopkeepers, one union leader (ex-labourer), one journalist, one merchant tailor, one labour contractor (ex-stevedore), one shoemaker, one ex-tram driver, one dental technician, one sect leader (the sole 'pastor' of the sect).

But this time the Secretaries of State and the Colonial Office recognized the necessity of a transfer of executive powers to representatives of the elected members. The problem was how to accomplish this change without damaging the working administration and how to confer the powers at a rate which would permit a growth in experience and responsibility at the same time.

With typical British political pragmatism no attempt was made to find a single, universal formula. Each colony was treated as a special problem and the rate of advance varied considerably in the several units. Barbados, with its long and unbroken history of representative government, began the march to elected ministerial government by the voluntary act of the Governor in choosing Executive Council members from the majority party in the House of Assembly. This 'Bushe Experiment' of 1946 paved the way for an Executive Council dominated by elected members as regards all domestic policies including financial ones. The Governor proposed to pick the leader of the majority party in the House as a member of Executive Council and ask him to choose the other elected members to the executive body. At the same time he proposed to make these elected members quasi-ministers with the duty of representing administrative departments in legislature and Executive Committee but without ministerial authority over them. The Bushe Experiment was followed by a genuine ministerial system, achieved in 1954, with full responsible government as regards domestic affairs. No doubt Governor Bushe was the more willing to introduce his experiment because of the strong electoral position of the Labour Party, the ability and moderation of its leader, Grantley Adams, and the veto power over legislation still possessed by the nominated Legislative Council.

In Jamaica the early development of a two-party system provided the necessary legislative base for a ministerial executive as soon as the ministers could be trained in their duties and responsibilities. Hence the series of reforms in rapid succession from the first real breakaway from the Crown Colony system in 1944 when five elected quasi-ministers were chosen by the House of Representatives. These were increased to eight and promoted to real ministerial status in 1953. The 'minister's conference' acting much like a cabinet was introduced by Chief Minister Manley in 1955 and the Executive Council transformed into a Council of Ministers without any official members in 1957, thus giving Jamaica responsible, cabinet government in local affairs.

In Trinidad the tardy development of strong political parties slowed the advance to ministerial government. It was not until 1950 that Trinidad was given an Executive Council with half of its membership (five) chosen by the legislative from among its elected members. These were given ministerial responsibilities but could not control Executive Council decisions against the combined vote of all the other members because the Governor had both an original and a casting vote. The elected ministers were chosen by the votes of a combination of official, nominated and elected members in the legislature and the largest single party delegation received no seat in Executive Council. The ministers therefore were political independents rather than a pre-cabinet of party colleagues working to carry out a coherent policy programme. The victory of the People's National Movement in 1956 changed this situation to one comparable with Barbados and Jamaica. The Executive Council now was dominated by a bloc of party members under the guidance of their leader as Chief Minister.

In some of the other colonies the replacement of official by elected control of the executive came about much more slowly. As late as 1954 there were no elected members in the Executive Council of British Honduras. In that year the elected members of the legislature were allowed to elect four of their number to sit in Executive Council which also contained three officials and two nominated members under the chairmanship of the Governor. The elected members of the Council were given quasi-ministerial responsibilities.

When British Guiana took its leap in 1953 from an Executive Council of the Governor, three officials and five nominees to one with a majority chosen by the all-elected House, this was done upon the supposition that the party system would remain inchoate and fragmented for some time to come and that no disciplined party bloc, therefore, would be able to control the Executive Council. The unexpected electoral victory of the PPP led to the trouble described earlier and the suspension of the constitution. The Renison constitution of 1956 restored Crown Colony government with an elected element but a much less advanced type of Executive Council containing five elected members. These are named by the Governor from the legislature, not elected by that body, and their departmental responsibilities are assigned by the Governor. Furthermore, they are balanced in Executive Council by three officials and two nominated unofficials.

THE WORK OF THE EXECUTIVE COUNCIL

Executive Councils spend most of their time in considering details of administration and arriving at decisions regarding administrative policy and proposed government bills. Agenda are prepared before meetings by the Colonial Secretary and pertinent documents are circulated among the members. At the meetings, usually held at least weekly, the method of procedure is not unlike that of a cabinet meeting. In Jamaica the Chief Minister now summons and presides; elsewhere this function is still in the hands of the Governor. Topics for discussion are introduced either by the presiding officer or a minister designated by him and after the discussion he announces the decision arrived at, usually without a vote having been taken. The Colonial Secretary or Chief Secretary (if present) makes a note of the decision and sees that the appropriate officials are informed of it and that subsequently it is executed. Recently it has become customary in several colonies to have the routine secretarial part of this duty performed by the 'Governor's Secretary and Clerk to the Executive Council,' appointed by the Governor.

CHOOSING THE PREMIER

Once ministerial government had been instituted, it depended upon the party situation whether the ministers would all be members of a single party as in Jamaica and Barbados or a collection of independents as in Trinidad. In either case the Governor retained the right to assign portfolios. The selection of a Chief Minister or Premier created additional problems. How should he be chosen? Various suggestions were made: by the Governor who should name a 'Leader of the Executive Council' (suggested by the Trinidad Constitutional Reform Committee); by the ministers from among themselves (advocated by the Waddington Commission). These suggestions were based upon the assumed absence of strong political parties. Once party control had become established in the legislature, the problem solved itself. The formally chosen leader of the majority party in the legislature was the obvious and only practical choice and, whether required by law or not, the Governor would have to consult him in making other ministerial appointments.

TYPES OF EXECUTIVE COUNCILS

It was noted earlier in this chapter that the Secretaries of State have adopted a pragmatic approach to the question of the control of the executive power by the elected element and have not tried to find a formula of universal application. It may be observed further that practical modifications of practice have occurred and have become habitual. It had long been the convention that measures involving a charge upon the colony's funds must be approved by the legislature but it also became customary for the Secretary of State to instruct

M

the Governor that he should not sign bills or financial resolutions that had been opposed unanimously by the elected legislators.[1] Of course this was a limitation upon the Governor but not upon the Secretary of State who might, if he saw fit, insist upon the passage of such measures.

Despite considerable variation in the time-table of constitutional advance in the several colonies and in the precise details of the different constitutions, it is possible to make a list of the various types of Executive Council and place them in the order of their historical occurrence, a sequence followed almost universally. The important stages are as follows:

1.   The Executive Council consists entirely of officials, some ex-officio and others nominated by the Governor.

2.   Unofficial persons nominated by the Governor are added to a Council otherwise official in membership.

3.   A few elected members of the legislature chosen by their fellow members are added to the Council which retains a majority of non-elected members, both ex-officio and nominated officials and nominated unofficials. At this stage the elected members may be appointed to committees concerned with the work of the administrative departments, each committee being chaired by the appropriate permanent official.

4.   The Governor refrains from nominating officials to the Council which then consists of the Governor, the three other principal officials, ex-officio (Colonial Secretary, Attorney General and Financial Secretary) plus several elected members of the legislature chosen by that body. At this stage the elected members may be given quasi-ministerial status, representing departments in discussions in both Executive and Legislative Councils but without administrative authority which remains with the permanent officials.

5.   This stage may be telescoped with the previous one. The elected members, now forming a majority of the total membership of the Executive Council can outvote the official members and decide policies if all or nearly all are in agreement. At this point the Governor, if not already so equipped, is given the reserved power to legislate positively over the adverse vote of his Executive Council. (This is not the case in Barbados which never became a Crown Colony.)

6.   The quasi-ministers become full ministers with administrative authority over their departments. Composing the majority of the membership of the Executive Council they decide upon policies and proposed legislation with the assistance and advice of the Governor and principal officials who still sit in the Execu-

[1] This was the case in Trinidad, for example, since 1922. See Charles Reis, *The Government of Trinidad and Tobago* 3rd rev. ed. (Port of Spain, 1947).

tive Council. This stage may not yet amount to full responsible government in that the ministers may owe their positions in part to the votes of official and nominated members of the legislature, in that they are chosen individually and lack cabinet solidarity, and although removable by legislative action (usually a two-thirds absolute majority) they are not bound to resign as a 'government' by a vote of no confidence.

7. Differs from the previous stage in the approximation to cabinet government provided by the creation of the office of Chief Minister or Premier chosen from the elected membership of the legislature by the Governor in much the same way as a British Prime Minister is chosen by the Sovereign. The other ministers are then chosen by the Chief Minister. This stage is practical and workable only when political parties are well enough developed to enable either a one-party or a firm coalition government to be formed. At this stage the Governor and other officials who still sit in the Executive Council will tend more and more to become advisory members rather than to try to dominate decision-making. Effective responsible government may exist at this stage because the ministers, as a group, must be able to control policy in the legislature or they will have no alternative to resignation.

8. This is substantially a refinement and formalization of the previous stage. The officials including the Governor withdraw from the Executive Council which is renamed Council of Ministers and is presided over by the Chief Minister. The Governor is still empowered to summon and preside over emergency meetings of the Council.

9. The final stage, not yet achieved in the West Indies, is that of full self-government or Dominion status in which the Governor in practice may not refuse to accept ministerial advice. Although still appointed by and responsible to the Crown, his appointment will be made only with the approval of the local government and his position will approximate that of the British monarch in relation to the exercise of executive and legislative powers. The Statute of Westminster will apply as a voluntary limitation by Parliament upon its sovereign power to legislate for the territory, which power will not hereafter be exercised except at the request of the government of the territory.

Throughout all the stages, from 1 to 8, the Governor must intervene if an attempt is made by the colonial government to enter fields denied it by the constitution. Whether or not he has the reserved power to legislate contrary to the desire of his ministers or legislature, the Secretary of State may interfere at any moment by new instructions to the Governor or by order-in-council with or without an accompanying Act of Parliament. In other words, the maximum amount of self-government possible in a colony remains self-government 'on a leash', no matter how long and relaxed the leash may be. Dominion status (stage 9) is actually different in kind, legally considered, from all the preceding stages.

The new federal executive is constructed at the level of stage 7 in the above list. It is somewhat less advanced than that of Jamaica in that the Governor General is expected normally to preside over meetings of the Council of State and in the presence at these meetings of three officials as consultants. There is also a limitation upon the Prime Minister's choice of ministerial colleagues in that he must pick three of them from the Senate.

LEGISLATURES*

Territory		Official	Membership Unofficial		Total
			Nominated	Elected	
Barbados	House of Assembly	—	—	24	24
	Legislative Council (Upper House)	2	12	—	14
British Guiana	Legislative Council	3	6	14	23
British Honduras	Legislative Assembly	3	3	9	15
Jamaica	House of Representatives	—	—	32	32
	Legislative Council (Upper House)	1	14	—	15
Leeward Islands:					
Antigua ⎫ St. Christopher- ⎬ Nevis-Anguilla ⎭	Legislative Council	Administrator+2	3	8	14
Montserrat	Legislative Council	Administrator+2	2	5	10
Virgin Islands	Legislative Council	Administrator+2	2	6	11
Trinidad & Tobago	Legislative Council	2	5	24	31
Windward Islands:					
Dominica ⎫ Grenada ⎬ St. Lucia ⎪ St. Vincent ⎭	Legislative Council	Administrator+2	3	8	14

*Tables from the British Information Services Reference Division, I.D. 1282, December 1957.

EXECUTIVE COUNCILS

Membership

Territory	Official	Unofficial Nominated	Elected	Elected Ministers or 'Members'
Barbados (a)				
(Executive Committee)	Governor+2	4	5	Premier+4
British Guiana	Governor+3	None	5	5
British Honduras	Governor+3	2	4	3 ('Members')
Jamaica (b)		2 (from		
(Council of Ministers)	None	Upper House)	10	Chief Minister+9
Leeward Islands:				
Antigua	Governor or Administrator+2	1	4	3
St. Christopher-Nevis-Anguilla	Governor or Administrator+2	1	5(c)	3
Montserrat	Governor or Administrator+2	1	2	2 ('Members')
Virgin Islands	Governor or Administrator+2	1	2	2 ('Members')
Trinidad & Tobago	Governor+2	None	8	Chief Minister+7
Windward Islands:				
Dominica				
Grenada	Governor or Administrator+2	1	4	3
St. Lucia				
St. Vincent				

(a) Under new constitutional arrangements endorsed in October 1957 by both Houses of the Barbados Legislature, the general direction and control of government in internal matters will pass from the Executive Committee to a Cabinet, meeting under the Chairmanship of the Premier and composed entirely of members of the majority party in the House of Assembly.

(b) Under new constitutional arrangements introduced in November 1957, the general direction and control of government in internal matters has passed from the full Executive Council to a Council of Ministers meeting under the chairmanship of the Chief Minister.

(c) Includes one member for Nevis, if a representative of that island is not included in the first 4 elected members.

CHAPTER VIII

LOCAL GOVERNMENT

T H E West Indian colonies vary considerably in their history of local government. Those with an old English tradition, such as Jamaica and Barbados, have enjoyed a measure of local self-government from Old Representative days to the present. They contrast sharply with Trinidad, for instance, which had no such background.

Whatever the local government system, its concern was with minor matters, principally roads and poor relief. The exciting and important political decisions were made by the central government and naturally the interest of the reformers and radicals was focussed upon the centre. As we would expect, therefore, reforms in local government and an increase in its political democratization have lagged behind these same reforms in connection with the central governmental structure. It is probably correct to say that such reforms have been the result of outside ideas and pressures rather than any strong public demand at the local level. To some extent these pressures have come from British sources, official comments, Royal Commission reports and the like advocating a widened public participation in local government. But probably the important factor in recent changes has been the extension of political party activities into the local government arena and the general political advantage to be gained from such an extension if the local government councillors could be added to the number of active party politicians. Whatever the reasons, it would have been remarkable had a legislature and executive substantially controlled by elected members not moved to take away the control of local government boards and councils from their political opponents, the conservative, propertied class.

JAMAICA

During the pre-emancipation period rural local government in Jamaica was left to the Justices of the Peace under the Custos Rotulorum, the chief magistrate. The JP's and Custos were appointed by the Governor and chosen from among 'men of substance', in other words, the planter class. The Custodes and Justices of the Peace plus the Rector and ten vestrymen elected annually by the freeholders of the parish made up the Vestry which assessed the local rates and approved the expenditure of the money on upkeep of church, gaol and roads. The Assembly, controlled by the same planter class, tended to add to the powers of the Justices of the Peace and the Vestries. For a time stipendiary magistrates or Special Justices were used in Jamaica. These were Englishmen trained in the law who were given rather extensive police power. Sixty-three of these magistrates were appointed originally, with the idea of using trained professionals to oversee the fair and legal execution of the emancipation and apprenticeship laws. The Assembly resented the presence of these magistrates and was able, by refusing appropriations for their salaries, to destroy the institution in time. Their powers then slipped into the hands of the nominated, unprofessional Justices of the Peace who identified the law with the interests of the planters and did much to destroy the confidence of the freedmen in the fairness of local law enforcement.[1]

The introduction of Crown Colony rule led to a revamping of local government arrangements by a law of 1866. This law replaced the Vestries by Municipal and Road Boards appointed by the Governor. In 1870 the Church of England was disestablished and in 1885 the Municipal and Road Boards were replaced by Parochial Boards. Each parish (for this purpose a local government unit rather than a religious community) was given a board to consist of the Custos, the person representing the district in the legislature and from thirteen to eighteen other persons elected by voters with a taxpayer franchise.

Down to 1956 local government remained in charge of the Parochial Boards with special arrangements for the parishes of Kingston (including Port Royal) and St Andrew which were combined as the Corporate Area with a composition and powers similar to a big Parochial Board but with the additional power to assess rates subject to the approval of the Governor in Executive Council and with representation on the Water Commission, along with appointees of the Governor, to manage the sewerage and water supply of the urban part of the Corporate Area.

The elected members of the Parochial Boards were chosen from single-member districts for a three-year term. In time universal adult suffrage was extended to the local government electorate and the only restriction on Board candidacy was a literacy requirement. The Board members were unpaid, receiving only indemnification for actual travelling expenses. It is claimed that for this reason poor men sometimes refused nomination as they could not afford the time spent on parish business.

[1] See P. D. Curtin, *The Two Jamaicas* (Harvard: Oxford, 1955) pp. 74, 75.

The Board elected its own chairman, vice-chairman and secretary annually and prepared an estimate of expenses to be sent to the Minister of Local Government and by him to the Governor in Executive Council for final approval. The Board was thus far from autonomous financially. Its principal work concerned roads and poor relief. Each Board had at least three committees: Finance, Roads and Works, and Poor Relief. The latter had powers by statute to spend the funds supplied for this purpose by the central government.

The Board worked with the Superintendent of Parochial Works, his assistant and staff (all appointed by the Board) and the Medical Officer of Health and a dentist appointed by the Minister of Local Government. The opportunity for patronage here was limited by the need for special skills on the part of the appointees and it would not appear that party patronage has been the chief factor in appointments.

There was an element of patronage in the distribution of 'Christmas relief' work. The Board drew up a plan of proposed work (this is mainly clearing brush from roadsides, filling holes, cleaning ditches, and the like) and got it approved, possibly with changes, by the Minister of Local Government. The House Members (who are ex-officio Board members) had influence in getting allocations for their constituencies if they were of the majority party.

Party designation was a factor in Board elections. Usually each of the two big parties had a candidate in every election district and there were always some independents as well. It would appear that the local prestige acquired by membership on a Parish Board was the principal motive of candidates for this duty.

This system seemed to work reasonably well. The Custos, who usually held office for life, was rather like the English squire of an earlier day. He was a man of high standing in the community both socially and otherwise, usually a white man, and because of his long service on the Board often had a good deal of influence on its decisions though possessing only the same voting power as all other members.

The Board, of course, was essentially an agent of the central government and had no real autonomy. It could be dismissed by the government for corruption or dereliction of duty among the members or staff. This power was exercised twice; the St Catherine Board in 1950 and the Trelawney Board in 1954 were replaced by centrally-appointed commissioners who operated the parish government until the next elections.

The voters were much less interested in parish elections than in those for the House of Representatives and usually not more than one-third of the electorate voted in local government elections. It was alleged that the poor quality of some candidates put forward by the parties was a reason for the low poll.[1]

Legislation was passed in 1956 making several changes in the local government system. The Custodes and members of the House of Representatives lost their ex-officio seats on the City Council. They had, in fact, ceased to be active participants in City Council meetings. The two Custodes had not attended meetings for years past and the MHR's had also ceased to attend. The rural Custodes also were removed from the Parish Boards, now renamed Parish Councils, but the MHR's were retained on these bodies with the stipulation that they might not be chosen chairman or vice-chairman. Statutory provision was made also for the appointment of a finance committee for each Council. In the case of important parishes the Governor was empowered to confer the title of mayor of the parish town upon the chairman of the Council. Membership was increased in several Councils which now number from thirteen to twenty-one and the City Council was increased to twenty-five.

In 1956 four hundred and ninety-one candidates secured nomination to contest the municipal and parochial elections. There were ninety-two independents among them but all others were party candidates: two hundred and twenty-four of the PNP, one hundred and sixty-seven of the JLP, and eight of minor parties. This is an indication of the extent to which the parties have begun to concern themselves with local government elections.

TRINIDAD

Trinidad has three municipal boroughs, Port-of-Spain, San Fernando and Arima. These have been given local governments according to the English pattern, Councillors, who must meet a property qualification, are elected for staggered three-year terms, about one-third of their number retiring each year. They are elected from multi-member wards by adult franchise. Until 1955 the voters in borough elections could be inscribed on the burgess roll only by meeting a low property qualification as property owners, renters or lodgers. This doubtless was an advantage to conservative independents and the Party of Political Progress Groups which long enjoyed much success in Port-of-Spain. The Councillors pick a smaller number of Aldermen either from their own ranks or from qualified outsiders. If a Councillor is chosen Alderman another election is held to fill his seat. The complete Council then picks a

[1] See editorial, Kingston *Daily Gleaner*, issue of March 23, 1956.

Mayor and Deputy Mayor from among themselves for a one-year term.

The Borough Council is concerned with electricity and water supply, markets, garbage disposal, street lighting and cleaning, the enforcement of building regulations, construction and maintenance of roads. Its revenue is derived from house tax, water rates, licence fees, market dues, wharf and cemetery dues and a rebate of motor licence fees from the central government.

Formerly local affairs outside of the boroughs were handled by Wardens, one for each county. These are career civil servants appointed by the Governor from lists prepared by the Public Service Commission. County Councils existed but with advisory powers only. In 1952 an ordinance was passed giving these bodies executive powers and, in effect, relegating the Warden to the position of adviser and administrator of the Council's decisions. The County Council's functions are similar to, but much less extensive than those of the Borough Councils. The seven counties were assigned Councils varying in number from eight to fourteen. Each elects its chairman and vice-chairman and the chairmen for the standing committees on public health, and finance. The vice-chairman of the Board is always chairman of the other standing committee on roads. The finance committee not only draws up annual estimates for the consideration of the entire council but concerns itself with everything not handled by the other two committees. In preparing estimates the finance committee is assisted by the Warden as County Treasurer. In the final stage, after Council approval, the estimates must be approved by the Executive Council of the colony. The accounts are audited by the central official, the Director of Audit. None of the counties possess sufficient revenue (from land taxes, licences and fees) to meet expenses and the difference, about eighty per cent, is made up out of general colonial revenue.

It was the intention of the central government to encourage still further decentralization by suggesting that the County Councils assist in the establishment of village or district councils to which could be entrusted some of the County powers.

The scheme outlined above was intended to stimulate democratic action and civic interest at the local level, to serve as a school of democracy and perhaps as a training ground for future legislators.[1] The only requirement for election to the County Council is the ability to speak and write English and all adults enjoy the franchise.

[1] See *The County Councils Ordinance, A Description of the Measure by* Sir John Imrie, Commissioner for Local Government, Colony of Trinidad and Tobago, May, 1952. Of the twenty candidates for federal seats listed in the *Sunday Guardian* (issue of 2 March, 1958, p. 14) eight had had city or borough council experience and one was chairman of a county council.

It is perhaps too early to estimate the significance of this recent attempt to introduce local self-government in Trinidad and Tobago. The quality of the Councillors in the early stages has not been high. Some of the Wardens were little inclined to hand over actual control to a body they considered unfit to exercise it. It was alleged that some Councillors were more interested in their travel and expense allowance, small as it is, than in civic affairs and were only too anxious to vote for needless inspection trips and the like to qualify for these payments. It may be assumed that it will be some time before the Councils are well prepared to undertake the real management of local affairs but in the meantime the Warden and his staff are prepared to carry on their daily work of administration. The County Councils and any village or district councils they recognize are without any background of local self-government and a tradition of civic responsibility must be established if they are to function as really useful local government bodies.

Meetings of two County Councils attended by the writer were characterized by noisy and sometimes pointless argument which ended in an exchange of personalities and the angry withdrawal from one meeting of a Councillor. The potentially most controversial item, a list of successful bidders on road contracts was accepted without argument or inquiry. The County Councils seemed as yet (in 1954) uncertain as to the extent of their authority in relation to the Warden and unclear as to their relationship to village councils. In one meeting the gallery consisted mainly of several very young men, one of whom was dressed in 'saga boy' costume, the Trinidadian equivalent of a 'zoot suit'. These young men wanted to be recognized as a village council and they all wore green berets decorated with red celluloid buttons as a sort of uniform of office.

It would seem that County Councillors are motivated not only by the personal aggrandisement to be derived from holding elected office but also by the attraction of the travel allowance and sometimes by the possibility of swinging contracts for road building to friends who will pay for this service. Others consider election to the County Council as the first step towards election to the Legislative Council.

Until recently the Council elections were dominated by independents who sometimes formed temporary election alliances and also in Council meetings where a majority bloc might be formed to control the chairmanship and the meetings in general. Party designation is becoming more important in local elections. In 1955, for the first time, six of the ten candidates for four vacant places in the San Fernando Borough Council had party designation or support and parties were active in the County Council elections of

1956. There were 273 candidates in 1953 and 233 in 1956 for the seventy-two seats. Electioneering is vigorous and sometimes disorderly, especially in the East Indian districts. Some candidates in 1956 were threatened with violence and one had his car damaged by a shotgun blast which narrowly missed him.

At Council meetings there is still a good deal of unparliamentary language and behaviour. It is not unusual for members to exchange insults and for some to leave the meeting before adjournment. In one case, reported in the Press in June, 1956, the chairman felt compelled to rebuke several Councillors for 'worthless and shameful conduct' including an invitation from one to another to 'come outside and fight' and a threat by the challenged Councillor to fetch a gun and 'blow up' his opponent.[1] Councillors are often extremely parochial, adopting a jealous attitude towards the provision of amenities in wards other than the one represented by the Councillor. They delay the execution of recommendations likely to offend some voters. They have bombarded the Commissioner for Local Government with appeals against their Executive Officers (the Wardens) and with demands that they receive salaries like the Legislative Council.

It is easy to be scornful of these beginnings of local government. But it must be remembered that Trinidad's rural areas had never enjoyed any kind of self-government, that the new Councillors were not only ignorant of parliamentary procedure but had had no experience in the processes of group decision-making, that it was hard to find able and worthy candidates for the Council and that the electorate was also totally inexperienced and, as regards the majority, not much interested in Council elections. A local observer has claimed that there has been some degree of progress in the understanding and performance of their duties by the Councils, even after the first year of 'executive responsibility'.[2]

BARBADOS

Down to 1958 Barbadian local government has been in the hands of parish vestries elected annually by voters meeting a property requirement. The vestries have been headed ex-officio, by the Anglican rector. This system began with the establishment of eleven parishes in the seventeenth century whose vestries undertook both ecclesiastical and civic duties in accord with canon and common law. As time went on the Barbadian legislature passed a number of laws

[1] See Trinidad *Sunday Guardian,* issue of June 3, 1956, p. 2.
[2] See articles by R. G. Kentworth in the Trinidad *Sunday Guardian,* issues of February 23 and March 13, 1954.

assigning various duties to the vestries and defining the requirements for the franchise and vestry membership. Parish boards and
commissions were also established, each with a particular function
to perform under vestry supervision. Among these functions were:
repair and upkeep of church property and payment of church
officers (churchwarden, vestry clerk, etc., but not the clergy who
are paid out of general colonial revenue), poor relief, public sanitation, parish roads, graveyards, grants to certain charities and a
miscellany of other matters. Vestry income was derived from an
ownership tax, a trade tax, and other minor taxes as well as pew
rentals, dog licences and the income from bequests. The heaviest
vestry expenditures were for poor relief and parish roads. The
vestries had some limited borrowing powers and received subventions from the central government, principally for roads.

It is obvious from the above brief summary that the Barbadian
local government system was the result of unplanned and haphazard
growth over the centuries. It was criticized adversely by all who
examined it including the Moyne Commission. That it should have
survived so long without basic change is evidence of the English
conservatism of Barbados and the fact that until recent times
virtually the entire population adhered to the Anglican faith.

In 1948 Sir John Maude, a British local government expert, was
asked to investigate the vestry system. His 'Report on Local
Government in Barbados, 18 February, 1948' listed faults and made
recommendations. He criticized adversely: the division of such a
small area (twenty-one miles by fourteen) into eleven separate local
government districts, the combination of civil and ecclesiastical
functions, the assumption that the local rector should, by reason of
his cloth, head the local government body, a franchise so limited
that less than three per cent of the population actually voted in
local government elections, an irrational, complicated and unfair
local tax system, inadequate supervision of parish business by the
central government. Maude advised that the island be divided into
three local government areas: the city of Bridgetown and the
Northern and Southern (rural) Districts. Bridgetown should have
the standard type of English city council elected from three wards.
Each rural district should have a district council on the English
model. Public health should be handled by an island-wide service.
The tax system should be overhauled and simplified and assessment centralized.

The Maude Report was discussed in the Press and the legislature
and in 1952 the government introduced a bill to reform local government in line with Sir John Maude's suggestions. The bill proved to be
highly controversial because it extended adult suffrage to city and

district elections.[1] This bill was rejected by the Legislative Council. Reintroduced in the following session, it was accepted by the Legislative Council with amendments and became law as the Local Government Act, 1954. Additional legislation was enacted concerning public health, poor relief and assessment of real property. Still further amendments are in process and the new system was put into effect in 1958. The possible disestablishment of the Church of England is under consideration by a select committee.

BRITISH GUIANA

The villages of British Guiana resulted from the breaking up of a number of sugar estates following emancipation. Freedmen combined their resources to purchase blocks of land and these were usually broken up into individual cultivator's plots and a residential area near the highway. Because of the irrigation-drainage system of cultivation peculiar to British Guiana it was necessary to handle the plots in this way with communal co-operation as regards irrigation and with the farmer's houses located in a village on higher land. Later, when some of the East Indians had completed their indenture as estate labourers, these too began to leave the estates in some cases, and establish rice and cattle farms. They also congregated in villages and, in time, the coastal plain of the colony bore a chain of villages along the main highway, some Negro, some East Indian and some mixed in population.

As long ago as 1892 a small measure of self-government was provided for these villages. A central Local Government Board was established and under this a number of inspectors to visit the villages and have general oversight of village government. Then in 1932 the colony was divided into several districts, five of which are in the coastal region, each with a District Commissioner with the duty of representing the colonial government in his district and co-ordinating the activities of the various departments as well as serving as a general adviser to the villages. They have oversight of public assistance disbursements and, to some extent, carry on the work of the old Immigration Agents in helping the East Indians in connection with their dealings with other government departments.

A local government ordinance was passed in 1945 reorganizing the entire rural local government system. Under this ordinance the Local Government Board has ten members: three ex-officio, including the Commissioner of Local Government (an office created in 1938), the Director of Medical Services (both permanent central

---

[1] The chief reason for the opposition in Legislative Council to the bill is discussed, *above*, p. 94.

officers) and the President of the Village Chairmen's Conference (chosen by the Conference). The other seven members are appointed by the Governor for two-year terms and must include two members of a village council or a country authority, one person nominated by the British Guiana Sugar Producers' Association and four other persons chosen at will by the Governor.

The Board has general oversight and approval of the budgets of local authorities. It can veto or amend these budgets. It can create new village and country districts out of the rural districts which have no self-government and are administered by the District Commissioner. In emergencies the Board can veto any decision by a local authority and supersede the local authority entirely. This is done only in emergencies when local government has broken down or the village council has brought about a disorderly situation.

Country districts represent the first step towards a measure of self-government. Their affairs are administered by Country Authorities consisting of several members and a chairman, all nominated by the Board.

Country districts can become village districts if most landowners in the district want the change and if the community is literate enough. The Board established forty per cent adult literacy as the minimum required for change from country to village status. There were forty-six of each type of council in 1955.

Village Councils are semi-elected bodies. One-third of the membership are still appointed by the Board but two-thirds are elected by registered voters who are owners of real property assessed at not less than fifty dollars. Elections are for a two-year term and the Village Chairman and Deputy Chairman are chosen annually by the Council. The elected members (but not the voters) must be literate in English.

Country and village authorities perform the same functions. Their principal work is in assessing property and collecting rates to pay for the cost of maintaining irrigation dams and canals, village roads, the earthworks necessary to the piping of drinking water, pasture lands, village sanitation and other local needs. Their collections are insufficient to cover the cost of sea dikes, drainage and fresh water pumps, pipes, and so forth and these costs are borne by the central government. In their work they have much to do with the District Commissioner who receives the rates collected and approves the payment of wages or other obligations incurred by the authority during the previous week. He often attends the meetings of the local authority (which is supposed to meet at least monthly). He may speak and advise but not vote in these meetings. The Commissioner of Local Government has taken the position that the

District Commissioners should refrain from giving too much advice and should encourage self-reliance on the part of the Village Councils.

In connection with the ever-present problem of drainage and irrigation the local authority is a central Drainage and Irrigation Board exists which includes among its members the Commissioner of Local Government and two representatives of village councils. The central government assigns districts to the Board which it is then required to take over as regards its subject. It administers irrigation and drainage in these areas securing the money for maintenance work from the local rates. This caused loud complaints among the villagers and in 1952 the Local Government Board decided to allow local proprietors and authorities to undertake maintenance work themselves in some cases, presenting estimates of cost for this work to the Board for approval.

As early as 1901 a Village Chairmen's Conference was held. This is a voluntary association for the exchange of ideas at an annual meeting. The Governor sometimes lends the prestige of his presence to this gathering and the Commissioner of Local Government is usually among the speakers. In the five coastal Districts there are voluntary Unions of Local Authorities which also hold meetings, usually quarterly. They also provide an opportunity for the discussion and exchange of ideas on local government problems often taking their subjects for discussion from the District Commissioner's opening address. These meetings also provide an opportunity for officials who are specialists in some field of administration to explain problems and policies in their speciality.

Some villages have also formed Community Councils which are advisory bodies containing representatives of the local authority and every village club, group or association. These Community Councils are supposed to work with the Rural Betterment staff of the Social Welfare officials who work with the District Commissioners but are responsible to the Commissioner of Local Government in his aspect as Social Welfare Officer. The Community Councils were frowned upon in the beginning by the local authorities who feared that there might be political activity on the part of the new bodies which might try to develop into ratepayers' associations. It is claimed that the Community Councils in some cases have shown signs of developing into organizations which will be useful in community planning and the encouragement of civic spirit.[1]

[1] 'Some Aspects of Community Development in British Guiana', mimeographed document issued by D. L. B. Wickham, Commissioner of Local Government and Social Welfare Officer. (August, 1952) pp. 7, 8.

Naturally the PPP campaign of 1953 and afterwards, conducted as it was in the villages, had its effect not only on central but on village elections as well. The elected part of a number of village councils came to consist of a solid delegation of PPP adherents. This did not matter from a colony-wide standpoint as the District Commissioner and the Board have sufficient authority to prevent misuse of power by village councils. It did provide the party with additional local machinery and opportunities for propaganda.

In 1954 the Secretary of State appointed Dr A. H. Marshall, City Treasurer of Coventry, to report on local government in British Guiana. Dr Marshall advocated a simplification of the pattern. The city of Georgetown and borough of New Amsterdam should retain municipal status with councils largely elected but with a minority of nominated members. The ninety-two village and country councils should be replaced by not more than eighteen rural district councils, also containing both nominated and elected members. There should be provision for the gradual disappearance of the nominated element. The Marshall suggestions were accepted in principle by the government and Dr L. C. Hill, a British local government expert, was appointed towards the end of 1956 on a two-year contract to oversee the reorganization necessary to establish the new system.

BRITISH HONDURAS

Until recently local self-government in British Honduras was confined to Belize which had a city Council elected on a rate-payer franchise. Other towns had their affairs administered by the District Commissioners and a Town Board of five members all appointed by the Governor.

Under People's United Party control, the legislature passed an ordinance in 1955 providing for universal adult suffrage in municipal elections. The six district towns were given boards of seven members, three nominated and four elected. In January, 1956, elections were held under the new law. The PUP supported by its General Workers' Union won more than half of the elected places but the towns of El Cayo and Benque Viejo, inhabited by Spanish-speaking Mayans and mestizos, chose Councillors of their own people without party affiliation. It is conceivable that this may mark the emergence of Mayan political communalism.

N

CHAPTER IX

PARTIES AND POLITICIANS

A GREAT political party is an association of politicians, politically active citizens and ordinary voters, acting together for a variety of reasons but primarily because they share a broad, social attitude. The party's chief function is the reduction of a welter of specific, differing demands and shades of opinion to an integrated and widely acceptable programme of action and the provision of machinery for the selection and organized electoral support of candidates pledged to this programme. A great party can continue to perform this function long after the issues that created it have passed into history and its original leaders have been replaced many times. Such a party becomes an institution in its own right, with historic, 'ancestral' heroes, an emotionally evocative name and a permanent organization devoted to the perpetual existence of the party. To continue its existence and remain important, the party must be able to accept and digest new ideas as to the objectives of governmental action, be able to shift emphasis from old to new issues, and continue to be a satisfactory instrument for blunting the sharper differences between its supporters and emphasizing their basic agreements. Parties of this kind usually are the product of a lengthy history of self-government in a community that accepts the secular state and contains no social cleavages deep and serious enough to jeopardize the continuity of representative government.

Great, stable, highly institutionalized parties like those of the United Kingdom and the United States have not yet had time to develop in the West Indies. No West Indian party is old enough to have outlived all the issues that brought it into existence. Almost all are headed still by the founder-leader. In some places the party pattern is one of bewildering complexity. In a kind of political kaleidoscope parties form only to vanish after elections, merge with other parties or re-form under another name. Many are one-man parties with a designation invented by a candidate who wants to avoid the colourless title of independent or, by the name chosen, to associate himself with 'progress', 'labour' or some other attractive abstraction.

The inchoate state of party development in some West Indian units may be illustrated by reference to the 1957 elections in the remote and poor island of Dominica where the majority of the rural inhabitants are illiterate and speak only French patois. In 1957 an attempt was made to introduce parties, hitherto almost unknown, although there had been two previous elections. the first in 1950, under universal suffrage. One of these new parties, the Labour Party, was founded by an unusual type of West Indian politician, Mrs Phyllis Shand Allfrey. Mrs Allfrey is the white, Dominica-born daughter of a former Commissioner of Prisons and grand-daughter of Sir Henry Nichols, a celebrated physician and founder of the local botanic gardens. She had achieved some celebrity as a writer and when a child, despite parental prohibition, had learned to understand and speak the patois of the peasantry. After a twenty-year absence in England, where she became a Fabian Socialist, Mrs Allfrey returned to Dominica in 1955 and founded the Labour Party whose base was provided by about seven thousand union members. Later another party which copied the name of the Trinidad People's National Movement was organized by a coloured lawyer and landowner, Clifton A. Dupigny. This PNM tried to ally itself formally with Dr Williams's party but was rejected. This was essentially a middle-class party. All the other candidates were well-known politicians who stood as independents. In the elections three Labour Party, two PNM and three independent candidates were elected. As soon as the results were announced, one of the PNM members resigned from the party and declared himself independent. An old-line independent, Frank A. Baron, was able to get three other independents to form a ministry with the aid of the nominated members.

The fluidity of party membership and even of leadership is illustrated by the recent history of the Labour Party in the island of St Lucia. John Compton, a barrister, although elected in 1954 as an independent was able, after joining the Labour Party, to take over its direction. He was the only elected member with a university education.

Ephemeral or not, these parties are provided with a programme and with an elaborate constitution calling for a full complement of elected officers and central and constituency organizations. The constitutions are largely ignored in practice, as a rule, and the party remains the autocratically directed group supporting its founder-leader. Parties of this character, to borrow St Clair Drake's phrase, are typical of 'transitional democracy', the period in which an in-experienced electorate is learning how to operate representative institutions.

Characteristic of this stage of political evolution in the West Indies is the greater effectiveness of the emotional as compared with the intellectual or reasoned appeal based upon practical proposals for solutions to social and economic problems. There are several reasons for this. In the first place, the mass voter has had little formal education. He is illiterate or barely literate. He is likely to have strong feelings of frustration and resentment at his low economic and social status but not much knowledge of the world in general or understanding of the total situation, historic and economic, in which he finds himself. It is difficult if not impossible for him to analyze critically the concrete proposals of the various parties and candidates. He can and will respond enthusiastically to appeals designed to play upon his fears, hates and longings: denunciations of the wickedness of 'colonialism', the rapacity of the upper class, and promises of a new day when the 'barefooted man' will be master of his own destiny and ruler of his own land. This type of appeal is particularly effective in the emotional atmosphere of the mass-meeting, and open-air mass-meetings are the chief electioneering institution in the West Indies. The individuals composing the crowd at such meetings respond in a different manner than they would in a face-to-face discussion with the speaker. The individual's emotional threshold is lowered and manifestations of emotion in the crowd are 'contagious'.[1] A high level of enthusiasm, hatred of the enemy and worship of the leader can be induced by the skilful orator who knows the right note to sound. On the other hand, it is extremely difficult to induce the members of the crowd to follow a closely reasoned, intellectual argument to its logical conclusion. It is possible, of course, that a crowd may respond with enthusiasm to an orator for reasons having little to do with the actual content of his message. Dr Eric Williams, in his series of lectures at the 'University of Woodford Square', employed arguments and used a vocabulary which must have been beyond the comprehension of a good many of his auditors. It appears evident that his great popularity was based upon something other than intellectual conviction. This is indicated by the fact that he received the votes not only of many middle-class, educated voters but also of the 'marabuntas', the local epithet for the very poor inhabitants of Port-of-Spain's Shanty Town and John John slum districts.

The enthusiasm so quickly inspired at the mass meeting may fade just as quickly. Parties which have no effective grass-roots organization which have little contact with the electorate except at mass meetings have trouble in building and keeping a sizeable

---

[1] The intensification and release of prepotent, primitive responses by the crowd situation is discussed in F. H. Allport, *Social Psychology* (Harvard: Oxford, 1924) Chapter XII, and in E. D. Martin, *The Behaviour of Crowds* (New York, London, Harpers, 1920).

corps of loyal voters whose support can be depended upon. The mass meeting follower can switch allegiance overnight. Politicians therefore are compelled to try to anticipate changes in mass preference. Hence the 'shopping around' before elections and the coy flirtations between parties and potential candidates before a final decision as to the pre-election alliance.

Not all West Indian parties are covered by the above description. The oldest and strongest among them already show signs of institutionalization. In some cases the constitution has more than a paper existence and a real effort is made to build and maintain genuine primary groups and constituency organizations whose prime loyalty is to the party and its programme rather than mere subservience to the charismatic leader. These groups are encouraged to discuss the political situation and the party policies and strategy and to engage actively in the political conversion of others. At the constituency level they participate in the choice of candidates. All, however, are conditioned by their recent origin and by the nature of the electorate. None is older than the labour disorders of the depression 'thirties and the founder-leader in many cases is still the keystone of party unity. To be successful the leader must have the qualities and employ the techniques that enable the crowd to regard him as an embodiment and projection of their aggressive drives.

The West Indian social milieu which has determined many of the characteristics of the political parties has been described earlier in this study. The factors which have been historically significant for party development may again be summarized as follows: the plural society resulting from an export agriculture, plantation economy; an upper class differentiated from the rest by race and colour and deficient in local attachment and loyalty; a society with few interests beyond the acquisition of money; the absence of cultural inter-class bridges; a small middle class chronically concerned with social status; a society poor in associational life, and with the few significant associations that exist, organized autocratically; centrally-controlled, officially administered local governments; officially dominated central governments; almost all authority and high status enjoyed by a tiny minority of white and coloured officials, planters, merchants and professionals with the rest of the population seemingly doomed to permanent poverty and social rejection.

The problems facing West Indian governments are the result of these conditions and others derived from them. They include: a standard of living for the majority little above subsistence level; population pressure due to high birth rates along with severely restricted possibilities of emigration and an inflexible economy with consequent unemployment and underemployment; and a society divided by race-class antagonisms and diffused loyalties almost to the point of anomy.

There are two principal positions that can be taken in relation to the issues arising from these conditions. It is possible to consider as of primary importance the maintenance and prosperity of existing commerce and agricultural enterprise and oppose any change that might disturb existing trade channels. Those holding this view tend to frown upon expanded governmental welfare activities and enterprise as involving increased taxation and favour a very gradual advance in constitutional arrangements as less likely to shake the social and economic order. This conservative position is unacceptable to the great majority of West Indians. The popular position is that taken by those who advocate expansion of welfare activities and other policies calculated to benefit the poor and a rapid achievement of complete self-government.

It is possible to classify West Indian parties and politicians into those of the Right and the Left depending upon their general stand in regard to these propositions, noting that the wide unpopularity of their position compels those of the Right to modify verbally or disguise their conservatism. The Left parties were naturally the first to be formed because the conservative position was represented adequately in the pre-party assemblies. Right parties were founded to try to counter the threat to the existing order by those of the Left. The oldest Left parties were made possible by two circumstances: the constitutional reforms after World War I which provided for a lowering of suffrage requirements and an increase in the elected element in the legislatures, and the labour disturbances of the depression period. These circumstances facilitated the rise of a new type of West Indian politician as the champion of the working man.[1] All this took place while the well-to-do middle class still monopolized the elected legislative seats. Usually elected as independents, these members did not regard themselves as representatives of the poor. Their electorate was restricted by property or income requirements and interest in elections was slight. Many potential voters did not bother to exercise the franchise and it was not unusual for candidates to be unopposed at the polls. Politics had not yet become a concern of the lower classes whose demands were latent, unformulated and without public expression.

The oldest Left parties were founded or became important as a direct result of the labour disturbances. In Jamaica, the People's National Party and the Jamaica Labour Party were founded at this time as were the Barbados Labour Party and the British Empire

[1] These events are described *above*, pp 38-41.

Workers' and Citizens' Home Rule Party in Trinidad. In several colonies a single party of the Left was soon able to outstrip its rivals and become unbeatable at the polls. There could be little real competition as to programme because all parties dependent upon the mass vote had to advocate much the same things. The relative success of Left parties depended rather upon the qualities of its leadership and its success in establishing trades union connections. The leaders, to begin with, were rarely of black, working-class origin. Few poor Negroes had yet been able to acquire the necessary experience, celebrity and prestige required to achieve party leadership. No doubt this explains the statement by the Jamaican nationalist, Roberts, who wrote that 'mixed blood' was a requirement for political leadership.[1]

The one community-wide association found in most of the colonies that represented the common man, welcomed his membership and gave him a sense of collective strength was the labour union. Often it would be an omnibus union, admitting all categories of labour, skilled and unskilled. Here, at last, was an instrument suitable for the articulation and expression of the hitherto latent demands of the lower-class West Indian. In the 'thirties the West Indian trades union movement was in its infancy and parties and unions grew up together. In Jamaica, for instance, although an ordinance permitting unions which was based upon British law had been enacted as early as 1919, only four unions were registered during the following twenty years and these included a tiny fraction of the labour force. Then the misery and turbulence of the depression era brought about a mushroom growth of labour unions. Alexander Bustamante neglected his money-lending business to become, almost overnight, a famous agitator and champion of labour. Norman Manley too gained fame as the court-room defender of Bustamante and others. Grantley Adams in Barbados acquired his reputation by activities similar to those of Manley. These middle-class spokesmen for the 'barefooted man' thus gained the necessary celebrity and inspired the general confidence in their motives and abilities which enabled their ready acceptance as leaders of the new unions or of mass political parties or of both.

Bustamante began his career as a labour agitator and union leader but both Manley and Adams started out as politicians connected with political parties which disclaimed class connections. It was soon evident that political victory could not be won merely by the secular appeal of socialism and constitutional reform. The successful political leader had to appear not only as the spokesman

[1] W. Adolphe Roberts, *Jamaica, the Portrait of an Island* (New York, 1955), p. 134.

for the majority of the population but as one who had achieved concrete benefits for them. West Indian parties of the Left were or soon became labour parties tied firmly to a union base. When Bustamante formed his Jamaica Labour Party and took with him his big trades union, pulling it out from under Manley's party, the latter had to set about the creation of a rival union. Adams was able to achieve the predominant voting power of his party only after the founding of the Barbados Workers' Union. In some of the less advanced colonies where there were no trained union organizers and where labour was difficult to organize, would-be political leaders still thought it worth while to appeal to the working-class voters by establishing unions consisting of little more than a name and a list of officers, with few if any dues-paying members.[1]

The party-trades union connections of the Left parties came about, therefore, in either of two ways. Some of these parties began with a general appeal to all nationalists or socialists and then found it advisable to find or create a trades union base for the party. Others originated as the political extension of pre-existing union activities. In the first category are Jamaica's PNP, the Barbados Labour Party, the PPP in British Guiana and the PUP in British Honduras. The second category includes the Jamaica Labour Party, Butler's BEW & CHRP in Trinidad and a number of parties in the smaller islands.

It is generally the case that in West Indian union-party relationships, the party dominates politically. Greater prestige and power is attached to party leadership and the top leadership of the union-party combination gravitates to the political side. Unless the political leaders also occupy the positions of union officers, these are delegated to the second team. At the same time, except perhaps in the case of some of the phantom unions created as vote-catching devices, the attitudes and some of the policies of the political leaders are conditioned by the need to retain the support of the union members. As is the case with labour parties in other countries, this may serve at times to exaggerate class antagonisms.

POLITICAL LEADERS

It may be generalized that nearly all outstanding politicians, even in the most politically sophisticated communities, have some charismatic appeal. For a part of their followers, at least, they have a measure of the divinity that doth hedge not only kings but other

---

[1] Some of the comments in this chapter have been made previously by the present writer. See 'Some Characteristics of West Indian Political Parties', *Social and Economic Studies*, 3, 2 (Sept., 1954), 186-196.

chieftains. This phenomenon is more evident and obvious in societies that are passing through a stage of rapid reconstruction. When a prolonged economic or political crisis has resulted in the destruction of most of the respect for and willing submission to the former dominating class, there occurs a dissolution of social bonds, a social fission which is painful to all classes. This is accompanied by the collapse of a portion, at least, of the social and political myths upon which the society is constructed. There is an immediate and urgent need, unless anarchy result, for the establishment of a new social myth and a new class of leaders to formulate and defend the myth upon which the society can again be rebuilt in orderly fashion. The new leaders are likely to inspire strong emotional attachments and to be elevated upon pedestals the height of which will be proportional to the depths of despair and social disintegration which provided their opportunity for leadership. The leaders of the Left parties in the West Indies arose under these conditions and it is hard to distinguish the secular from the charismatic appeal they have for their supporters.

Left party leaders can be distinguished, however, by the degree of emphasis they place upon rational argument and specific reform proposals *versus* the general promise of the New Jerusalem coupled with attacks upon the old order. They can be distinguished also in terms of their rejection or acceptance of a socialist solution for West Indian problems. There are also some differences in the degree of local nationalist and anti-imperialist feeling they display. These distinctions are not linked. In other words, some leaders who depend heavily upon charisma and demagogic techniques are socialist, others are not. And the degree of local nationalism including the presence or absence of outright anti-British sentiments will repend upon the particular colony and its recent history rather than upon any other consideration.

As a rough generalization it may be stated that the greatest reliance upon the charismatic appeal is made by party leaders who have risen through the trades unions and who are of Negro or dark-coloured origin and who have had little, if any, formal education. Their proposed reforms are couched in vague terms or are visionary and sometimes self-contradictory. Their general stated objectives, of course, are substantially the same as those of all Left politicians: local nationhood and promoting the welfare of the working class. As their political careers depend upon their remaining important as a symbol of lower-class aspirations and sentiments, they are concerned mainly with words and actions calculated to maintain this position. Some examples may be cited in illustration.

The most remarkable of the West Indian demagogues is Sir

Alexander Bustamante (né Clark). He is a tall man of good physique and the face of an ageing actor, with thick eyebrows, a mane of white hair and a well-shaped aquiline nose. At the beginning of his political career he abandoned his previous role of perfumed Spanish grandee and appeared instead as the fearless labour leader and man of the people. Disdaining middle-class finery he went about hatless and with two revolvers strapped to his belt. His speeches were sprinkled with constant references to his 'rise from the gutter'. This may have been to establish identity with the lower classes and counteract the possible disadvantage of his light colour and actual middle-class origin. He is a fluent and effective speaker both in English and the crude Jamaican dialect of the poor and ignorant. His mass support has come from the dock and waterfront workers of Kingston and from sugar estate labourers who are members of his autocratically-controlled Bustamante Industrial Trade Union. By adopting a vigorously anti-socialist position he was able to appeal to religious and business people as their bulwark against the 'godless communism and ruinous socialism' of the People's National Party. With the attainment of unquestioned domination of both union and party, Bustamante changed his mode of dress, except for the white bow tie which had become his sartorial trade-mark. Despite the tropical heat of Kingston, he now favoured dark suits of tight, English cut. On formal occasions he appeared in grey cutaway and top hat, carrying a furled umbrella, his wavy white hair trimmed to moderate length. He now had something of the manner and appearance of an elder British statesman, suitable to a man of substance with gubernatorial ambitions. Despite this elegance, he seldom failed to take advantage of any opportunity to keep reminding the lower classes that he was of them and for them. For example, when a cocktail party was given at the Myrtle Bank Hotel some years ago in honour of Lord Lyle of the Tate and Lyle sugar firm, Bustamante, who was present in the hotel but not as a guest of the party, suddenly and for no apparent reason, called a waiters' strike just as the drinks were about to be served. He called off the strike a half-hour later, but the picture of upper-class Jamaicans and the great Lord Lyle himself compelled to wait upon their 'Busta's' whim no doubt delighted BITU members all over the island.

Bustamante's personality is engaging and his constant boasting is entertaining rather than offensive. He has a vivid sense of the theatrical and can always capture and hold the attention of a Jamaican audience although he has been less successful in other places. His debating technique is often to start by ridiculing the opposition and then shift suddenly from a light-hearted joking attack to one that is angry and highly emotional. Like other master demagogues he can sense the emotional tone of a crowd and improvise an appeal designed to play upon this prevailing feeling.

Tubal Uriah Buzz Butler of Trinidad, an uneducated Negro of Grenadian working-class origin, got his start as an agitator during the depression labour troubles and acquired martyrdom, as did Bustamante, by suffering arrest and imprisonment for incitement to violence. Butler's *persona* is that of a Biblical prophet. His speeches are heavily larded with scriptural quotations and he employs an extensive if sometimes mystifying vocabulary reminiscent of that used by the American cult-leader, Father Divine. His role of prophet is manifested physically by dignified clothing and a white beard. He refers to himself as 'the Chief Servant'. Although, in the long run, Butler was eclipsed in competition with better trained and more skilful union leaders because he relied too much upon his prophetlike appearance and strange oratory and was absent from Trinidad for long periods without providing for adequate party organization, he was one of the first successful demagogues in the southern Caribbean. As such, he was the inspiration of several ambitious politicians in other islands.

Eric Gairy of Grenada was an avowed disciple of Butler and also has employed the religious appeal. His *persona,* however, has been that of the successful man of affairs, dressed elegantly, driving an impressive motor car, and with a superior, even arrogant manner. He too can boast of minor martyrdom, having been exiled from Grenada for a short time following small-scale riots, house burnings and animal maimings used in recruiting members for his Mental and Manual Workers' Union, now named Grenada Trades Union. He has shown more flexibility than his mentor in seizing opportunities to widen his appeal and acquire a measure of general acceptance, once office had been won.

No doubt mixed motives underlie political ambition in all societies. Personal prestige, power, and a relatively high income may all be involved as well as a burning desire to right wrongs and steer the ship of state on a correct course. In the West Indies, with its rather rigid, colour-class social structure, there can be no doubt that the opportunity to achieve personal goals, especially celebrity and social acceptance, provide a strong motive for a political career. In no other way can class barriers be overcome so quickly as by gaining elective office.[1] The other routes, by outstanding profes-

[1] As noted in the case of the Boston Irish by the fictional politician, Skeffington, in Edwin O'Connor, *The Last Hurrah* (London: Reinhardt, 1956) p. 220. . . . 'the main reason I went into politics was because it was the quickest way out of the cellar and up the ladder'.

sional achievement, require long and costly training and years of hard work. The significance to politics of these personal motives, especially powerful in the case of intelligent, ambitious, but un-educated Negroes, is that when their personal ambitions have been satisfied, their enthusiasm for extreme and socially explosive re-forms is likely to wane. They must, of course, retain the pose of a fighting leader of the Left, but their lack of basic fanaticism makes it possible for the official side of government to secure moderation and compromise in their policies.

This type of leader has certain practical advantages in an emer-gent democracy. He can satisfy his followers and retain their support by securing reasonable social and constitutional advances, and by the psychic 'lift' they get from self-identification with him, the charismatic leader. At the same time, he does not insist upon the unobtainable and learns to tolerate the opposition. Parliamentary government remains workable and time is provided for growth in the understanding and use of its institutions so that group decision-making and executive responsibility can become thoroughly estab-lished.[1]

Although a nationalist-socialist programme and a labour union base have been the usual accompaniments of Left party success, there are several exceptions. Two notable ones are the Jamaica Labour Party and the People's National Movement of Trinidad. Bustamante's economic conservatism and his reluctance to press for constitutional reforms has been mentioned already. These features of his policies, not popular in themselves, he could overcome and to some extent disguise by his oratorical skill, the dazzling effect of his charisma, and his reputation as a fighter for labour. The astonishing electoral victory of the Trinidad PNM in 1956 did not depend upon a socialist philosophy, disavowed by the leader, Dr Williams, nor upon a union base, although the party did have some union connections. Its appeal was reformist and strongly nationalist and anti-colonial. It also developed the most complete organization at voter level so far seen in Trinidad. Agitational and enrolment centres were set up in every constituency. Williams's lectures delivered throughout the island caught the public imagina-tion and he and his party were swept into office despite a desperate, eleventh-hour alliance of nearly all the other parties and outstand-ing independents. It may be too soon to say whether the PNM has at last established the party system as an integral part of Trinidadian politics or whether Williams represents the island's most successful charismatic leader since Butler's heyday. That 'Williams the Con-

<hr />

[a] As Apter notes in connection with Ghana. See David E. Apter, *The Gold Coast in Transition* (Princeton: Oxford, 1955), p. 306.

queror', as he was dubbed by a calypsonian, has charismatic appeal for many is indicated by his clean sweep in the poorest districts, by the fact that urban campaign crowds often refused to listen to any PNM speaker but Dr Williams, and by the disorderly behaviour of PNM supporters towards rival candidates.

PARTY ORGANIZATION

Formal party constitutions in the West Indies resemble those of democratic parties in other western countries. Local party units of prescribed size are entitled to send delegates to an annual conference which is the all-powerful party legislature, choosing the officers and the executive committee. The practice, however, is usually rather different from the formal scheme.

The Jamaica Labour Party scarcely bothered with the organization at the voter level provided for in its constitution. Bustamante relied instead upon a whirlwind pre-election campaign. The People's National Party, on the other hand, tried to organize its constituency groups and keep them active, each based upon a number a primary groups scattered throughout the constituency. There were, indeed, some three hundred and fifty of these primary groups in being by 1946. But the number of active groups varies greatly from time to time. In theory members of these groups are supposed to busy themselves with recruitment and party propaganda and pay dues of threepence per month, one penny going to the central party organization. Many of the enrolled members fail to pay their dues. Approximately one delegate per twenty-five active members is chosen to attend the party conference. Constituencies with at least twenty active primary groups may select their own legislative candidates but few qualify for this privilege, the choice of candidate necessarily remaining with the party leadership. The PNP executive at various times has dropped ineffective legislators and prevailed upon the constituency concerned to accept another candidate. It was admitted by a party officer in 1953 that at that time only some four or five out of thirty-two constituencies had a really effective and working primary group organization. These groups are supposed to meet weekly and devote each meeting to a selected topic: local party business, a guest speaker, a social evening, or a discussion of the PNP *News Letter*. Three or four times a year they may hold a fund-raising dance.

The care taken in the Crown Colony system to keep personnel administration and the control of the civil service in the hands of permanent officials means that no party, even with a legislative majority and all the ministerial posts, can do much to build a machine based upon civil service appointments. The enthusiasm of the unpaid party workers tends to flag between elections and the job of maintaining the loyalty of the voting public falls almost entirely upon the party leader and his colleagues in the legislature and the associated labour union.

The Trinidad People's National Movement, as mentioned earlier, patterned its organization upon that of the Jamaican PNP. The PNM has emphasized the constituency group as the key organization in keeping the rank-and-file alert and informed. These groups hold frequent meetings to hear from their officers and party members who have been elected from the constituency to local or central bodies. For example, an all-day meeting was held in the constituency of Port-of-Spain South East in May, 1957, to hear from the constituency chairman, the party leader, Dr Williams, who presented a general political review, and the two members of the city council from this district. Port-of-Spain South had a similar meeting in July, 1957, to hear from the PNM leader of the city council, Dennis Mahabir, the constituency secretary, and Dr Patrick Solomon, Minister of Education and Culture.

The PNM constituency conferences select their candidates subject to the subsequent approval of the party's executive council. There is an annual party conference which elects the officers including the party chairman but not the parliamentary leader. He is chosen by the party delegation in the legislature. As parliamentary leader he is also leader of the party. A key body is the executive council which meets monthly or oftener. This consists of the party officers and twenty-five members elected by the annual conference plus two members from each constituency, chosen by the constituency conference. This body approves candidates, acts as the connecting link between the party and the parliamentary group, and decides how to spend the party funds. Between meetings of the council, affairs are handled by the executive committee, meeting at least weekly. This 'presidium' is composed of the party officers, the parliamentary leaders, three members of the parliamentary delegation, chosen by themselves, and eleven members of the executive council chosen by that body. This machinery has been used to fend off old-line politicians who sought to board the band wagon and to find acceptable candidates. It was used after the elections to discipline by suspension or expulsion some members who failed to hew to the party line.

The party leader always enjoys in fact a more influential position than that outlined in the constitution. He is likely to have the final word as to candidacies and be able to secure the expulsion of those who challenge his leadership. He has the chief voice in defining party policy and determining party strategy. As students of party government have observed in connection with other countries, this is the general tendency. It may well be that a scarcity of well-qualified persons among the elected politicians of the Left parties in these small West Indian colonies has contributed to the towering position usually occupied by the party leader. He may virtually be compelled to decide many questions himself because the consultative bodies provided in the party constitution are not well able to provide quick and correct decisions. Hence the tendency is to ignore these bodies in practice. The annual conference of the Barbados Labour Party has not been convened for several years and the party's policy council, supposed to contain some conference-chosen delegates, has come to consist of the BLP House members only. As the policy committee selects the party candidates, the legislators form a self-renominating group. Adams, of course, can always muster enough support to secure the expulsion of opponents that emerge within the parliamentary delegation. His disciplinary powers are somewhat limited by the fact that certain individual members are popular enough to be elected without BLP designation, and by the absence of party-controlled electoral machinery in the constituencies. Indeed, in 1955, several elected members of the BLP broke with Adams. Four of them along with a man who had been defeated in a bid for the presidency of the Barbados Workers' Union, formed the Democratic Labour Party. The BWU leader, Frank Walcott, who had not been given a ministerial appointment by Adams, also broke away and won election as an independent. The new DLP claimed to be 'democratic socialist' in contrast with the 'dictatorship' of the BLP. The DLP constitution calls for the election of a general council by secret ballot and the choice of the leader by the parliamentary group at every session of the legislature. Its leadership includes some well-known and able politicians such as J. Cameron Tudor, a former president of the Oxford Union, and Errol W. Barrow, a nephew of Duncan O'Neale, founder of the Democratic League. Despite these defections, the BLP was able to capture fifteen out of the twenty-four seats in the 1956 elections.

The usual connection between a West Indian labour party and its supporting union is less formal than that between the British Labour Party and the Trades Union Council. As a rule the union, as such, is not represented directly on party bodies. The connection is maintained by the device of interlocking directorates. Although the revised constitution of the Jamaica Labour Party (1951) provided for BITU representation on both the Island General Council (annual conference) and the Central Executive of the party, the real connection is provided by the autocratic leadership of both party and union by Sir Alexander Bustamante, who is president for life and treasurer of the BITU and leader for life of the JLP.

Although Manley never held office in the union created to provide a base for his party, Nethersole, Glasspole and others of the top leadership in the PNP held all the principal positions in the NWU until they resigned to accept ministerial appointments. Adams was president of the BWU from its founding in 1941 until he became Premier of Barbados in 1953.

THE EXTREME LEFT

Communist and crypto-Communist parties have been unsuccessful in the West Indies with the exception of the Jaganite People's Progressive Party in British Guiana. This contrasts with Communist success in all the French Caribbean Overseas Departments. The PPP victory in British Guiana was due not to the ideology of its leaders but to the fact that these leaders were the first to combine the key appeal of the Left with a thorough party organization in the constituencies, a grass-roots campaign unmatched in the colony's history and the support of the strongest and most active labour unions. Factors contributing to this victory were the energy and enterprise of the PPP leaders, the absence of any other strong party and an over-abundance of weak, independent candidates.

Elsewhere Communist-led parties have fared badly. Even in Trinidad which, like British Guiana, had not seen the development of a colony-wide labour-socialist or labour party, the crypto-Communist West Indies Independence Party in years of effort were unable to acquire any influence with the electorate. Its failure may be explained in part by the relatively high degree of prosperity enjoyed in Trinidad and by inexpert and unimaginative party leadership.

An example of a Communist attempt to capture the leadership of an existing party by a combination of boring-from-within and *coup d'état* tactics, is provided by the history of the Jamaican PNP in the years 1944 to 1951. Following Bustamante's victory in November, 1944, Manley sought to build a labour base for his party as quickly as possible. He asked for and received the co-operation of trades unionists of the extreme Left, both Communists and 'fellow-travellers'. These union leaders and others worked hard and greatly increased the voting power of the party. Indeed, the PNP polled a majority of all votes cast in the 1949 elections although its strength was too heavily concentrated in the Kingston area and only thirteen of its candidates were elected to seventeen of the JLP. Immediately after the elections several of the successful JLP candidates approached Manley with the suggestion that they switch parties and so give him a majority if he would promise them ministerial posts. Manley refused to entertain this politically immoral suggestion and was promptly attacked by his left-wing colleagues as a 'traitor to his party'. The insurgents hoped to win enough rank-and-file support to replace Manley as party leader by Ken Hill, who is said at this time to have been Moscow's choice for British Caribbean leader. The Hill faction had already gained control of the Trades Union Council and had formed several 'paper' party groups, whose dues they paid and who could be depended upon to send obedient delegates to the party conference. By their votes and those of genuine delegates who resented Manley's refusal to welcome the JLP turncoats, they were able to elect a majority of the party executive. At this juncture (December, 1951) Manley ordered a probe of Communist activities in the Trades Union Council after charges had been made by two former Hill henchmen who had broken with the TUC and formed their own union.[1] By convening a special party conference Manley was able to secure backing for the expulsion of Hill and several of his supporters. The National Workers' Union then severed connections with Hill's TUC. Despite the expulsions, Manley's close association with these extremists from 1938 to 1951 gave some appearance of justification to the charge of Communism brought against him and his party by the JLP. This charge may well have cost him some middle-class support. As late as 1953 Bustamante referred to the PNP as . . . 'these Communists or whatever they are'.[2]

After their expulsion the Communist group fell apart. Ken Hill set up a one-man party of his own, concentrating on a racist appeal in his poverty-stricken West Kingston constituency. Richard Hart, another of the expellees, founded the People's Educational Organization to operate both as a study group and a political party co-operating with Ferdinand Smith's Jamaica Federation of Trade Unions and the Caribbean Labour Congress. These labour organizations were not successful in penetrating or undermining the non-Communist unions and Hart's educational efforts were bound to be painfully slow in showing any results. His few students have been semi-literate labourers who lack the educational background needed to grasp Marxist theory.

All parties and movements of the extreme Left in the West Indies have suffered from lack of funds and to some extent, from police

---

[1] The official account of this incident and the advice of the tribunal appointed by Manley as to the expulsion of Arthur Henry, Richard Hart, Ken Hill and Frank Hill, is contained in *PNP News Letter;* 1, 16 (Feb.-March, 1952).

[2] Conversation with the present writer, November 12, 1953.

restrictions and interference. In Jamaica, Hart has been given some help by both American and British Communists. Upon one occasion, at least, a sizeable gift in American currency is known to have been received by the PPP in British Guiana. It is hard to say how much police attentions have inhibited the activities and growth of these parties. In British Guiana, at least, previous police restrictions did not destroy the voting strength of the Jaganite PPP in the 1957 elections.

THE RIGHT

Individual conservatives are able to win election as independents in colonies which still have a weak and inchoate party system, but avowedly conservative parties are in a hopeless case in the West Indies. They can expect votes only from members of the tiny upper class and that part of the middle class not attracted by one of the Left parties. Even in the more prosperous colonies the entire middle class does not include more than ten per cent of the population. Only a crypto-Right party like the Jamaica Labour Party can hope to receive mass support. Non-labour conservative parties can expect opposition status at best. Most of these parties came into existence reluctantly. Their leaders were the heirs of the class that had long dominated both the nominated and elected part of the legislatures when the franchise was restricted, parties were unknown, and electoral victory went to respectable independent candidates. When Left parties began to be successful after the introduction of universal adult suffrage, the conservative independents felt compelled to organize a counter-alliance of some sort lest they disappear from the political scene.

Examples of such parties are the National Party in British Honduras and the Electors' Association in Barbados, now renamed the Progressive Conservative Party. Under a restricted franchise in 1950, the Electors' Association won ten out of twenty-four seats in the House of Assembly, but did poorly under universal suffrage in subsequent elections. Parties of this stripe seem to suffer from a general lack of energy and drive and their leaders from a feeling of frustration. The reasons for this are obvious. They are constantly denying allegations that they represent only the white man and the employer. Their rank-and-file supporters are taunted as tools of the bosses and sometimes are even subjected to intimidation. Paradoxically, these 'rich men's parties' suffer from poverty because the business community, while it may share the party's aims and vote for its candidates, can see little point in wasting money in a lost cause. Many business men prefer to use their political funds to buy the friendship of Left leaders who have a good chance of attaining power.

Another party of the general Right category was the Party of Political Progress Groups, of Trinidad. Its name (like that of the Electors' Association) indicates its original formation as a 'good government' pressure group to support selected independent candidates at a time when the only half-way successful Left party was that led by the labour demagogue Butler. The POPPG had a relatively high proportion of white members and depended chiefly upon urban, middle-class support.[1] It was charged by its opponents with being under the influence of the Roman Catholic Church. After the elections of 1956, in which all nine POPPG candidates were defeated, it joined forces with the People's Democratic Party and the Trinidad Labour Party to form the Democratic Labour Party, as the local branch of the federal party of this name led by Sir Alexander Bustamante.

FEDERAL ELECTION ALLIANCES

The effect of the federal elections of 1958 was to stimulate first, an intercolonial alliance of 'labour-socialist' parties, some of them ideologically Left and others pseudo-Left, demagogic parties, combined as the West Indian Federal Labour Party. This alliance received the official blessing of the British Labour Party delivered personally by its Parliamentary Deputy Leader, James Griffiths. The creation of the FLP led to a counter-move by Bustamante who announced the formation of the Democratic Labour Party as a non-socialist alliance and made an inter-island speaking tour on its behalf.[2] Both new federal parties have reflected the federal idea in their internal organization. They represent alliances of parties rather than unified parties with island branches. Their constitutions provide for the admission of parties rather than individuals and the expulsion of parties that fail to follow the leader in the federal legislature. To begin with, there was no possibility of creating federal parties in any other way than by alliances of existing island parties. Naturally, the scramble to share in the control of the new federal parliament led inevitably to the inclusion in both the FLP and the DLP of parties having little in common except a desire not

[1] According to the secretary of the POPPG, its members in 1955 were 15% of European ancestry, 20% mixed, 60% Negro and 5% others, mainly East Indian and Chinese. This compares with a general population, as of 1946, composed of 2.7% white, 14% coloured, 46.8% Negro, 35% East Indian, 2% other.

[2] For further comment see the present writer's 'Political Aspect of Federation', *Social and Economic Studies*, 6, 2 (June, 1957), 247-261.

to be left out of the federal picture. When a leading party in an island joined one of the new alliances, this led normally to the membership of its opposition party or parties in the rival alliance, ideology playing a minor part.

Federal political issues can crystallize only after a federal government has been in existence for some time. The federal pre-election campaign of 1958 of necessity was fought over local issues and personalities. The only truly federal matter to be discussed at any length was the permanent location of the federal buildings. The PNM in Trinidad insisted upon taking over the leased American base at Chaguaramas and their opponents, the DLP, automatically expressed preference for another location. In other places the PNM's sister parties of the FLP paid little attention to this discussion.

The two rival alliances backed a majority of the one hundred and eight candidates who contested the forty-five seats to be filled by the votes of an electorate of about 1,415,000. The Manley-Adams-Williams axis known as the FLP presented a complete slate of forty-six candidates, one for every seat plus the alternate candidate to be elected in Montserrat. The rival DLP alliance concentrated its efforts with thirty-eight candidates. There were also sixteen independents and eight nominees of local parties in the contest. The tendency of the most experienced politicians to remain in the local arena compelled the choice of a number of candidates who were virtually unknown to the voters. After considerable hesitation Sir Grantley Adams agreed to enter the federal race, the only top party leader to do so. He became at once the obvious FLP choice for Prime Minister. The rival DLP aspirant for this office was generally considered to be Ashford Sinanan of Trinidad.

Pre-election forecasts had predicted a sweep for the FLP alliance but in both big islands the DLP did far better than had been expected, winning by a score of eleven to five in Jamaica and six to four in Trinidad and Tobago. It required the small island vote to give the FLP its majority of twenty-four to nineteen, with one seat in Jamaica still unfilled because of the invalidation of a number of votes in that constituency. A subsequent recount gave the seat to the DLP increasing its strength to twenty. In Trinidad the PNM had retained and even increased its total voting strength since winning the unit elections of 1956, but its vote was too much concentrated in the urban districts and the East Indian vote was almost solidly DLP.

Before the federal legislature assembled there was much speculation about the possible switching of allegiance on the part of certain of the newly elected members, particularly the two from Grenada who are members of Gairy's Grenada United Labour Party. (Gairy himself had been disqualified by law from entering the contest.)

Although elected as FLP candidates they felt that they were in a good position to demand favours as the price of their continued loyalty to the alliance, because their defection and that of one or two others might have enabled the DLP to control the selection of the federal ministry. Sir Grantley Adams charged that various successful candidates had been approached and offered ministries if they would declare for the DLP. In the outcome the two GULP members remained within the FLP fold and one of them secured election to the post of Deputy Speaker. Sir Grantley Adams was chosen Prime Minister by the narrow margin of twenty-five to nineteen votes. He received the support of the single member of the uncommitted Barbados National Party as well as that of one or two others whose permanent allegiance remained doubtful.

PARTY FINANCES

The exact sources of party funds are difficult to establish in many cases. Most rank-and-file members of Left parties are in no position to contribute much if anything on a regular basis. The spending scale of West Indian parties is modest, as will be evident from the description of electioneering techniques given hereafter. Nevertheless, money is needed for office space, typing assistance, loudspeakers, lights and other equipment for street meetings, as well as for the partial support of a party newspaper that cannot pay its own way.

Some ambitious candidates who can afford the luxury will spend considerable sums out of their own pockets to secure election. One is said to make a door-to-door campaign and leave money at every house. The usual custom is to provide several 'sprees' with free food and drink for all who come and are willing to listen to a campaign speech. In the Trinidadian phrase, electioneering consists of 'rum, roti and ranting', 'roti' being a popular local delicacy of East Indian origin. This kind of campaign expense is borne by the candidate himself and its employment is typical of the campaigns of independent politicians.

The larger Left parties all require active members to contribute small sums regularly, ten cents a month in the case of the PNM of Trinidad, but it is said that most members are soon in arrears. In any case the amount raised in this way is never sufficient. All elected members of the Jamaican People's National Party are required to hand over part of their salaries to the party for use in the constituencies. The party leader, N. W. Manley, is said to contribute a large share also of his income as a barrister to the party treasury. The party has a few 'angels' who make contributions from time to time, especially in periods of financial stringency. The PNP, unlike other West Indian parties, has been able from its inception to count upon a sizeable and steady income from sympathizers in the United States. Manley has conducted an annual fund-raising tour in the United States and is said to collect from ten to fifteen thousand dollars per trip, with the aid of the Jamaica Progressive League.

Bustamante claims that he finances the Jamaica Labour Party principally out of his personal funds and that few other contributions and no large ones are received. His political opponents allege that substantial monetary support is given the JLP by Kingston businessmen. Adams's opponents in Barbados also charge that the BLP is in receipt of money from Bridgetown business interests.

Union funds are a principal source of party financing in many cases. Many West Indian union treasurers are notoriously lax bookkeepers. Whether with or without the approval of union members, there can be no doubt that substantial amounts of union money are diverted to personal as well as political uses by many leaders.

The extreme Left, Communist and crypto-Communist, uses similar methods and in addition has received a certain amount of foreign aid, chiefly from the British Communist Party. Literature is supplied free and money gifts are sometimes smuggled in by party couriers in the merchant marine. It was alleged with some supporting evidence although denied by the party, that cash gifts were made to the People's United Party of British Honduras by the Arbenz government of Guatemala. At most, foreign aid is meagre and parties of the extreme Left are poor. Their lower class supporters can contribute little and their chance of attaining power is too remote to attract 'angels'. An exception to this generality is the PPP of British Guiana.

One other source of party funds may be mentioned. At certain times and places pressure may be brought to bear upon businessmen and contributions extracted from them by methods akin to blackmail. This is said to have been done by the PUP in Belize before that party's first electoral victory by the simple threat to have the party members boycott a store if the owner did not subscribe to the party funds.

ELECTIONEERING

All West Indian parties must depend mainly upon the spoken word to spread their message and keep their leaders in the public eye. With an electorate containing a high percentage of illiterates and semi-literates, a small newspaper circulation, and with radio unavailable in many places either because there is none or because the station is government-owned and political time is not for sale, politicians must rely, as they have from the beginning, upon the street meeting as their chief electioneering device.

Although it places a physical strain upon the politicians who must appear and speak, night after night, all year long, the street meeting cannot be neglected. The small size of most of the units makes it possible to reach almost the entire population by this means. Nor is it only the party faithful who are reached. At least a portion of every audience consists of auditors who are present because they cannot afford other entertainment and who enjoy both the music and oratory available without charge at the street meetings. Indeed, a stranger may well be astonished at the capacity of the West Indian crowd not only to endure but actually to enjoy a meeting of three hours' duration with no seats available for the audience. These meetings are held from time to time during the entire year and with increasing frequency as election day approaches. Even when the elections are a distant prospect they are still held because party leaders want to maintain the enthusiasm of their supporters, because only thus can the party attitude be made clear on issues as they arise, and because opposition meetings must be countered.[1]

The typical West Indian political street meeting is held in the evening at a convenient crossroads or in a public park or square. It sometimes opens with prayer. The speakers are always preceded by mass singing. Accompaniment is provided by gramophone records amplified over a public address system and a song leader conducts. Sometimes hymns are sung; often they will be special party songs with new lyrics to an old tune. Until after the expulsion of the extreme Left element, the Jamaican PNP regularly sang 'The Red Flag' at its street meetings. It still employs the clenched fist salute of Popular Front days, during the singing of the party's 'national' anthem: 'Land of Our Birth'.

After a degree of rapport has been established by the mass singing, the speeches begin. There are always several speakers starting with the less important ones and culminating usually with the leader of the party himself. There is more mass singing between speeches and the meeting may conclude with prayer or song or both.

The political street meeting has an extra-political function for many West Indians. It provides a free show for those who cannot afford any other kind. It brings a note of colour and excitement

---

[1] More than a year before a general election, the Jamaica *Gleaner* (issue of November 17, 1953) contained notices of four political street meetings to be held within a two-day period.

into the lives of people who lead a drab existence. It provides not only the emotional release of singing and cheering but helps to create a quasi-society, the party, whose members can feel themselves to be a kind of élite, self-identified with that great man, the party leader. These functions, performed to some degree by political parties everywhere, are especially important in a society like that of the West Indies.

While the spoken word remains the prime means of political persuasion, there are difficulties in connection with its use in some places. In the rural parts of certain colonies the language in common use is not English and not even a creole dialect of English. In some of the Windwards the local dialect is a French patois, poor in vocabulary and expressive only of simple and uncomplicated ideas. To quote the journalist, Adrian Espinet, the crowd at a political meeting in Dominica may well consist of . . . 'illiterates or near illiterates lost in the dark crevices between two broken languages'.[1] The street meeting, then, must rely generally upon a simple, emotive appeal, as was noted earlier in this chapter.

The worship of the leader and hatred of his opponents stimulated at these meetings sometimes produce mob reactions directed against the political 'enemy'. In the earlier stages of the PNP-JLP contest in Jamaica PNP meetings were sometimes broken up with considerable violence. PNP adherents, or those who were assumed to be such because of middle-class appearance, were jostled in the streets by JLP partisans. Bustamante boasted that Manley did not dare to hold a meeting in downtown Kingston. The Jamaican party struggle is comparatively quiet and orderly today but Bustamante himself was howled down recently in Port-of-Spain by a crowd of PNM supporters. Concerted singing of calypsoes and hymns to drown out the speaker and the throwing of rotten eggs disturbed a number of political meetings in Trinidad during the first federal election campaign. It has been charged that not only intimidation but actual murder has punctuated the electoral struggle in Trinidad, especially in the East Indian districts, which some candidates dare not visit without a bodyguard.

Intimidation, disorderly behaviour and the use of violence in West Indian politics at its worst has never approached in scale or organization the systematic destruction of electoral freedom that distinguished the fascist march to power. It might, perhaps, have done so in some colonies had it not been for the presence of police

[1] Trinidad *Sunday Guardian,* August 11th, 1957, p. 22. Creole dialect has evolved from slave-English which dispensed with inflexions, auxiliary verbs, etc., and added new suffixes. It was a *lingua franca* like pidgin English in the Orient. A shop in Belize, closed for inventory, displayed the notice: 'We de tek stok'. This could be understood by its customers.

directed by politically neutral colonial officials. It was to overcome this obstacle that the PPP in Britain Guiana proposed the establishment of a municipal police force under the command of a minister.

The Press is also an instrument of party propaganda of varying value in the several colonies according to the degree of prosperity and literacy they enjoy. Even in the small islands, Left parties consider it worth while to publish a paper, usually a weekly, which serves the dual purpose of union and party organ. The party and the union may thus incur expense for few of these papers are self-supporting. Possibly the prestige value of this medium is sufficient justification for its use, as well as the felt need to challenge in print the big, general newspapers, most of which are likely to take a rather conservative editorial line and which fail to give adequate coverage, from the standpoint of the Left parties, to the activities and pronouncements of their leaders. The Jamaican PNP uses both a party newsletter sent to all its branches as well as the weekly newspaper, *Public Opinion*. In British Guiana the PPP had a wide circulation for its little paper, *Thunder,* which was sent to all party members. This gave currency to issues of international Communist interest as well as the local struggle and familiarized the party faithful with the Communist vocabulary. It reached many villagers who seldom saw the Georgetown newspapers. Broadly speaking, however, the printed word is much less important in the West Indies than the spoken message in its effect upon political behaviour. There is little pamphleteering although, of course, party manifestoes are often printed in pamphlet form and distributed.

NON-PARTY GROUPS

Political parties sometimes represent the extension into the electoral field of power conflicts between groups distinguished from each other by race, tribe, caste, religion or some other characteristic. This situation is sure to occur in a plural society and it contains obvious threats to the successful operation of a representative democracy. Rigid political communalism, if co-extensive with the electorate, will inhibit the formation of secular parties. Success in politics will depend upon reflecting exactly the communal interests and prejudices. Compromise is rendered difficult and relative party strength may be frozen for long periods because a party can grow only with an increase in the size of the community upon which it is based. In such a case the government formed by one or a coalition of two or more of these communal parties may not be able to meet the challenge of urgent social problems and a breakdown of representative government may occur because the legislators and executives are prevented by communal loyalties from attacking the problems in commonsense fashion.

Fortunately, West Indian social communalism has not resulted in such extreme political manifestations. Despite the history of group antagonism between the coloured middle class and the black working class, black political communalism did not develop to a serious extent largely because of the successful self-identification of middle-class, coloured politicians with the emergent labour parties from the beginning. This forestalled any significant black political communalism directed against the large coloured minority. Nor did racial communalism develop against the small white minority. The general disappearance of the whites from the electoral arena rendered this unnecessary. White exclusion from party politics has been due not to black communalism but rather to voluntary withdrawal and to the inability of the Negro voter, whose vote is indispensable in most constituencies, to believe that a white candidate can possibly identify himself sincerely with the working class or truly understand its problems. Whites have been successful in certain territories, Trinidad, Barbados and Dominica for example, when their association with the labour movement has denied the assumption that they would display class or colour bias. Indeed, the general admiration of upper-class, white standards of speech, education, dress and manners may have worked to the advantage of both coloured and white politicians. Certainly, fanatical black racism has developed only sporadically and usually quite apart from politics. It has not been the basis of successful political appeals.

Negro tribalism is non-existent. It is now too far in their background to influence politically even the small number of Negroes who came to the islands in the post-emancipation period when there was no deliberate de-tribalization policy. Even in their case the dominant European culture overshadows West African culture except in some aspects of music, dancing, folklore, magic and religion.[1]

Only in the case of the East Indians is there a tendency to act politically, to a significant degree, in terms of racial and religious communalism. This East Indian communalism is important only in the colonies of Trinidad and British Guiana where East Indians compose about half the population. Even here there is no party that openly avows a communal identification. Leaders who have worked hard to establish this identification, such as Bhadase Sagan Maraj in Trinidad, have always been careful to include candidates

[1] See J. G. Moore and George E. Simpson, 'A Comparative Study of Acculturation in Morant Bay and West Kingston, Jamaica, *Zaire* Vol. 11 (Louvain, 1957) 979-1019, and Vol 12 (1958) 65-87.

of other racial backgrounds in the party list. That East Indian voters vote 'East Indian' cannot be denied. The strength of East Indian communalism in Trinidad is the obvious explanation for the failure of the victorious People's National Movement to win rural seats in the 1956 elections. Maraj's People's Democratic Party won five seats: all three in Caroni County where the populuation is predominantly East Indian, one in Victoria and the other in St Patrick. Only one of the PNM victories could be said to have been gained in a purely rural constituency, Ortoire-Moruga.[1]

Purely religious affiliations, not involving race, are not of much political significance in the West Indies. People in general are religious and politicians are careful to maintain a respectful attitude towards religion but religious leadership has not, as a rule, provided entry to a political career. As might be expected, bishops and clergy of both the Church of England and the Roman Catholic Church have tried sometimes to influence the political behaviour of the faithful. The Anglican Bishop of Barbados has always been a member of the nominated Legislative Council. The clergy have not engaged in active electioneering but in 1956 the Roman Catholic Archbishop of Trinidad spoke publicly in favour of the election of independents as opposed to party candidates and so, by clear implication, opposed the PNM whose slogan was 'vote the party'. Evidently the Archbishop's advice was ignored by many Roman Catholic voters.

Apart from direct electoral advice by the clergy there are some parties which are said to be under clerical influence. As noted earlier, this was alleged of the Party of Political Progress Groups in Trinidad. The allegation seems mainly to have been based upon the fact that many of the party's leading figures were of the Roman Catholic faith. In British Honduras the education of the great majority is provided by Jesuit schools and as a result of Jesuit missionary activities the bulk of the population is now Roman Catholic. Political leaders of all kinds belong to this faith. The original programme of the victorious People's United Party was based upon Roman Catholic doctrine in its declared opposition to lay schools and birth control. At the same time there would seem to be no evidence of direct clerical control of PUP politicians and the latter deny that they ask for or accept clerical advice in political

[1] Professor Gordon Lewis of Puerto Rico, in an article in the Jamaica *Daily Gleaner,* issue of January 7, 1957, argued that the East Indians obviously did not all vote communally and certainly did not vote as a racist bloc in the Trinidad elections of 1956, as evidenced by the PNM poll of about one-third of the votes cast in the Caroni constituencies. Thomas Wright in the *Daily Gleaner,* January 14, 1957, asserted that some religious communalism was involved, the Christian and Muslim East Indians tending to support the PNM and the Hindus, the PDP.

matters. Doubtless their piety would operate to prevent their embracing policies in any way contrary to Roman Catholic doctrine. In Jamaica where the Roman Catholic Church is not strong numerically, Father Feeny of Catholic Action was instrumental in the founding of a party to contest the 1944 elections. This was the Jamaica Democratic Party and its president was Abe Issa, Kingston's most prominent businessman. In the elections of 1944 all the JDP candidates forfeited their deposits and it is the general belief that the party had never been intended as a serious contender for victory but was a device to attract some middle-class votes away from the PNP in order to assist the JLP to win. The party dissolved after the elections. In St Lucia, with a population about ninety-three per cent Roman Catholic, the principal legislative leader of the St Lucia Labour Party, John Compton, is said not to have been given a ministerial portfolio because he is 'persona non grata with the Catholic Church'.[1]

Despite the strongly religious element in East Indian communalism there is no evidence that Hindu pandits have been influential with East Indian politicians or have tried to acquire anything like the political importance of Buddhist monks in some Southeast Asian countries or Muslim scholars in Pakistan. It is claimed, however, that some Trinidadian pandits have urged their congregations to support a particular party or candidate either out of conviction or in return for a money gift from the candidate.

The leaders of the lower-class cults, Revival Zionist, 'Pocomania', Shango, 'Shouter' and the rest (derived from a mixture of Christianity and West African polytheism and magic) rarely are active politically. Indeed, as George E. Simpson points out, these cults represent a withdrawal from society, which is found to be unsatisfactory, and the creation of a new society with its own peculiar hierarchy in which lower-class members can enjoy status and which is directed towards the after-life. In the course of studying these groups over a period of several months Simpson encountered only one example of partisan activity by a Pocomania pastor.[2] Even if their orientation were not so completely otherworldly these cults could not form a satisfactory base for a party or political movement because they are totally lacking in intergroup organization, even as regards those of identical doctrine and liturgy.

[1] Despatch in Trinidad Sunday Guardian, April 14, 1957.
[2] George E. Simpson, 'Jamaican Revivalist Cults', Social and Economic Studies, 5, 4 (Dec., 1956), 372, 373.

FEDERAL PARTIES

One of the agreements reached at the London Conference of February, 1956, was that the first elections for the new federal House of Assembly should be held in 1958. During the conference itself some of the West Indian party leaders began conversations regarding a possible federal election alliance. A meeting in Barbados in June, 1956, of the Standing Federation Committee provided another opportunity for the island leaders to continue the discussion. They met between sessions of the Federation Committee and on June 14th statements were issued announcing the creation of a federation of socialist parties jointly sponsored by N. W. Manley (PNP, Jamaica), Grantley Adams (BLP, Barbados), V. C. Bird (ALP, Antigua), R. L. Bradshaw and J. N. France (St Kitts Workers' League), E. M. Gairy (GLP, Grenada), Carl LaCorbinière (St L. LP, St Lucia), and W. H. Bramble (Montserrat Trades and Labour Union). Subsequently this federation adopted the designation of West Indian Federal Labour Party. It remains, however, a federation rather than a party. Its members are not individual voters but parties and despite the 'socialist' label there is little in common between some of the member parties.

It is far from clear as to the amount of control that can be exercised over this grouping of parties by Manley as leader. Manley's decision to remain as Chief Minister of Jamaica and not to contest a federal seat, resulting in the choice of Sir Grantley Adams as first Prime Minister of the West Indies, is a further complication of leadership. Mr Manley remains president of the party and any serious differences between Manley and Adams might split the party into its island components. As Prime Minister, Adams will be in a position analogous to that of a weak, mediaeval king in relation to a powerful and independent baronage whose actions he is unable to control because the 'barons' cannot be dislodged from their island strongholds by the disfavour of the 'monarch'. The WIFLP will have to be held together chiefly by the favours that the leader can bestow such as ministerial and other appointments.[1] It is not so much a party as a pre-election alliance of the kind formed by independent candidates in the various colonies in the days before a real party system had developed.

The alliance thrown together to oppose the WIFLP represents an even more heterogeneous grouping of parties. Known as the Democratic Labour Party of the West Indies, it is headed by

[1] Some of these comments have appeared previously in the present writer's 'Political Aspects of Federation', *Social and Economic Studies*, 6, 2, June, 1957, 247-261.

Manley's ancient rival, Sir Alexander Bustamante. Its provisional constitution permits individual citizens to join by pledging allegiance to the party and vowing that they are not 'Socialists, Communists or Fascists'. Parties and other organizations such as trades unions may become affiliate members. In fact, of course, the DLP is also an alliance of parties. It claims to be anti-socialist and opposed to 'undue' encroachment of federal powers over the units. In addition to Bustamante, who visited Trinidad in April, 1957, to launch the party, its prominent figures include Albert Gomes and Bhadase Maraj of Trinidad and E. T. Joshua, labour leader of St Vincent. It is obvious that these leaders and the rest of the UDP leadership have little in common beyond their opposition to the parties and leaders of the FLP, Manley, Adams, Williams and others.

Clearly, the formation of genuine federal parties must await the actual operation and growth of federal government. If the federal government should become the principal location of political power in the West Indies there can be no doubt that federal parties will develop, the unit branches of such parties being not only ostensibly but practically subordinate to the federation-wide organization and leadership as in Canada, Australia and other federal systems with the parliamentary form of government. But the development of these truly national parties cannot occur in advance of the need to deal with actual federal problems. To begin with the federal ministry had to rely upon an alliance of unit parties and leaders and so long as the real basis of party strength and organization remains tied to the government and politics of the unit, party leaders will hesitate to abandon the local for the federal arena. To do so, especially in the case of parties held together by a single personality, is to encourage the rise of rival leaders and divisions within the party. It was generally necessary, therefore, to find a second team of candidates to contest the federal seats while the leader and his principal lieutenants continued to hold the fort at home. One reason probably for the federal defeat in Trinidad of the PNM was the fact that its second string consisted largely of untried and unknown candidates opposed by experienced politicians who had been defeated in the local PNM victory of 1956.

Sir Grantley Adams provides the exception to this general rule. In his case the risk may have seemed worth taking for several reasons. In Manley's absence he was virtually certain to become Prime Minister. The recent disaffection of his party's 'left wing', long threatened, had taken place without dislodging him from office in Barbados, so that he might be able to count upon a breathing spell of relative harmony within the BLP. Finally, the close proximity of Barbados and Trinidad would allow him to visit his home base frequently and keep in close touch with island party affairs.

SUMMARY AND CONCLUSIONS

Secular, institutionalized parties on the British model are not yet fully developed in the West Indies although there are indications that this is in process of accomplishment in Jamaica and other places.

Party leadership is almost totally charismatic in the case of the one-man, pseudo-Left parties and less so as regards other parties, both conservative and ideologically Left. Leaders representing the old colonial traditions and values have been eliminated, or nearly so, from elective politics and have tended to withdraw from party activity. Left party leaders are more rational, pragmatic and compromising in their policies in office than the over-simple, emotional appeal of the hustings would indicate. The pressures producing compromise are exerted by the official side and by business, agricultural and other special interests. Pressures are exerted by arguments and persuasion employed by officials in Executive Council meetings and in the daily contacts in connection with departmental business, by the social lobby which subtly identifies the politician with the upper class and sometimes by the purchase of good will by the representatives of special interests.

Left party leaders are usually either middle-class, coloured men of good, professional education (Manley, Adams, Williams), or coloured and Negro labour leaders who have entered politics by way of agitational union activities (Butler, Bradshaw, Joshua, Gairy). The achievement of political leadership is not dependent upon the class of the leader nor does the electorate display anti-intellectual prejudice. West Indian social mobility has been accelerated by the political results of universal suffrage, including the vaulting of the colour-class barrier by Negroes.

In the early stages, when the party system is still inchoate, 'parties' may be little more than the name invented by a candidate to designate his followers or the name of an election alliance entered into by several independent candidates. These pseudo-parties are temporary election devices and perform no aggregative function. Candidates and parties flirt coyly with each other almost up to election eve. Some candidates ride the coat-tails of a charismatic leader into the legislature and then resign from his party or refuse to accept party discipline. All candidates pay lip service to the key objectives but few present a concrete programme for their accomplishment. They reflect the fragmented nature of West Indian society, its low degree of secularization and its weak and diffuse loyalties. The continued existence of quasi- and pseudo-parties along with a large number of independents almost compels the voter to choose between them according to some non-party criterion such as race, religion or personality, and militates against the rise of genuine parties.

A serious weakness of these temporary parties and of independent candidates lies in their inability to build a permanent organization through lack of money or jobs to support a machine. This is the reason why the few parties that have shown the ability to survive electoral defeat have been allied with labour unions which do possess permanent organizations and funds. Well-led parties that manage to organize at the constituency level can usually defeat the pseudo-parties and all but the strongest independents. But even in such cases, the leader is usually indispensable to the party's success. His overwhelming importance may well dispose him to manage the party autocratically in disregard of the party's official constitution. He is further constrained to behave autocratically because he can seldom be sure of the loyalty of all of his lieutenants, some of whom may be awaiting a favourable opportunity to supplant him. He therefore tends to discourage the advance of secondary leaders whose popular appeal might come to rival his own and to pick his ministerial team from among the less active and ambitious of his supporters. This may tend to discourage and disappoint the ablest lieutenants and induce them to break away and found splinter parties. It also works to prevent the institutionalization of his party which remains dependent upon and identified with his personal leadership and may disintegrate when he leaves the political scene.

Great political parties are slow to develop. They require not only time and history but a degree of political sophistication on the part of their active members which is still rare among West Indian partisans. They also require, on the part of the leaders and legislative delegation, an understanding and respect for the usages of parliamentary democracy, along with the self-restraint and public responsibility these usages imply. Constitutional advances have come thick and fast in the past fifteen years of West Indian history but many West Indian politicians have also gained substantially in maturity during this same period. If party organization is still often sketchy, party objectives less than crystal clear and party leadership still sometimes irresponsible, it remains a fact that the fears of the colonial conservative have not been realized. Since the general adoption of universal adult suffrage both voters and politicians have learned a great deal about the operation of representative democracy. It is not unduly optimistic to foresee a steady development of stable, responsible, effective party government in the West Indies.

CHAPTER X

FEDERATION

THE idea that administrative economies and internal advantages might flow from a federation of the West Indies is a very old one. Indeed the Leeward Islands were first federated in the reign of Queen Anne and this federation lasted from 1705 until 1798. The Wood Report mentioned federation as advantageous but impossible at the moment because not backed by public opinion. In 1929 the unofficial members of the Legislative and Executive Councils of Antigua petitioned the Secretary of State to consider the possibility of combining all of the British islands of the Eastern Caribbean, from St Kitts to Trinidad under a single Governor and legislature with local government organs for the individual islands. In 1930 the West Indian Sugar Commission proposed an administrative union of the Leewards and Windwards.[1] The Secretary of State for the Colonies, Lord Passfield, proposed the appointment of a Commission to investigate these proposals. This was done in 1932 and the Commission's report favoured a common Governor for the Leewards and Windwards but the retention of substantial autonomy by the several units. This was to be a tentative step towards a wider and more complete federation.[2] This scheme was not carried out because of the consideration that a federation of the small islands would increase rather than cut expenses and because Trinidad was strongly opposed to any kind of union with these poverty-stricken territories. Lord Swinton, then Secretary of State, decided to drop the matter. But the idea of a West Indian nation was not entirely defunct. It had a strong attraction for many politically conscious West Indians as the Moyne Commission discovered during its tour of the area in 1938 and 1939. Their report, therefore, expressed the opinion that an eventual union of all British Caribbean possessions should remain an ideal goal of policies.[3] The Moyne Report also noted that mere economy in administration was not the only factor to be considered. It suggested as a first step the enlargement of the Leeward federation to include the Windwards. This suggestion

[1] *Report of the West Indian Sugar Commission*, Cmd. 31517 (1930).
[2] *West Indies Report of the Closer Union Commission*, Cmd. 4383 (1933).
[3] *West Indian Royal Commission Report*, 1938-1939, Cmd. 6607 (1945).

again foundered because of local disagreements about customs duties and other matters.

Despite the obstacles in the way of political amalgamation individuals and institutions in the several colonies were glad to meet and discuss their common objectives and problems. The Development and Welfare Organization created in 1940, largely as an outcome of the Moyne Report, convened a member of intercolonial conferences to consider area problems and sometimes to devise a co-operative attack upon them. Regional co-operation was furthered also by the activities of the Caribbean Commission, first established as the Anglo-American Caribbean Commission in 1942 by Great Britain and the United States to study regional problems. This body was joined in 1945 by France and the Netherlands, the two other Caribbean powers. Because it was the creature of the metropolitan powers it remained largely outside of the political developments in the colonies and was not considered by the local governments as an organ of theirs. Nevertheless its Research Council (established in August, 1943) did provide them with useful information and its West Indian Conferences (established in January, 1944) were especially significant in aiding the growth of a West Indian community. These conferences, meeting at least biennially, are attended by two representatives from each colonial unit. The decisions arrived at, although advisory only, have resulted in action by the Commission and sometimes by the metropolitan governments. The conferences provided a forum for Caribbean debates and decisions on area matters by intercolonial agreement.[1]

Of greater significance as a pre-federal institution was the Regional Economic Committee created as a result of a resolution passed by the Montego Bay Conference. The REC was established by an instrument adopted by the several colonial governments in 1951. Its deputy chairman was the Economic Adviser to the Comptroller for Development and Welfare (Professor Beasley) and its members are representatives of ministerial or comparable rank from the various governments. Its chief concern has been with the Trade Commissioners in Canada and Great Britain, economic surveys, inter-island shipping, air services, local borrowing and other problems assigned to it by the member governments. It was a body of politicians rather than civil servants or experts and its meetings at times reflected this fact. Inconclusive debates, the intrusion of local selfishness and 'politics', led to Press criticism of the

[1] See annual reports of the Caribbean Commission, published since 1943, and R. T. Bunche, 'The Anglo-American Caribbean Commission: An Experiment in Regional Cooperation'. American Council Paper No. 7, 9th Conference of the Institute of Pacific Relations (Jan. 1945).

REC. In fact, however, it was a valuable training ground for federal politics. It helped the island politicians to become better acquainted and accustomed to the problems and processes of intercolonial debate and co-operation.[1]

Another local move in the direction of federation was taken by the Caribbean Labour Congress, founded in Barbados in September, 1945, which held its first important conference in Jamaica in September, 1947. Of the thirty-four delegates from fifteen colonial units, twenty-seven were officials of trades unions and labour parties. This meeting of the Congress passed resolutions advocating a Caribbean federation with Dominion status based upon units with full responsible government. This was contemporaneous with the Montego Bay Conference and intended to influence its deliberations.

By the end of World War II the British government had decided to press for West Indian federation as vigorously as West Indian opinion would permit. The reasons for this decision are obvious enough. It is plain that with rare exceptions these little colonies could never hope to attain economic self-sufficiency or any meaningful degree of international status. United, they might just be able to reach this goal. It was, on the other hand, unthinkable that they should remain Crown Colonies forever. Even if it were practical from any point of view for the Overseas Service to retain the sovereign powers of final decision and to use as much force as necessary to repress the manifestations of a growing local nationalism, the resulting disorders and the political repercussions in Great Britain and other countries would render inconceivable any such policy. This being the case, the British government was faced with the problem of overseeing the development of West Indian self-government in orderly fashion and the encouragement of an eventual West Indian state and nation which might in due course take its place among the Commonwealth Countries. The chief difficulties were created by population pressures and poverty. Unlike Ghana, many of these colonies have not paid their own way in many years. In 1952-53, for example, not a single West Indian colony was able to balance 'true' revenue and 'true' expenditure. The total deficit for the area was approximately $BWI 8,725,999. All had an adverse balance of trade which, however, was almost entirely offset by CD & W grants of $BWI 8,391,000.[2] The local indifference and actual opposition to federation has been due in large part to this economic situation. The fear that federation would mean

[1] An evaluation of the REC is contained in Lloyd Braithwaite, 'Progress Towards Federation, 1938-1956', *Social and Economic Studies* 6, 2 (June, 1957) 166 ff.
[2] 'Financial Aspects of Federation of the BWI Territories', Colonial Development and Welfare Organization, January 1953.

the loss of British grants and at the same time throw the burden of the poorer colonies upon the more prosperous ones has been expressed time and again. It was not until assurances were given that British assistance would not cease with the beginning of federation that some West Indians were won over to its acceptance.

The Secretary of State for the Colonies, Oliver Stanley, sent a dispatch to the West Indian governments in 1945 urging further consideration of federation. All the recipients of this dispatch except the Bahamas agreed to the proposal which was renewed in 1947 by Stanley's successor as Secretary of State, Arthur Creech Jones. Accordingly, the first of the steps that were to result in the achievement of federation was taken at the Conference held at Montego Bay, Jamaica, from September 11 to 19, 1947. All the West Indian colonies were represented by delegates chosen by the legislatures accompanied by the legal and financial officials. All possible views were aired at this conference which was presided over by the Secretary of State, himself. Several delegates thought federation should not be considered until the economy of the area had been improved. Bustamante demanded local gains in self-government as a more pressing need. He objected to the idea of advanced Jamaica associating with politically backward colonies. Gomes advocated federation and self-government throughout simultaneously. Adams favoured federation with immediate Dominion status of the pre-1931 variety. V. C. Bird of Antigua was strongly in favour of federation as permitting economic improvements through regional planning. In general, the small island delegates were pro-federation. Manley differed sharply with Bustamante and noted a growth in federal sentiment corresponding to the proliferation of inter-colonial consultative bodies. Eventually the conference accepted the general desirability of a federation on the Australian model with residual powers in the units. It also recommended the creation of a Standing Closer Association Committee of delegates from the colonial legislatures and a chairman and secretary to be appointed by the Secretary of State. This Committee should consider fiscal and tariff policies, the unification of currency and other matters including the details of the federal constitution. The British Guiana delegation alone would not accept federation in principle.[1] Subsequently the Regional Economic Committee was established as well as Trade Commissioners in Canada and Great Britain. The federal idea may also have received impetus with the opening of the University College of the West Indies at Mona, Jamaica in

[1] Conference on the Closer Association of the British West Indian Colonies, Montego Bay, Part I, Cmd. 7291 (1948); ibid., Part II, *Proceedings,* Col. No. 218, 1948.

October, 1948, with a student body drawn from all over the West Indies.

The Standing Closer Association Committee began its meetings in November, 1948, and presented its report in October, 1949[1] The Report contained a detailed plan of a federal constitution along with the reasoning which led to the adoption by the Committee of the various provisions. It was discussed by the several colonial legislatures over a period of two years and eventually accepted in principle by all except the two mainland colonies and the British Virgin Islands, one of the Leeward Presidencies.

The proposed constitution would provide a strictly limited amount of central authority, the residual powers remaining with the units. It would appear that a weak federation was considered the optimum obtainable in view of the strong local loyalties and intercolonial suspicion and jealousy. The Report contained a hint that its authors recognized this fact and were leaving it to future changes in the allocation of powers to remedy the initial lack of central authority.[2]

The Report advocated a bicameral legislature, the primary chamber elected by universal adult suffrage which by now was in use in the larger islands and was probably soon to become universal or nearly so in the rest. The second chamber, however, was to embody the nominated principle, because all powers should not belong to a single elected chamber. To have two elected chambers would place the chambers in possible opposition and with equal claims to represent the people. A nominated body would be revisionary, advisory and in the final analysis, subordinate to the popular chamber. These arguments may be taken at face value or it may be that they represent a rationalization of the old colonial office attitude of caution and reluctance to trust West Indian popular government without the safeguard of legislators chosen by the Governor. In the more primitive systems these nominees sit as part of a unicameral legislature. In the more advanced forms they are segregated in their own chamber as in Jamaica and Barbados. But this feature of the federal constitution seemed to some West Indians to smack of the Crown Colony writ large even though Canada could be cited as offering a Dominion example.

The allocation of seats in the elected chamber proved to be a difficult problem. In the end no precise mathematical formula was used to derive the number of members from population statistics. The assignment contained an element of the arbitrary.

[1] *Report of the British Caribbean Standing Closer Association Committee,* 1948-49. Col. No. 255, 1950. (The Rance Report).
[2] Col. No. 255, 255, para. 38.

The Council of State or executive authority reflected the Crown Colony principles employed in Executive Councils of an advanced type. Eight members would be appointed on the nomination of the Prime Minister but the other six would be named by the Governor General, three being officials. Furthermore, the Governor General would also retain the power to reserve for the approval of the British government all bills relating to defence and all bills repugnant to any future Order in Council relating to the federation in a number of matters including internal and external public safety and the financial stability of the federation.

This was still, therefore, a Crown Colony constitution of an advanced type but slightly less advanced than the constitutions now in force in some of the territories.

The next step was taken once again upon the initiative of the Secretary of State who convened a conference of West Indian leaders in London in April, 1953. In the meantime all the colonial governments except those of the two mainland colonies had accepted the Rance Report in principle, so these colonies sent observers rather than delegates to the London Conference. Meetings were held for more than two weeks, April 13th to 30th, and the result was a plan for federation amending the Rance Report plan in several respects. Among the more significant changes was the assignment of government borrowing and income tax to the list of concurrent powers, even though it was provided that no income tax might be collected by the federal government for the first five years of its existence. A strong assertion was placed in the preamble to the effect that the federation should encourage the greatest possible freedom of movement of people and things. The subject of 'immigration, emigration and deportation' was put in the list of exclusive federal powers and was provided that this legislative power might not be used to restrict the movement of West Indian nationals on economic grounds. A Trinidad representative objected vigorously to these allocations of power because his colony had long been a mecca for unemployed Barbadians and Grenadians who could be excluded or admitted conditionally under existing Trinidadian law. This difference had to be resolved at another conference. The Rance Report had recommended that members of local legislatures should not be eligible to sit in the federal chambers. This was reversed by the 1953 Conference only to be restored by the 1956 Conference. The two other matters of importance decided in 1953 concerned the agreement of the British government to continue to supply needed financial assistance through the federal government which would allocate it to the units. It was provided, however, that if the original aid given was insufficient more would be forthcoming only upon conditions of Treasury control. At the same time the Secretary of State offered a gratuity of £500,000 towards the cost of establishing the federal capital. Finally, it was agreed that the Rance Report had made insufficient provision for constitutional amendment, leaving that matter to be handled by Order in Council just as the constitution itself would be created. It was felt that this might produce the kind of stalemate found in Canada, where differences between the federal and provincial governments as to proposed amendments have prevented action altogether because the British amending authority will hesitate to act unless there is substantial unanimity of demand. It was provided, therefore, that there would be no constitutional changes for the first five years and then a constitutional convention would be called to consider revisions. Thereafter changes would be made by a two-thirds majority in the House of Representatives and the approval of at least six unit legislatures by a similar majority, followed by reference to the British government.

The London plan was debated and accepted in the island legislatures but not everywhere with enthusiasm or heavy majorities. In Trinidad the large East Indian minority remained fearful of a political union which would place them in a permanent minority position. The Trinidad legislature voted on the federation scheme on December 12, 1954. It was favoured by the three ex-officio members, the four nominated members, three ministers and five other elected members. Against it were six elected members (four being East Indians and two members of the Butler party). Three East Indian members did not vote, one of whom was presiding as Deputy Speaker and another a minister who had been informed that he must resign his portfolio if he opposed the plan.

The differences between the units on freedom of movement, with Trinidad hesitant about it and Barbados insistent upon it, were resolved at a conference on this subject alone held in Port-of-Spain, Trinidad.[1] The Trinidadians at this conference showed a willingness to compromise. The local prejudice against 'small islanders' was not strong enough to justify intransigence and the possible collapse of the plan for federation.[2] It was agreed that immigration

[1] *Report of the Conference on Movement of Persons within the British Caribbean Federation.* Col. No. 315 (1955).
[2] This prejudice was strongest, probably, during the wartime rush to Trinidad to work on the construction of the American bases, at which time a calypsonian expressed the feelings of the Trinidad working class in this lyric :
   Small island, go back where you really come from,
   Small island, go back where you really come from,
   You come Trinidad in a fishing boat
   And now you wearin' a Saga coat!
   Small island, go back where you really come from.

restrictions based on health and security precautions would remain in the hands of the unit governments but that restrictions on any other grounds would fall within the concurrent powers and that after five years the federal legislature would have veto power over unit immigration legislation.

Further preparatory work was done by commissioners appointed by the Secretary of State to report on civil service, fiscal and judicial problems. These reports had to be tentative in some respects because although the main lines of power allocation were established, the precise need for particular administrative agencies for example, would have to await the actual functioning of federation to see whether or not the federal government chose to legislate in all the fields covered by the concurrent powers.[1]

It was now time to take the final step before the actual launching of the federation. Once again the Secretary of State called a London Conference. His opening speech emphasized two considerations: that full Dominion status could not be hoped for by any single West Indian territory (this aroused some resentment in Jamaica) and that the British government realized fully that financial assistance would need to be given to the West Indian federation for some time to come. The freedom of movement issue being out of the way the big issue now was customs union, two other minor but difficult ones being the degree of independence the federation should enjoy from the Colonial Office and the site of the federal capital. The Jamaican delegation, headed by N. W. Manley, was the most aggressive and persistent in its demands for two changes: that colonial status should be ended regardless of any continuing need for financial assistance and that the proposed Council of State should have no official members. The Secretary of State agreed in principle with the divorce of financial aid and colonial status, noting the essential economic interdependence of all modern states and citing the Colombo Plan as a possible model for future action in the West Indies. The democratization of the constitution was agreed to as well. The three ex-officio officials in the Council of State were replaced by three nominated officials who would be present at Council meetings as advisers without a vote. The Prime Minister also would be empowered to pick the three Senators on the Council of State. As to the nominated principle in the Senate itself, there was the further provision that in making his nominations the Governor General should consult the unit legislatures in advance.

[1] The Plan for a British Caribbean Federation. Report of the Fiscal Commissioner, Cmd. 9618 (1955); Ibid., Report of the Civil Service Commissioner, Cmd. 9619 (1955); Ibid., Report of the Judicial Commissioner, Cmd. 9620 (1955).

The antagonists on the customs union issue were Trinidad and Jamaica. The former was not greatly dependent upon customs duties for its income which were derived largely from oil royalties and company income taxes and it was beginning to enjoy a measure of industrialization with a potential export market not only in the small islands of the Eastern Group but also in South America. It was, therefore, strongly in favour of free trade. Jamaica, with few possible export markets for manufactures, a larger internal market and its few industries existing only because of the tariff wall or even a complete embargo on imports (as in the case of rum and until recently of matches), and an income depending heavily upon customs duties, was strongly protectionist. Once more the solution was found in an agreement in principle and a postponement of its realization. Jamaica agreed to accept the ultimate desirability of free trade and to the inclusion of a statement of this objective in the preamble, with final decision as to details to await the report of a Commission on Trade and Tariffs. Another commission composed entirely of non-West Indians was entrusted with advising on the ticklish issue of the federal capital site, final decision to remain with the Standing Federation Committee composed in the same way as the Conference and to remain in being until federation should be a reality.[1]

This Standing Federation Committee assembled in Jamaica in January, 1957, and devoted its time chiefly to a discussion of the capital site. It is possible that no committee of outsiders or West Indians could have produced recommendations on this subject that would not have aroused resentment in many quarters. In any case the Site Commission managed to annoy a large number of West Indians. Their animadversions on Trinidadian politics, their references to East Indian communalism, their preference for the most British of the islands Barbados, known elsewhere as 'Bimshire' (the white man's county), their references to tropical heat, all irritated the West Indians. In the end the Committee chose Trinidad, which had been the Site Commission's third choice.[2] West Indian nationalism was also insulted by the appointment of an Englishman to the post of Chief Justice of the Supreme Court in view of the fact that for many years the principal judicial posts in the West Indies had been held by West Indians some of whom were men of outstanding judicial attainments. A small triumph of local nationalism was the decision to abandon the designation of 'British

[1] *Report of the Conference on British Caribbean Federation*, Cmd. 9733 (1956).
[2] British Caribbean Federal Capital Commission Report, Col. No. 328, 1956.

Caribbean Federation' in favour of 'the West Indies'.

The necessary Act of Parliament empowering the establishment of the federation by Order in Council was passed on August 2, 1956, and the Order in Council itself in 1957.[1] According to the Act, the Order-in-Council had to be laid before Parliament before going into effect. This was done in July, 1957, and it was approved without amendment.

The first Governor General, Lord Hailes, was appointed as of October 1, 1957.[2] He arrived in the West Indies in January, 1958, and his first duty was to fix the date for federal elections. The choice of Lord Hailes as Governor General did not arouse much enthusiasm either in Great Britain or the West Indies. A relatively minor Conservative politician, his most important previous post had been that of Chief Whip of his party in the House of Commons.

The preamble of the constitution pays homage to the principles of religious freedom, freedom of movement of persons and goods within the federation and the desirability of establishing as soon as possible a customs union and internal free trade.

The federation to be known simply as the West Indies, consists of the following units: Antigua, Barbados, Dominica, Grenada, Jamaica, Montserrat, St Christopher, together with Nevis and Anguilla, St Lucia, St Vincent, and Trinidad and Tobago. It is provided that British Honduras and British Guiana may enter the federation if they so desire.

The federal legislature is bicameral, the Senate having nineteen members, two appointed by the Governor General from each territory except Montserrat which has one. In making these appointments the Governor General acts on the advice of the unit Governors who normally accept the advice of their ministers.[3]

The House of Representatives has forty-five members: seventeen from Jamaica, ten from Trinidad and Tobago, five from Barbados, two from each of the others except Montserrat which has one voting member and a non-voting alternate. All are elected by universal adult suffrage. Small units with two seats to fill use the entire

[1] British Caribbean Federation Act, 1956.
[2] Appointed by the Sovereign under Sign Manual and Signet to hold office during the royal pleasure and act according to Royal Instructions and the law.
[3] Following the first federal election Sir Alexander Bustamante protested to the Governor of Jamaica, Sir Kenneth Blackburne, against any recommendations for federal Senators from Jamaica being made before the elected government had been formed in the federal legislature. The Governor replied that he was bound to accept the advice of his Council of Ministers (headed by Bustamante's opponent, Manley) . . .'unless he was of the opinion that he should act contrary to that advice'. See Trinidad *Sunday Guardian*, March 30, 1958, p. 2.

territory as a two-member constituency. Barbados also operates as a five-member constituency. Both Trinidad and Jamaica were divided into voting districts. In Trinidad these are single-member districts, the island of Tobago electing one member. Jamaica used its existing parishes as constituencies as well as its three counties. The Jamaican voter, accordingly, casts two ballots, one for the parish and one for the county constituency.

Membership in either federal chamber precludes membership in the legislature or Executive Council of a territory. Election disputes are settled by the federal Supreme Court. The chambers elect their own presiding officers who have a casting vote only. The Senators are appointed for five-year terms and the House is elected for a similar period unless sooner dissolved.

Legislative subjects are listed as exclusive (denied to the unit legislatures) or concurrent (on which both federal and unit legislatures may legislate). The residual powers, not mentioned on either list, belong to the territories. The exclusive list is not a long one. It includes federal audit, borrowing, defence, financial aid to governments or persons, exchange control, immigration, emigration and deportation, income tax on federal officers, legal proceedings between the federation and a territory or between territories and other obviously federal interests such as the various federal agencies and the University College of the West Indies.[1] The concurrent list is extensive and detailed, covering a long list of subjects from aliens, atomic energy and aviation to trades unions and weights and measures. As federal law supersedes unit law in case of conflict, it will be possible for the federal government gradually to assume control of many important matters. A limit to the speed with which this may be done is attached to several items. Although customs and excise is on the concurrent list, articles 94 and 95 of the constitution require the federal government to rebate to the territories any federal excise collected in excess of a specified total sum. Movement of persons is on the concurrent list but subject to articles 45, 50 and 51 providing that after five years the federal legislature must act positively to approve territorial laws on this subject or these laws will lapse. In effect this gives control of movement of persons to the federal legislature after 1963. Postal services are also under concurrent control. It is obvious that this service will be taken over by the federation but it is provided that after a federal postal system is instituted the federal government will pay to the units their average postal revenue (computed upon the preceding five years)

---

[1] The exclusive list is given in the West Indies (Federation) Order in Council, 1957, (Third Schedule) Part I. The concurrent list is given in *Ibid.*, (Third Schedule) Part II.

for a period of five years. Income and profits taxes are also levied concurrently but here again the federal government may not exclude the units during the first five years.

The two federal chambers are of unequal powers. Money bills may be introduced only in the House of Representatives and the equivalent of the famous Standing Order No. 78 of the House of Commons is included. A charge on the revenue may be proposed only upon the recommendation or with the assent of the Council of State, effectively barring 'pork-barrel' bills and resolutions by private members. Money bills after passage in the House are considered by the Senate but if rejected there become law within one month of their rejection unless the House resolves otherwise. The Senate has more suspensory power in connection with non-fiscal matters which become law after Senate rejection only if passed in two successive sessions by the House. This gives the Senate a one-year suspensory veto over non-fiscal bills.

The constitutional Order in Council retains for the British government the right to enact legislation for the federation by Order in Council regarding defence, external relations and the financial stability of the federation.

The executive power resides in the Council of State. This is composed of the Prime Minister and the other ministers and is normally presided over by the Governor General. In his absence the Prime Minister takes the chair. The Prime Minister is chosen by the House of Representatives from its membership and formally appointed by the Governor General who also formally appoints the other ministers on the Prime Minister's advice. The Prime Minister is somewhat limited in his choice of colleagues by the stipulation that three ministers must be chosen from the Senate. The Council also contains three non-voting members. These are permanent officials picked by the Governor General.

The Governor General ordinarily will act in accord with the advice given him by the Council of State. If he differs with his Council in proposals relating to defence, external relations or the financial stability of the federation he must refer the matter for final decision to the Secretary of State.

There will be a Federal Supreme Court consisting of a Chief Justice and three or more Federal Justices, appointed by the Governor General after consultation with the Prime Minister.[1] The Supreme Court will have original jurisdiction in cases concerning the federation or more than one territory. It will also serve

[1] The first Chief Justice was appointed by the Governor General under instructions from the Secretary of State before the federal elections were held and consequently was appointed without local consultation.

as an appeals court from the superior courts of the units and also from the Virgin Islands and British Guiana. The legislature will decide whether or not appeals from Supreme Court decisions may be taken to the Judicial Committee of the Privy Council.

In the first five years of existence the federation will derive its revenue chiefly from an assessment upon the unit governments according to a schedule whereby Jamaica pays 43% of the total, Trinidad 39%, Barbados 9% and the others lesser amounts down to 0.27% for little Montserrat. The total may not exceed $BWI 9,120,000 for any year. The federal government is entitled also to retain any 'seigniorage' or profits from the issue of currency. If its collections from the units and any revenue from excise duties or postal service totals more than the maximum sum mentioned above, it must be rebated to the territories.

The federal civil service will be appointed according to standards and rules established by the Public Service Commission of three to five members, one being chairman, appointed by the Governor General. Except for the Attorney General, the Clerk of the Senate, the Clerk of the House and Trade Commissioners or other representatives abroad of the federation, virtually all public servants will be appointed by the Public Service Commission.

The constitution may be amended by Order in Council and in any case a conference will be convened within five years to review the constitution and suggest changes.

COMMENTARY

It is much too soon to evaluate the federal system of the West Indies or to be certain of its effects upon the political, economic and social life of the area. To some extent it is an artificial union, urged from outside and resting upon no overwhelming local demand. Unlike Canada in 1867, for example, no military threat exists upon its frontiers. Traces of intercolonial jealousy and selfishness still exist. The extreme isolation of some units is another obstacle in the way of West Indian nationhood as are the extreme differences in size and population. The Jamaican, at least, has long thought of himself as Jamaican rather than West Indian. These wide variations in size made it impossible to assign seats precisely according to population in the House of Representatives. Even though under-represented, Jamaica with its block of seventeen seats out of forty-five may be able to exert a predominant influence at times if the other units are divided. A truly national outlook which will outweigh island loyalties still has to be developed. In this instance the state is hardly the natural expression of a pre-existing nation. The nation, rather, will have to develop as the result of political union and common action.

The economic ties between the islands are slight. All are essentially concerned with export agriculture and even when one is a specialist in crops not much grown elsewhere, such as Grenadian nutmegs and cocoa, there is no internal West Indian market for these products. In this respect the islands differ sharply from the thirteen American colonies with their complementary economies.[1] Indeed it is the two stand-outs, British Honduras with its lumber, and British Guiana with its rice which have for sale the products needed in the West Indies. As some of the units, probably Trinidad and Jamaica, develop a greater degree of industrialization there may be sharp disagreements at the federal level between those desiring to protect a home market for manufactures and the free-trade objective of those concerned with agricultural exports.[2] At the same time it is true that the vitality of the Regional Economic Committee and the numerous other intercolonial organizations proved that there was a felt need for inter-unit co-operation and to this extent political federation was the natural outcome of the increasing realization of the desirability of tackling area problems by area-wide action.

The West Indies starts with the advantage of not having the problems of some federal unions. All the units have essentially the same legal and political system even if some are more advanced than others. There is no sharp communal division along religious and language lines as in Canada. East Indian communalism is a local rather than a federal problem. Otherwise the population is substantially homogeneous and the existence of creole dialects and patois is relatively unimportant and due to diminish with improved education. One West Indian institution exists of great emotional value—the West Indian cricket eleven. As regards the test matches the West Indian transcends completely his island loyalty. The colour-class complex remains, of course, to affect West Indian society as it does that of the units.

The attempts to construct federal parties or election alliances has been discussed in the previous chapter. It is still too early to say whether or not the Prime Minister of the West Indies will be able to exert sufficient discipline over his ministers to enable the Council of State to function in the manner of a British cabinet or whether

---

[1] David Lowenthal, 'Two Federations' *Social and Economic Studies* 6, 2 June, 1957. 190.
[2] Competitive industrialization also creates problems. Note the reaction in Trinidad to the proposed oil refinery in Jamaica. See article by Dr A. R. Richards in Trinidad *Sunday Guardian*, issue of Sept. 7, 1958: 'Jamaica and Federation. Present Policy Threat to Whole WI Economy'.

these ministers as leaders of island-based parties may not rather resemble an intercolonial conference like the Regional Economic Committee. If, however, the importance of federal decisions begins to overshadow those of the unit governments so that the real focus of power in the West Indies is seen to be in the federation, there is a probability that the federal parties will become the true parties and the unit branches of these parties really subordinate to the West Indian party leadership. Even for local elections the voters will incline to support or oppose candidates because of their federal party affiliation. This is a conceivable future development. In the meantime the federal governments must be composed of what is essentially a coalition of island parties even if these parties choose to adopt a federal name.

At all events, ready or not, the West Indies had little choice but to attempt federal union. As observed earlier, the approaching independence of many of the territories would have left them still in a position of economic dependence, colonies in all but name. Only if economic viability were achieved could political independence acquire any reality. Together this might be possible. Federation would not produce a magic improvement in the economy but in the long run it might enable a more rational exploitation of resources, a more intelligent investment of capital and a greater use of local capital, an elimination of uneconomic enterprise in some units and a combined weight as seller and buyer in the world markets that would enable better bargains to be made.

But for some the chief reason for federation was not economic. Federation, to these idealists, represented the realization of a great dream—the emergence of a new West Indian nation or at least the framework within which such a nation might grow. Certainly this was the case with some of the older federationists such as the late T. A. Marryshow of Grenada, who lived to become a federal Senator. They envisaged a local art and culture with its own character, not a feeble copy of European models. Already in the work of a few writers, Mittelholzer, Lamming, Mais, Selvon and others, in the spontaneous folk music of the calypsonians and the steel bands, in the West Indian versions of African dances, there were evidences of great artistic talent. Freed from the colonial stigma, full of a new feeling of national pride and self-respect they might hold up their heads as West Indians. Their flag may be new and without history but to them it has great symbolic meaning for it indicates that they are nearing the end of the long journey from slavery through colonialism to genuine national independence and a place, however modest, among the nations of the world.

SELECT BIBLIOGRAPHY

HISTORY AND POLITICS

W. L. BURN, *The British West Indies* (London, Hutchinson & Co. Ltd., 1951).

ALAN BURNS, *The History of the British West Indies* (London, Allen & Unwin, 1954).

J. A. FROUDE, *The English in the West Indies* (New York, 1888).

Vincent Todd Harlow and Frederick Madden, eds., *British Colonial Developments, 1774-1834; Selected Documents* (Oxford, 1953).

FREDERICK MADDEN, ed., *Imperial Constitutional Documents, 1765-1952* (Oxford, 1953).

WILLIAM LAW MATHIESON, *The Sugar Colonies and Governor Eyre, 1848-1866* (New York, 1936).

LORD OLIVIER, *The Myth of Governor Eyre* (London, Hogarth Press, 1933).

————, *Jamaica, the Blessed Island* (London, Faber & Faber, Ltd., 1936).

J. H. PARRY AND P. M. SHERLOCK, *A Short History of the West Indies* (London, Macmillan & Co., 1956).

L. J. RAGATZ, *The Fall of the Planter Class in the British Caribbean, 1763-1833* (New York and London, 1928).

————, *Guide for the Study of British Caribbean History (1763-1834)* (Washington, 1932).

R. L. SCHUYLER, *The Fall of the Old Colonial System* (New York, 1945).

T. SOUTHEY, *Chronological History of the West Indies* (3 vols., London, 1827).

ERIC WILLIAMS, ed., *Documents on British West Indian History, 1807-1833* (Port-of-Spain, 1952).

H. V. WISEMAN, *A Short History of the British West Indies* (London, University of London Press, 1950).

HUME WRONG, *Government of the West Indies* (Oxford, 1923).

GEOGRAPHY

SIR C. P. LUCAS, *Historical Geography of the British Colonies*, vol. II *The West Indies* (Oxford, 1888-1920).

RAYE R. PLATT, *et al.*, *The European Possessions in the Caribbean Area* (New York, 1941).

COLONIAL POLICY

JOSE DE ALAMEDA *et al.*, *Colonial Administration by European Powers* RIIA (London, 1947).

ERNEST BARKER, *The Ideas and Ideals of the British Empire* (Cambridge, 1941).

GEORGE BENNETT, ed., *The Concept of Empire: Burke to Attlee, 1774-1947* (London, A. & C. Black, Ltd., 1953).

SIR A. BERTRAM, *The Colonial Service* (Cambridge, 1930).

PAUL BLANSHARD, *Democracy and Empire in the Caribbean* (The Macmillan Co., New York, 1947).

M. J. BONN, *The Crumbling of Empire* (London, Allen & Unwin, Ltd., 1938).

Q

SIR B. BOURDILLON, *The Future of the Colonial Empire* (London, SCM Press, 1945).

ROBERT BRIFFAULT, *The Decline and Fall of the British Empire* (New York, 1938).

C. E. CARRINGTON, *The British Overseas* (Cambridge, 1950).

W. R. CROCKER, *On Governing Colonies* (London, Allen & Unwin, Ltd., 1947).

————, *Self-Government for the Colonies* (London, Allen & Unwin, Ltd., 1949).

H. E. EGERTON, *A Short History of British Colonial Policy* (12th edn., London, Methuen & Co., Ltd. 1950).

E. W. EVANS, *The British Yoke: Reflections on the Colonial Empire* (London, Hodge & Co., Ltd., 1949).

LORD HAILEY, *The Future of the Colonial Peoples* (London, 1944).

————, *The Labour Party and the Colonies* (London, 1946).

W. K. HANCOCK, *Argument of Empire* (London, 1943).

————, *Empire in the Changing World* (London, 1943).

HANSARD SOCIETY, *Problems of Parliamentary Government in the Colonies* (London, 1953).

RITA HINDEN, *Common Sense and Colonial Development* (London, Gollancz & Co., Ltd., 1949).

————, *Empire and After* (London, Gollancz & Co., Ltd., 1949).

H. V. HODSON, *Twentieth-Century Empire* (London, Faber & Faber, Ltd., 1948).

SIR CHARLES JEFFERIES, *The Colonial Empire and its Civil Service* (Cambridge, 1938).

————, *Partners for Progress* (London, Harrap & Co., Ltd., 1949).

A. CREECH JONES, *Labour's Colonial Policy* (London, Anti-Slavery Soc., 1947).

———— AND RITA HINDEN, *Colonies and International Conscience* (London, Gollancz & Co., Ltd., 1945).

PAUL KNAPLUND, *James Stephen and the British Colonial System, 1813-1847* (Madison, Wis., 1953).

KLAUS E. KNORR, *British Colonial Theories (1570-1850),* (Toronto, 1944).

THE EARL OF LISTOWEL, RAWLE FARLEY, RITA HINDEN AND COLIN HUGHES, *Challenge to the British Caribbean,* Fabian Research Series No. 150 (London, 1952).

W. M. MACMILLAN, *Warning from the West Indies* (London, Faber & Faber, Ltd., 1938).

NICHOLAS MANSERGH, ed., *Documents and Speeches on British Commonwealth Affairs, 1931 1952* RIIA (2 vols., London, 1953).

GEORGE R. MELLOR, *British Imperial Trusteeship, 1783-1850* (London, Faber & Faber, Ltd., 1951).

HERMAN MERIVAL, *Colonization and Colonies* (Oxford, 1949).

FRANK A. NORMAN, *Whitehall to West Indies* (London, John Lane, 1952).

SIR COMO PARKINSON, *The Colonial Office from Within* (London, Faber & Faber, 1947).

MARGERY PERHAM, *Colonial Government* (London, Faber & Faber, Ltd., 1950).

Principles and Methods of Colonial Administration: Colston Papers Based on a Symposium Promoted by the Colston Research

Society and the University of Bristol in April, 1950 (vol. III, London, 1950).

MARY PROUDFOOT, *The U.S.A. and Britain in the Caribbean Islands* (New York, 1954).

LORD SAMUEL, *The British Colonial System and its Future* (London, Anti Slavery Soc., 1943).

JOSEPH SCHUMPETER, *Imperialism, Social Classes* (Oxford, Blackwell, 1955).

JACK SIMMONS, ed., *From Empire to Commonwealth: Principles of British Imperial Government* (London, Odhams, 1949).   ,

KATHLEEN M. STAHL, *British and Soviet Colonial Systems* (London, Faber & Faber, Ltd., 1951).

W. M. STRAUSS, *Joseph Chamberlain and the Theory of Imperialism* (Washington, 1942).

CONSTITUTIONS AND CONSTITUTIONAL HISTORY

SYDNEY D. BAILEY, *Constitutions of the British Colonies* (London, Hansard, 1950).

SIR CECIL CLEMENTI, *A Constitutional History of British Guiana* (London, Macmillan, 1937).

HEWAN CRAIG, *The Legislative Council of Trinidad and Tobago* (London, Faber & Faber, Ltd., 1952).

SIR IVOR JENNINGS AND C. M. YOUNG, *Constitutional Laws of the Commonwealth* (2nd edn., Oxford, 1952).

CHARLES REIS, *The Government of Trinidad and Tobago: Law of the Constitution, Commemorating 150 Years of British Rule,* 1797-1947 (3rd rev. edn., Port of Spain, 1947).

AGNES M. WHITSON, *The Constitutional Development of Jamaica,* 1660-1729 (Manchester, 1929).

MARTIN WIGHT, *British Colonial Constitutions,* 1947 (Oxford, 1952).
————, *The Development of the Legislative Council,* 1606-1945 (London, Faber & Faber, Ltd., 1946).

HUME WRONG, *Government of the West Indies* (Oxford, 1923).

ECONOMIC PROBLEMS

CARIBBEAN COMMISSION, *The Promotion of Industrial Development in the Caribbean* (Port-of-Spain, 1952).

N DEERR, *The History of Sugar* (2 vols., London, Chapman & Hall, Ltd., 1951).

ANNETTE B. FOX, *Freedom and Welfare in the Caribbean: A Colonial Dilemma* (New York, 1949).

BERT F. HOSELITZ, ed., *The Progress of Underdeveloped Areas* (Chicago, 1952).

INTERNATIONAL BANK FOR RECONSTRUCTION AND DEVELOPMENT, *The Economic Development of Jamaica* (Baltimore, 1952).
————, *The Economic Development of British Guiana* (Baltimore, 1953).

N. S. CAREY JONES, *The Pattern of a Dependent Economy : The National Income of British Honduras* (New York, 1953).

W. ARTHUR LEWIS, *Industrial Development in the Caribbean* (Trinidad, 1951).

W. M. MACMILLAN, *Warning from the West Indies: A Tract for Africa and the Empire* (London, Faber & Faber, Ltd., 1938).

K. MANDELBAUM, *The Industrialization of Backward Areas* (Oxford, 1945).

LORD OLIVIER, *White Capital and Coloured Labour* (London, Hogarth Press, 1929).

T. S. SIMEY, *Welfare and Planning in the West Indies* (Oxford, 1946).

KATHLEEN M. STAHL, *The Metropolitan Organization of British Colonial Trade* (London, Faber & Faber, Ltd., 1951).

SOCIOLOGICAL PROBLEMS

W. L. BURN, *Emancipation and Apprenticeship in the British West Indies* (London, 1937).

SIR ALAN BURNS, *Colour Prejudice* (London, Allen & Unwin, Ltd., 1948).

R. COUPLAND, *The British Anti-Slavery Movement* (Oxford, 1933).

GEORGE CUMPER, *Social Structure of Jamaica*, (Mona, Jamaica, 1949).

————, *Social Structure of the British Caribbean* (*Excluding Jamaica*) (Mona, Jamaica, 1950).

I. M. CUMPSTON, *Indians Overseas in the British Territories* 1834-1854 (Oxford, 1953).

E. J. DINGWALL, *Racial Pride and Prejudice* (London, 1946).

W. E. B. DUBOIS, *Colour and Democracy*: *Colonies and Peace* (New York, 1945).

E. FRANKLIN FRAZIER, *The Negro in the United States* (New York, Macmillan, 1949).

MELVILLE J. HERSKOVITS, *The Myth of the Negro Past* (New York, 1941).

———— AND FRANCES S. HERSKOVITS, *Trinidad Village* (New York, 1947).

MADELEINE KERR, *Personality and Conflict in Jamaica* (Liverpool, 1952).

WILLIAM P. LIVINGSTONE, *Black Jamaica* (London, 1900).

PHILIP MASON, *An Essay on Racial Tension* (RIIA, London, 1954).

WILLIAM L. MATHIESON, *British Slave Emancipation* (London, Longman's Green & Co., Ltd., 1932).

————, *British Slavery and its Abolition*, 1823-1838 (London, 1926).

RENE MAUNIER, *The Sociology of Colonies* (2 vols., London, Routledge & Kegan Paul, Ltd., 1949).

MARGARET MEAD, *ed.*, *Cultural Patterns and Technical Change* (UNESCO, Paris, 1953).

DWARKA NATH, *A History of Indians in British Guiana* (London, Nelson & Co., Ltd., 1950).

LORD OLIVIER, *White Capital and Coloured Labour* (London, Hogarth Press, 1929).

A. H. RICHMOND, *The Colour Problem* (Penguin Books, London, 1955).

A. G. RUSSELL, *Colour, Race and Empire* (London, 1944).

VERA RUBIN, *ed.*, *Caribbean Studies*: *A Symposium* (pamphlet, Inst. Soc. and Econ. Research, UCWI, Jamaica, 1957).

WILLIAM GRANT SEWELL, *The Ordeal of Free Labour in the West Indies* (New York, 1861).

M. G. SMITH, *Caribbean Affairs, A Framework for Caribbean Studies* (pamphlet, Extra-Mural Dept., UCWI, Jamaica, n.d.).

RAYMOND T. SMITH. *The Negro Family in British Guiana* (London, Routledge & Kegan Paul, Ltd, 1956).

J. A. THORNE AND J. H. KIMBALL, *Emancipation in the West Indies* (New York, 1938).

J. D. TYSON, *Report on the Condition of Indians in Jamaica, British Guiana and Trinidad* (pamphlet, Govt. of India. Simla, 1939).

ERIC WILLIAMS, *Capitalism and Slavery* (Chapel Hill, 1944).

————, *Education in the West Indies* (Port-of-Spain, 1950).

LABOUR ORGANIZATION

WALTER BOWEN, *Colonial Trade Unions* (London, Fabian Society, 1954).

G. ST. J. ORDE BROWNE, *Labour Conditions in the West Indies* (London, HMSO, 1939).

CENTRAL OFFICE OF INFORMATION REFERENCE PAMPHLET 3317, *Labour in the United Kingdom Dependencies* (Dec., 1956).

CD & W ORGANIZATION BULLETIN NO. 28 (1949) *Summary of Labour Legislation in the British West Indies.*

INFORMATION BULLETIN OF CARRIBEAN AREA DIVISION OF ORIT OF ICFTU, MONTHLY (BARBADOS).

W. A. LEWIS, *Labour in the West Indies* (London, 1939).

OFFICIAL DOCUMENTS

Report of the Hon. E. F. L. Wood, MP, *on his visit to the West Indies and British Guiana, 1922 Cmd. 1679.*

Trinidad and Tobago Disturbances, 1936: Report of the Commission Cmd. 5641 (1938).

MAJOR G. ST. J. ORDE BROWNE, *Labour Conditions in the West Indies* Cmd. 6070 (1939).

Papers Relating to the Disturbances in St Christopher Cmd. 4956 (1935).

West India Royal Commission Report Cmd. 6607 (1945).

———— *1938-39: Recommendations Cmd. 6174 (1940).*

———— *1938-39: Statement of Action Taken on the Recommendations Cmd. 6656 (1945).*

West Indian Conference (Report) 1st session, 1944 Col. No. 187.

Trade Union Organization and Industrial Relations in Trinidad, a report by F. W. Dalley (1947) Col. No. 215.

The Colonial Empire (1939-1947) Cmd. 7167 (1947).

Development and Welfare in the West Indies a series of Colonial Office documents issued for the years: 1943-44, 1945-46, 1947-49, 1950, 1951, 1952, 1953, 1954, 1955-56.

Report of the Closer Union Commission Cmd. 4383 (1935).

British West Indian Colonies: Closer Association Cmd. 7120 (1947).

Conference on the Closer Association of the British West Indian Colonies, Montego Bay, Jamaica, 11th to 19th Sept., 1947
Part I: *Report Cmd. 7291 (1948).*
Part II: *Proceedings Col. No. 218 (1948).*

Report of the Commission on the Unification of the Public Services in the British Caribbean Area, 1948-49 Col. No. 254 (1949).

Report of the British Caribbean Standing Closer Association Committee, 1948-49 Col. No. 255 (1950).

Report of the Commission on the Establishment of a Customs Union in the British Caribbean Area, 1948-50 Col. No. 268 (1951).

Colonial Regulations, 1951 Col. No. 270 (1951).

An Economic Survey of the Colonial Territories, 1951 Vol. IV Col. No. 281-4 (1953).

The Colonial Territories Command documents issued annually, covering the twelve month period between April 1 and March 31.

Industrial Development in Jamaica, Trinidad, Barbados and British Guiana: Report of a Mission of United Kingdom Industrialists, October to November, 1952 Col. No. 294 (1953).

Report of the British Guiana Commission, April, 1927 Cmd. 2841 (1927).

Report of the British Guiana Constitutional Commission Cmd. 2985 (1927).

Memoranda prepared by the Elected Members of the Combined Court of British Guiana in reply to the Report of the British Guiana Commission Cmd. 3047 (1927).

The Constitution, Suspension Ordered on October 8, 1953 pamphlet issued by Bureau of Public Information, BG, containing statement by Her Majesty's Government, two broadcasts by H.E. the Governor, Sir Alfred Savage, and a white paper issued by Her Majesty's Government.

Report of the British Guiana Constitutional Commission, 1954 Cmd. 9274 (1954).

Annual reports issued by the Colonial Office (including a map, photographs and a bibliography) for :
Barbados, British Guiana, British Honduras, Dominica, Grenada, Jamaica, the Leeward Islands, St Lucia, St Vincent, Trinidad and Tobago, Cayman Islands, Turks and Caicos Islands.

PERIODICALS

Caribbean Quarterly (Trinidad).
Colonial Review
Crown Colonist
New Commonwealth (successor to the *Crown Colonist*).
Jamaica Historical Review
Parliamentary Affairs
Political Quarterly
Round Table
Social and Economic Studies (Institute of Social and Economic Research, UCWI).
Times British Colonies Review (quarterly).
West India Committee Circular
Yearbook of the West Indies and Countries of the Caribbean (annual).

LOCAL PRESS

BARBADOS: *Advocate, Recorder.*
BRITISH GUIANA: *Daily Argosy, Daily Chronicle, Guiana Times News Magazine.*
BRITISH HONDURAS: *Billboard.*
JAMAICA: *Daily Gleaner, Jamaica Times, Public Opinion, Spotlight.*
LEEWARDS: *Union Messenger, Daily Bulletin, Crusader* (St Kitts).
TRINIDAD: *Daily and Sunday Guardian, Port-of-Spain Gazette.*
WINDWARDS: *West Indian* (Grenada), *Voice of St Lucia, Vincentian, Dominica Tribune.*

INDEX

90

U.S.A.

Nassau

GULF OF MEXICO

C U B A

20°

CAYMAN IS.

M E X I C O

Belize

BR. HONDURAS

JAMAICA

Kingst

GUATEMALA

HONDURAS

C A R I B

SALVADOR

NICARAGUA

N

COSTA RICA

CANAL ZONE

10°

P A N A M A

C

PACIFIC OCEAN

Cartography by permission of
Central Office of Information,
British Information Services

90°